CREATING DISCIPLE-MAKING MOVEMENTS: HOW THE MAKING OF HOLISTIC DISCIPLES IS CENTRAL TO THE MISSION OF CHRIST

Paul E. Johnson, D.Min.

Creating Disciple-Making Movements:
How the Making of Holistic Disciples
Is Central to the Mission of Christ

Copyright © 2012 Paul E. Johnson, D.Min.
All rights reserved.

You can write to the author at pjohnson@corban.edu.

A Dissertation Project Submitted to the
Faculty of Western Seminary, Portland, Oregon
In Partial Fulfillment of the Requirements
For the Degree of Doctor of Ministry

Additional copies of this volume are available for sale online at
www.BooksaMillion.com
www.BarnesandNoble.com
www.Amazon.com

*To the memory of my mother Mary Katherine Johnson,
my brother Larry Edwin Johnson and friend Dorothy Spratt,
as well as to my father Gordon W. Johnson.
Each one has demonstrated to me how to be Christ-like
and pursue the journey of being a holistic disciple
for the glory of the Father.*

CONTENTS

ABSTRACT, 1

CHAPTER 1 BACKGROUND, 2

TO THE STUDY, 2

    Central Problem, 5
    Thesis of the Study, 8
    Purpose of the Study, 9
    Research Methodology for the Study, 9
    Research Questions, 10
    Assumptions of the Study, 11

        Theological Assumptions, 11
        Philosophical Assumptions Supporting the Concept of Holistic Disciples, 13
        Philosophical Assumptions Supporting the Concept of Disciple-Making Movements, 14

    Delimitations and Limitations of the Study, 15
    Definition of Key Terms, 16
    Significance of the Study, 21
    Organization of the Study, 22
    Summary, 23

CHAPTER 2 LITERATURE REVIEW, 24

    Literature Review Methodology, 24
    Literature Addressing the Biblical Nature of a Disciple and the Mission of Christ, 25

        Introduction, 25
        Primary Resources on the Nature of a Disciple, 26
        Primary Resources on the Mission of Christ, 32
        Primary Resources on the Making of Holistic Disciples, 36
        Primary Resources on the Mission of Christ from Selected Examples in Church History, 43
        Primary Resources on Sixth to Seventh Century Irish Piety, 44

Primary Resources on Twelfth Century Cistercian Piety and Bernard of Clairvaux, 46
Primary Resources on Seventeenth and Eighteenth Century German Pietists, 49
Primary Resources on Dietrich Bonheoffer's Legacy, 52

Literature Review on Resources Related to the Mission of Christ, 55

Introduction, 55
Primary Resources on the Missional Church, 56
Primary Resources on Church Planting Movements, 59

Conclusion, 61

CHAPTER 3 THE MISSION OF CHRIST IN THE WORLD, 63

Introduction, 63
Theological Framework for Understanding the Mission of Christ, 64

Introduction, 64
The Theological Importance of Understanding Salvation History, 65
Hermeneutical Principles for Identifying the Mission of Christ, 66

The Mission of Christ in Relationship to the Kingdom of God, 69
The Unique Nature, Purpose and Task of the Mission of Christ in the World, 71

Introduction, 71
The Authority, Lordship, and Christ-Centered Mission in the World, 72
Christ Is the Lord of His Church, 75
Defining the Mission of Christ in the Church Age, 78
The Priority of Matthew 28:18-20 in Defining the Mission of Christ, 81

Christ-Saturated Mission—From *Missio Dei* to *Missio Christi,* 85

The Dual Objectives of Christ's Mission in the World, 87

> Introduction, 87
> The Mission of Building Christ's Church, 87
> The Mission of Making Christ-like Disciples, 89
> The Mission of Christ Is Measurable and Clear, 95
> Conclusion, 97

CHAPTER 4 THE NATURE OF HOLISTIC DISCIPLES, 99

Introduction, 99

Defining the Nature and Character of a Holistic Disciple of Jesus Christ, 99

> Introduction, 99
> The Contemporary Understanding for Making Disciples and Discipleship, 100
> Understanding the Two-Faceted Nature of Salvation, 105
> Understanding the Nature of a Holistic Disciple, 111
> Making Holistic Disciples: The Product and the Process, 117
> New Testament Terms Supporting the Holistic Disciple Concept, 123
> Becoming a Holistic Disciple Is a Choice, 128

The Motivation and Reproduction of Holistic Disciples of Jesus Christ, 129

> Introduction, 129
> Love of God and Others—The Motivation of a Holistic Disciple, 129
> The Importance of Godly Examples in Making Holistic Disciples, 132
> The Challenge of Reproducing Holistic Disciples, 135
> The Necessity of Others-Centered Service in the Making of Holistic Disciples, 137

A Holistic Disciple Is Created for a Life of Good
  Works, 140
Conclusion, 143

CHAPTER 5 THE NATURE OF DISCIPLE-MAKING
  MOVEMENTS, 145

Introduction, 145

The Growth of a Movement—Great Commission
  Best Practices, 146
The Two Objectives of Christ's Global
  Mission, 149
Contemporary Approaches That Prioritize the
  Planting and Growth of Churches to Fulfill
  Christ's Mission, 153
The Problem With Prioritizing Church Planting and
  Growth Over Disciple-Making, 157
Returning to the Center of Christ's Mission—
  Beginning with the End in Mind, 163
A Call for Creating Disciple-Making
  Movements, 166
Essential Components to Growing a Disciple-
  Making Movement, 170

Conclusion, 173

CHAPTER 6 HISTORICAL EXAMPLES OF THE MAKING OF
  HOLISTIC DISCIPLES AND DISCIPLE-MAKING
  MOVEMENTS, 176

Introduction, 176

Irish Piety in the Sixth and Seventh Centuries, 177
Cistercian Monasticism in the Twelfth Century, 188
German Pietists, 197
Dietrich Bonhoeffer, 207

Conclusion, 215

CHAPTER 7 AN ANALYSIS OF CURRENT MISSIONAL
  THOUGHT INTERPRETED BY THE THESIS OF THIS
  STUDY, 217

Introduction, 217
Central Tenets Used to Advance the Missional Church
  Concept, 218

> Introduction, 218
>
>> The Broad Theological Basis for Missional
>>   Church Ministry, 219
>> The *Missio Dei* Emphasis in Missional
>>   Ministry, 220
>> The Kingdom and Reign of God in Missional
>>   Ministry, 224

The Place of the Church in Missional Theology, 226
A Critique of the Missional Church Movement, 229

> Introduction, 229
> The Missional Church and the Mission of
>   Christ, 230
> A Critique of Missional Church Philosophy, 238
> Conclusion, 243

CHAPTER 8 SURVEY OF CONTEMPORARY AUTHORS CONCERNING THE MISSION OF CHRIST IN THE WORLD, 244

Introduction, 244
Question #1: The Nature of the Mission of Christ, 245

> Introduction, 245
> Summary of Responses, 246
> Conclusion, 251

Question #2 Missional Objectives to Fulfill Christ's
  Mission, 252

> Introduction, 252
> Summary of Responses, 253
> Conclusion, 258

Question #3 The Place of Missional Movements in Christ's
  Mission, 259

> Introduction, 259
> Survey of Responses, 260

Conclusion, 266

Conclusion, 266

CHAPTER 9 SUMMARY AND CONCLUSION, 268

Introduction, 268
The Validation of the Study, 269
Implications for Believers and Churches Today, 271
Conclusion, 274

APPENDIX A NEW TESTAMENT PASSAGES ON GOOD WORKS, 275

APPENDIX B RESEARCH SURVEY QUESTIONS, 287

APPENDIX C RESPONSES TO RESEARCH SURVEY QUESTIONS, 288

APPENDIX D TOKYO 2010 DECLARATION VISION STATEMENT, 320

Making Disciples of Every People in Our Generation, 320
Preamble, 322
Declaration, 324
Mankind's Need, 324
God's Remedy, 325
Our Responsibility, 325
Finishing the Task, 327
Our Pledge, 328

BIBLIOGRAPHY, 330

ABSTRACT

As obedient followers of the Lord Jesus Christ, it is vital to understand how Christ defined his mission for his followers in the world. The thesis of this study seeks to demonstrate that the center or core of Christ's mission is the making of holistic disciples (complete, mature and obedient), who are transformed into Christ's likeness and reproduce other holistic disciples. This study also presents the concept of disciple-making movements as the divinely ordained and most effective method of completing the mission of Christ as presented in the New Testament.

Along with biblical analysis, this research presents four stellar examples from church history of groups or individuals who pursued the fulfillment of the mission of Christ through the making of holistic disciples and, to some degree, disciple-making movements. This study also examines how the writings and perspectives of key contemporary writers on the missional church and discipleship compare with the author's understanding of the mission of Christ and his model for the making of holistic disciples and disciple-making movements. Finally, results from a brief survey are evaluated to determine how key contemporary authors describe the mission of Christ in the world today. It is the author's hope that this study will challenge believers to understand the unique mission of Christ in the world and to pursue the making of holistic disciples and the creation of disciple-making movements among all peoples for his glory.

CHAPTER 1
BACKGROUND
TO THE STUDY

The topic developed in this dissertation is a central concern for this author. Although Christ's mandate to *make disciples* is clear, an adequate understanding of the biblical teaching on the nature and character of a disciple and the need to pursue disciple making is largely misunderstood. Growing up in the church, the author equated the characteristics and practices of believers around him and the teaching he had learned on the spiritual life as the biblical model of discipleship taught in the New Testament. He had concluded that spiritual growth occurs automatically through a natural and passive spiritual process, much like the process of "osmosis." The author believed that faithfulness in personal spiritual growth, regular church attendance, orthodox doctrine, and regular ministry involvement automatically produces a disciple with Christ-like character. Yet these elements alone do not produce a mature or whole disciple.

During his years of study at Simpson College and Dallas Theological Seminary, the author grew significantly in his knowledge of the Bible and understanding of the spiritual life. The author has had the privilege, both in the classroom and church, of sitting under solid biblical preaching and teaching from men who taught God's word. He has been blessed with a rich spiritual heritage, biblical instruction and godly models of Christ-likeness. Yet, as the author grew in biblical knowledge and ministry skills, he began to equate these things with spiritual maturity and the essence of discipleship.

After seminary, the author and his wife joined CAM International (CAM) to pursue a ministry of church planting in central Mexico. After language training they began their ministry in Mexico on January 1, 1994. Veteran church planters provided the model for new missionaries to follow, filling their weekly schedules with Bible studies to both unbelievers and new believers. One church planter taught as many as twenty-five separate Bible studies per week with different families and individuals. This ministry model—to invest our lives with non-believers and new believers, teaching them essential biblical truth and basic doctrine through a series of Bible studies—was the standard ministry approach for many church planters.

Although people put their faith in Christ and participated in various biblical and theological studies, much of their cultural and contextual moorings seemed to hold them back from what we understood at the time to be a "mature believer." It became apparent that the nature of the training provided a good foundation but did not consistently make mature disciples who were growing in Christ-likeness in their cultural context. Believers who showed progress in their spiritual growth were seen as candidates for ministry leadership, based predominantly upon their biblical knowledge. Although developing Christ-like character was emphasized, the subtle message was that spiritual growth and leadership roles are for those who have attained and demonstrated a certain level of biblical/theological knowledge and ministry skill. This was the primary indicator of spiritual maturity and a growing disciple.

Over the last several years, CAM's leadership has observed that, overall, effective and biblical disciples have not been consistently produced through its varied ministries. Although the ministry was growing and the Lord was clearly working in many exciting ways, it seemed like a consistent understanding and an effective approach to developing mature believers and leaders was not regularly achieved. Disciple-making ceased to be reflected as an overall priority on most fields and related ministries and was associated only with ministries designed to equip new believers. Others did not see a need to prioritize disciple-making.

Through a careful Spirit-led process, CAM's leadership concluded that there is a need at all levels to return to the central ministry and priority of making Christ-like disciples. In 2007 CAM's leadership developed a new "ends statement" to refocus the priority of all missionary personnel to pursue the making of disciples. CAM's new end statement reads, "Because of CAM International there will be . . . among Spanish-speaking people worldwide a growing number of biblically mature believers who make disciples globally."[1] This emphasis on disciple-making coincided with the author's Doctor of Ministry studies at Western

---

[1] *"Ends Statement,"* CAM International, Dallas, Texas, 2008.

Seminary to reinforce his understanding and conviction on the importance and nature of disciple-making. As the author more accurately understood biblical discipleship, he became disturbed with a gnawing feeling that, for the most part, many in evangelical circles do not fully understand and prioritize the nature, process and product inherent in developing mature and complete Christ-like disciples.

In this study, the author seeks to present a biblical model of a disciple that results naturally in a process or movement that prioritizes the making of other disciples who love, live, look and long to be like Jesus Christ. The author hopes that a more complete and biblical perspective on the nature of disciple-making serves as a "clarion call" to define and pursue missional efforts that prioritize the making of holistic disciples and the creation of disciple-making movements.

Central Problem

The author believes that the making of disciples who grow into the likeness of Christ is the central priority of the Lord in the world today and the key purpose for which his church exists. The overriding command in Matthew 28:18-20 is to make obedient disciples of all nations and people. Christ's promise to "build" his church (Matthew 16:18) is solely founded on his disciples' efforts to make Christ-like disciples of others. Yet, it is crucial to ask: Is the making of Christ-honoring disciples the central priority and purpose of believers, churches and missional efforts today? Is the making of obedient and mature disciples the overriding strategy in cross-cultural ministry and mission agencies? Is the growing contemporary emphasis on the "missional" nature of the church, the "mission of God" (*missio Dei*), and the "missional church" based firmly upon the biblical mandate, to make obedient disciples who live to make more disciples?

Many ministries do not focus on producing healthy, obedient, and other-centered disciples who live for the sake of others. In the words of Engel and Dyrness regarding the state of world missions, "We have turned the great commission into a great commotion of words and more words as we have tried to make converts on the field. We have planted many churches, but we have not made disciples committed to the values of the Kingdom of Christ."[2]

Christ designed his commission to be successfully fulfilled as global progress is made towards a definable goal—that of making obedient disciples of all people. Disciples are to be trained so that they learn to "obey all that I (Christ) have commanded" (Matthew 28:19). However, the effectiveness of a church's effort to fulfill Christ's great commission is rarely defined or measured by the priority of making disciples who obey all that Christ has commanded. Success in the fulfillment of Christ's great commission has been reduced, redefined, and diluted in the understanding and practice of many evangelicals. When efforts to

---

[2] James F. Engel and William A. Dyrness, *Changing the Mind of Missions* (Downers Grove, IL: InterVarsity Press, 2000), 53.

fulfill the great commission are measured solely in terms of individual conversions to Christ, then the efforts and focus of the church, no matter how well intentioned, are not in full alignment with Christ's mission.

The making of obedient disciples involves a re-creation of our entire being that entails an intentional pursuit of holiness and transformation of character into Christ's likeness and a passion to live for and serve others for Christ's sake. Holistic or mature disciples who actively pursue transformation into the likeness of Christ in all aspects of their being will live, look, love, and long to be increasingly more like Christ. Their progress will be displayed both through their obedience to biblical truth resulting in personal godliness, and in their humble service to others, resulting in the making of other mature disciples. Healthy churches will be formed and holistic disciples will be made.

A growing number of evangelical authors are challenging church and mission agency leaders to be "missional," "externally focused," and "mission-shaped."[3] An entire issue of "Leadership Magazine" (Winter 2007) was titled, "Going Missional: Break Free of the Box and Touch Your World." In the article entitled "New Ownership", author Eric Reed presents his understanding of the word "missional":

> The word "missional" has been in the dictionary for 100 years, defined in the 1907 Oxford English dictionary as something that is of, or pertaining to, missionaries. But

---

[3] These are common terms used in literature describing the "missional church."

those who use the word today have broader applications, focusing on the church's role in culture.

It refers to a philosophy of ministry: those followers of Christ are counter-cultural, on a mission to change the culture. Missional refers to the specific activity of churches: to build the kingdom of God in all settings where church members are at work, rather than building up the local congregation, its programs, numbers, and facilities.[4]

In literature promoting the missional church and missional ministry, the disciple-making priority of Christ's great commission is often lacking. The missional church must find its biblical expression in the purposeful and ongoing commitment to develop obedient disciples intentionally, who form disciple-making movements.

Thesis of the Study

The thesis of this study is based on two propositions:

1. The teaching of the New Testament and stellar examples from selected periods in church history demonstrate that the biblical priority of intentionally making holistic disciples and pursuing disciple-making movements is the divinely ordained and central goal of Christ's great commission.

2. The majority of current literature on disciple-making and on the missional church, does not consistently demonstrate the priority of making holistic disciples and the pursuit of an intentional disciple-making ministry to strategically fulfill the mission of Christ (his great commission).

---

[4] Eric Reed, "New Ownership," *Leadership* (Winter 2007): 20.

Purpose of the Study

The purpose of this study is to demonstrate that the making of holistic disciples is the central goal and priority found in Christ's great commission, as taught in the New Testament and demonstrated in selected examples of church history. The making of holistic disciples and the creation of disciple-making movements is compared with the teaching of key scholars and advocates for the missional church ministry.

Research Methodology for the Study

This study follows a multi-method research approach, incorporating a combination of qualitative and quantitative systems of inquiry including both archival and self-reflective enquiry (action research) methods. Biblical studies on the nature of a disciple are based on exegetical qualitative research methods. Research into specific historical examples is conducted through archival research. Research focused on demonstrating how holistic disciple-making is central to the mission of Christ is pursued through archival research. Quantitative inquiry, archival and action research is implemented through a study of the principal literature on the topic and through surveys and interviews with twenty noteworthy authors. These research methods are employed to compare and contrast current missional thinking and theory with the biblical and historical model and the conclusions defined in the thesis of this study.

Research Questions

Six research questions guide the development of this project:

1. In biblical salvation history, what unique place and significance does Christ's mandate to make disciples have as the central priority of his great commission as defined in Matthew 28:18-20? This question is answered in Chapter Three.

2. What biblical passages and theological principles demonstrate the nature and validity of the concept of making "holistic disciples" as Christ's intended goal in his great commission? Chapter Four addresses this question.

3. What are biblically defined "disciple-making movements" and does this concept support the strategic outcomes of disciple-making and church formation intended by Christ to fulfill his great commission? This query is answered in Chapter Five.

4. How do selected examples in church history support and demonstrate the position that the center of Christ's mission is the making of holistic disciples that result in disciple-making movements? This question is dealt with in Chapter Six.

5. How does an understanding that the making of holistic disciples and disciple-making movements is central to the mission of Christ compare with the positions and teaching in contemporary literature focused upon the missional church and the mission of God in the world? This question is answered in Chapter Seven.

6. How do prominent contemporary authors, dedicated to the topics of spiritual formation, discipleship and the missional church, understand and prioritize the activities necessary to fulfilling the mission of Christ in the world? This question is addressed through the results of a survey analyzed in Chapter Eight.

Assumptions of the Study

The various assumptions that serve as a foundation for this study are broken into the following topics.

Theological Assumptions

There are seven theological assumptions that the author recognizes as central to the development of this study.

1. As Evangelical Christians, it is assumed that the Bible is true and relevant, the sole authority and source for determining the nature and character of a disciple and the mission of Christ's church in the world.
2. All Scripture should be interpreted from a literal, grammatical, historical and contextual understanding to determine its meaning.[5] The words, sentences, and grammar are studied within their context to discover their unique theological meaning.[6] God's message is revealed in Scripture progressively,

---

[5] Charles C. Ryrie, *Dispensationalism Today* (Chicago, IL: Moody Press, 1965), 87.
[6] Charles C. Ryrie, *Basic Theology: A Popular Systematic Guide to Understanding Biblical Truth* (Wheaton, IL: Victor Books, 1987), 114.

adding or changing aspects of what He communicated in one era compared to another era.[7]

3. From a dispensational perspective, the mission of God is centered in the post-resurrection mission of Christ. God's mission is focused solely and ultimately on the Person and work of Christ and his declared promise to build his church and authoritative command to make disciples of all peoples to the end of the age.

4. This study assumes that the central mandate of Christ's great commission is the purpose of the church and the calling of every believer. The teaching and commands related to Christ's great commission, therefore, serve to dictate and determine individual and corporate priorities of believers and Christ's church.

5. A holistic disciple is a mature, complete, or spiritually whole disciple. A holistic disciple is a believer who is pursing transformation into the likeness of Christ through faithfully obeying God's word and living sacrificially for the benefit of others as a disciple-maker. The priority of making holistic disciples is foundational to understanding the New Testament's teaching on the doctrine of regeneration, the doctrine of sanctification and spiritual maturity.

Key New Testament passages support the importance and development of disciple-making movements. Disciple-making movements accurately define the process, initiated and mandated

---

[7] Ryrie, *Dispensationalism Today*, 33.

by Christ, to reproduce disciples and build his church among all peoples.

The making of holistic disciples by God's design results in the purposeful and natural pursuit of "disciple-making movements" among the lost.

Philosophical Assumptions Supporting the Concept of Holistic Disciples

There are four assumptions about holistic disciples and disciple-making movements related to the fulfillment of the great commission in church history.

1. Although the word "disciple" and the command to "make disciples" does not occur in the New Testament after the book of Acts, it is assumed that the concepts are clearly taught and prioritized throughout the remainder of the New Testament. It is assumed that terms such as "complete," "perfect," "mature," "godliness," "holiness," "image," "likeness" and "formation" and the command to imitate Christ are apt synonyms for "disciple" and "disciple-making."
2. It is assumed that the making of disciples who obey all that Christ has commanded (Matthew 28:19) constitutes the essence of Christ's mission as taught in the great commission and delineated throughout the New Testament.
3. It is assumed that spiritual formation into the likeness of Christ is synonymous with the process of making holistic disciples

and therefore finds its purpose and ultimate expression in the life-long pursuit of holistic discipleship.
4. It is assumed that there are compelling examples from church history to demonstrate the priority of making holistic disciples and disciple-making movements as being central to the mission of Christ.

Philosophical Assumptions Supporting the Concept of Disciple-Making Movements

There are four philosophical assumptions to support the concept of disciple-making movements to fulfill the mission of Christ.

1. It is assumed that the making of holistic disciples will result, through obedience and spiritual transformation of individuals, in a divinely ordained process (or "movement") through which many disciples are made and churches are formed.
2. It is assumed that the making of holistic disciples resulting in disciple-making movements accurately delineates the process and most effective means for fulfilling his great commission in every culture, social context, and people group.
3. It is assumed that by prioritizing the making of holistic disciples, more believers will be equipped and biblically healthy churches reproduced to fulfill the great commission than through any other approach.
4. It is assumed that missional priorities and activities of believers and churches to fulfill Christ's mission should be evaluated

based on their alignment with and their prioritization of the making of holistic disciples and disciple-making movements.

Delimitations and Limitations of the Study

The sources for research and their relevance for this study have been limited solely to those which are pertinent to the thesis of this study. The outcomes of this study are delimited to the goal of creating an understanding of how the making of holistic disciples and disciple-making movements contributes to the fulfillment of the mission of Christ.

Cited written resources are limited to include prominent published and unpublished writings that address issues related to the topics of disciple-making, spiritual maturity and formation, the mission of the church, and the missional church. The research on church history is limited to the study of four individuals or groups that emphasized, to some degree, holistic disciple-making and disciple-making movements.

It is beyond the scope of this study to present a thorough biblical analysis on the process of discipleship. This information and focus has been adequately handled by many others. This study is limited to the concept of the making of "holistic disciples" which seeks to build upon much of what has been written related to disciple-making and discipleship. It is also not within the scope of this study to examine all literature that addressed the topics of disciple-making, discipleship, spiritual growth, and spiritual formation, and the mission of Christ. Only the most pertinent contemporary literature that treats some aspect of the thesis of this study will be researched and referenced. The survey section was limited to those scholars who could be contacted directly and were willing to answer the three questions that made up the survey.

The model presented in this study of a "holistic disciple" is not meant to provide a comprehensive, once and for all, analysis of biblical teaching on the nature, character and development of a disciple. This study is limited to the application of the model of a holistic disciple, as developed in the study and as compared and contrasted to selected examples from church history and with selected contemporary literature on these topics.

The literature reviewed and personal interaction pursued with prominent missional thinkers is limited to materials and conversations in English. A comprehensive and in-depth exegetical and historical study of the topics of spiritual formation, discipleship, the great commission, church history and missional thought is too broad a focus to be adequately dealt with in this study.

Definition of Key Terms

The following terms and phrases are used in this study with specific definitions in mind. The term "Bible" refers to the sixty-six canonical books of divine revelation that compose the Protestant Bible. The term "biblical" refers to that information found in the Bible and is descriptive, precedent, cultural and temporal in nature.⁸ "Scriptural" refers to information found in the Bible that is normative, authoritative, principle-based, and universally applicable in nature.⁹ The word "theology" refers to the study of God, his revelation of Himself, and his character, nature, will and purposeful involvement and expressed will towards his creation as revealed in the Bible.

The word "sanctification" is the divinely intended development of one's salvation that describes a lifelong pursuit of transformation into the likeness of Christ. It is characterized by holy and godly lives of believers who seek to obey God's Word and abide in Christ through dependence upon the power of the indwelling Holy Spirit.[10]

The term "great commission" refers to the post-resurrection teachings and commands of Christ to his followers summed up in the central command found in Matthew 28:18-20 to make disciples of all ethnic groups until the end of the age. The great commission is equal to "the mission of Christ" in the title and thesis of this study.

A "disciple" in its basic etymological usage in biblical Greek (μαθητης) designates a "learner."[11] In contemporary use, a

---

[8] Enoch Wan, "Ethnohermeneutics: Its Necessity and Difficulty for All Christians of All Times," Global Missiology, entry posted January 2004, <http://www.Globalmissiology.net/Research Methodology. html> (accessed Feb. 18, 2010).
[9] Wan, 1.
[10] Stephen D. Renn, ed., "Hagiasmos," *Expository Dictionary of Bible Words* (Peabody, MA: Hendrickson Publishers, 2005), 495.
[11] Michael J. Wilkins, *Following the Master* (Grand Rapids, MI: Zondervan Publishing House, 1992), 27.

"disciple" is a regenerated follower of Jesus Christ who enters into a life of growing as an obedient follower of Christ.[12] The term "discipleship" refers to the lifelong, intentional process of a disciple's spiritual growth as he is transformed into Christ's likeness in all areas of their person and life. The phrases "making disciples" or "disciple-making" refer more specifically to the intentional process of training a believer, from regeneration to glorification, to grow personally into Christ's likeness by obeying all that He has commanded (Matthew 28:19-20).

The term "spiritual formation" refers to the process of developing Christ's character in every aspect of one's being through personal effort and God's work of grace.[13] "Spiritual transformation" refers to the process of seeking to make the character, attitudes, thoughts, values, and will of Jesus one's own through obedience to Him.[14] In a practical sense, the terms "spiritual formation," and "spiritual transformation," can be understood as synonyms for the terms "sanctification" and "discipleship," and reflect the emphasis given to intentionally pursuing spiritual growth and change into Christ-likeness as found in the Epistles where the term "disciple" does not appear.[15]

The term "church planting movements" refers to "a rapid and multiplicative increase of indigenous churches planting

---

[12] Renn, 31.
[13] Bill Hull, *The Complete Book of Discipleship: On Being and Making Followers of Christ* (Colorado Springs, CO: NavPress, 2006), 19.
[14] Hull, 188.
[15] Hull, 32-35.

churches within a given people group or population segment."[16] Over the past decade "church planting movements" have gained a popular following as a philosophy of ministry that seeks to create an indigenous church planting effort to win the lost and initiating the greatest number of new church starts that do the same.[17] The author of this study created the phrase "disciple-making movements" as a corrective concept to "church planting movements." "Disciple-making movements" thus refers to the intentional pursuit of making and multiplying holistic disciples that leads by divine design to a movement of disciple-making and church planting among all peoples.

The term "holistic disciple" is central to the thesis of this study. The term "holistic" describes the character and nature of a mature, complete, or godly believer who is being transformed into the likeness of Christ. The term "holistic" is not used, as is commonly done, to describe the scope, range or character of one's ministry. "Holistic" does not refer to the ministry but to the person who is becoming like Christ. A "holistic disciple" is a believer who is seeking to be complete in Christ or Christ-like in all aspects of their being, motivations and behavior. Holistic disciples intentionally seek to obey and actively live out all that Christ has commanded. They are being transformed into his likeness, and are

---

[16] David Garrison, *Church Planting Movements* (Richmond, VA: Office of Overseas Operations International Mission Board of the Southern Baptist Convention, 1999), p. 7.
[17] Garrison, *Church Planting Movements*, 10.

therefore, like their Lord, compelled to live sacrificially through good deeds to serve and pursue the making of disciples of others.

The author uses the phrase "disciple-making movements" to delineate how Christ divinely intended his followers to fulfill his great commission to make disciples of all peoples. "Disciple-making movements" refers to an intentional process of reproducing holistic disciples who see as their key objective the making of other holistic disciples who live to serve the Lord and others. This concept underscores the fact that it is Christ who is building his church and that He has commissioned his followers who participate with Him by intentionally seeking to make holistic disciples who pursue the same goal. The concept of a disciple-making movement also best defines the essence and direction that should characterize the missional nature of a local church's ministry.

The term "mission of Christ" refers to the purposes and plans of Christ during the church age, as expressed in his post-resurrection commands in each Gospel account and in Acts 1, that are commonly referred to as the great commission. The term "missional" is an adjective "denoting something that is related to or characterized by mission, or has the qualities, attributes or dynamics of mission."[18] "Missional" refers to the qualities, attributes, dynamics and activities of believers as they relate to the mission of Christ centered on making disciples of all ethnic groups.

---

[18] Christopher J. H. Wright, *The Mission of God* (Downers Grove, IL: InterVarsity Press, 2006), p. 24.

The term "missional church" refers to the church that believes that it is sent by God into the world to pursue, as its primary purpose, the alignment of believers individually and corporately with God's missionary calling and purposes in the world.[19] The term *"missio Dei"* is Latin for the "mission of God." It is used to emphasize the understanding that mission is centered on a "sending God" who initiates, pursues and sustains his redemptive plan toward mankind. "The church is God's partner in what is his agenda"[20]

Significance of the Study

This study is important because it defines the essence of the mission of Christ that all believers are called and commanded to fulfill. That disciple is a holistic disciple, transformed into Christ's likeness. It is essential for church and mission agency leaders to prioritize a biblical disciple-making perspective. Holistic disciples are made and healthy churches planted through disciple-making movements. Holistic disciple-making and the propagation of disciple-making movements are Christ's divine design and should be the normative priority for believers and local churches. The great commission is designed to be fulfilled through the making of holistic disciples and disciple-making movements.

---

[19] Michael Frost and Alan Hirsch, *The Shaping of Things to Come* (Massachusetts: Hendrickson Publishers, 2003), 229.
[20] A. Scott Moreau, Gary R. Corwin, and Gary B. McGee, *Introducing World Missions: A Biblical, Historical, and Practical Survey* (Grand Rapids, MI: Baker Academic, 2004), 17.

This study seeks to make an important contribution in the overall discussion of the mission of the church. Christ, as the sovereign Lord, has all authority over his church. It is Christ alone who defines the nature and character of his mission and commands obedience to that mission from his disciples. The missional efforts of the church must be focused on the mission of Christ to ensure that the priority to make holistic disciples and disciple-making movements is central to their missional endeavors.

Organization of the Study

Chapter One of this study highlights the biblical, historical and philosophical rationale that has made this research project necessary. Chapter Two provides a review of literature that is pertinent to the thesis of this study. Chapter Three presents a biblical and theological understanding of the nature of Christ's mission and the central priority of disciple-making. Chapter Four includes a biblical study of the characteristics, process and priority of making of holistic disciples to fulfill the mission of Christ. Chapter Five examines the concept of how the mission of Christ is designed by him to be fulfilled through the reproduction of disciples and the subsequent forming of disciple-making movements. Chapter Six surveys four noteworthy examples selected from church history that demonstrate how holistic discipleship and disciple-making movements were pursued through their lives and ministries. Chapter Seven examines prominent contemporary literature concerning the missional nature of the church as compared with the thesis of this study. Chapter Eight analyzes the results from a survey taken by twenty scholars whose expertise is in the areas of discipleship, missions and the missional church related to the thesis of this study. The study will conclude with a brief summary of the entire project and some initial thoughts on how churches and mission agencies can align their ministries to prioritize holistic disciple-making and facilitate disciple-making movements to fulfill the mission of Christ.

Summary

Christ has commanded his disciples to make disciples who obey all that He has commanded. Disciples of Christ are to love, live, look and long to be like Jesus. Christ's character is formed in the lives of obedient disciples who live to be transformed into his likeness and serve others through good deeds. The heart of Christ's mission is not to "reach" people or even to multiply churches as an end in and of itself. The goal of the mission of Christ is to make holistic disciples who obey and live for Him. By doing so, more lost people will be reached, more disciples will be made, and more biblically healthy churches will develop.

Many evangelical leaders are encouraging believers and local churches to be missional. However, if the concept of missional ministry is not based on the mission of Christ and his ordained purpose for his followers, then the progress in Christ's mission is weakened.

CHAPTER 2
LITERATURE REVIEW

Literature Review Methodology

This chapter reviews and synthesizes accessible literature that either supports or challenges the core propositions of this study: [1] disciple-making movements, [2] the making of holistic disciples, and [3] both concepts as they relate to the mission of Christ.

The literature review can be considered a "theoretical review" that critically analyzes the common approaches to disciple-making and discipleship in contemporary evangelical ministries as compared to the priorities to make holistic disciples and disciple-making movements, based on the thesis of this study.[21] This chapter evaluates the contemporary literature that addresses making disciples, discipleship, disciple-making movements, and missional ministries to determine their relationship to the biblical goals presented in this thesis. The literature review therefore seeks to validate the thesis of this study as a legitimate and biblically prescribed perspective.

The literature review concentrates on doctoral dissertations and master theses, journal and Internet articles, and books that address some aspect of the thesis. The author has included a brief

---

[21] Randolph, Justus J., "A Guide to Writing the Dissertation Literature Review," in *Practical Assessment, Research & Evaluation*, 14:13 (June 2009), 3, http://pareonline.net/getvn.asp?V=14&n=-13.html (accessed June 2, 2010).

synopsis of the most credible four or five examples of pertinent and informative literature on the topic and thesis of this study.

The literature review is divided into five sections. The first section reviews the most pertinent literature that deals with the biblical nature of a disciple and the mission of Christ. The second section reviews the literature concerning disciple-making and discipleship that focuses in some way on the making of holistic disciples. In the third section the literature review concentrates on describing selected groups and individuals from four historical periods in church history who demonstrated, to some degree, the priority of disciple-making movements and the making of holistic disciples. The fourth section reviews the most influential literature defining the "missional church" and missional ministry in contemporary thought in light of the thesis. The last section reviews the literature that describes the concept of "church planting movements" to validate the need for the proposed concept in this study entitled "disciple-making movements." The chapter concludes with a summary and subsequent validation for this study.

Literature Addressing the Biblical Nature of a Disciple and the Mission of Christ

Introduction

The purpose of this study is to demonstrate that the central objective in Christ's mission is the making of holistic disciples who live to make holistic disciples of others, resulting in disciple-making movements. The basic biblical teaching identifying who a disciple is and the nature of discipleship has been thoroughly and adequately examined by scholars. However, in order to practically understand the nature and importance of making holistic disciples, it is necessary to understand the biblical teaching on disciple-making and how that ministry forms the heart of Christ's mission during this age.

Primary Resources on the Nature of a Disciple

The reviewed resources include:

The Complete Book of Discipleship[22]

In *The Complete Book of Discipleship*, Bill Hull develops a comprehensive understanding of discipleship by examining proven concepts from the practices of "classic discipleship," "spiritual formation," and "environmental discipleship" that together transform believers into fully developed disciples of Christ.[23] Hull's book makes the greatest contribution to the thesis of this study by biblically defining the mission of Christ and describing the teaching on the making of disciples and discipleship. He demonstrates that the making of disciples is central to the divine mission of Christ in the world. Hull helps the reader understand the

---

[22] Bill Hull, *The Complete Book of Discipleship: On Being and Making Followers of Christ* (Colorado Springs: NavPress, 2006).
[23] Hull, 18-20.

need to pursue discipleship by describing how a pervasive "non-discipleship Christianity" is prevalent in the church in America.[24]

Bill Hull provides a brief historical survey of how certain movements and believers through history have understood and pursued the making of disciples. He includes a brief study of Spener, and Bonhoeffer, two of the men previously identified by the church history scholars for exploration in the historical section of this study.

Hull's emphasis on the development of obedience and maturity in the disciple's life and the priority of pursuing transformation into Christ-likeness support the thesis of this study. His presentation of the essential character qualities and growth in maturity for a mature disciple and the importance of practicing spiritual disciplines in biblical discipleship reinforce the study's emphasis on making holistic disciples. Hull helps the reader to understand that the call of Christ to discipleship is not optional. The pursuit of transformation into Christ-likeness is to be the life-long pursuit of all believers and churches. He supports the concept that the integral qualities of a disciple are lives characterized by obedience, love and service.

---

[24] Hull, 41-43.

Following the Master[25]

Wilkins is a professor of New Testament language at Talbot School of Theology. He has studied disciple-making since his M.Div. thesis in 1977 and has written several books and articles on the topic of discipleship.[26] In this book, Wilkins describes how Jesus sought to develop his disciples so that they could understand and emulate his example in their future efforts to make disciples.

Wilkins presents an important survey of the major views on the nature of a disciple. It addresses who is a disciple, when one becomes a disciple, and if disciples are made or born. He concludes that a disciple of Christ is a believer in Christ who enters a life-long process of growing into the likeness of Christ. All believers are therefore disciples. Wilkins promotes throughout the book that discipleship is essentially the Christian life and should be the obedient pursuit of all believers.[27]

Wilkins presents a comprehensive study of the term and concept of "discipleship" and a thorough study of the use and meaning of the term "disciple" from ancient Greek and Roman, Old Testament and New Testament contexts. This information is helpful to understand how the concepts of a disciple, of making disciples, and discipleship were viewed in a first-century, Jewish

---

[25] Michael J. Wilkins, *Following the Master* (Grand Rapids, MI: Zondervan Publishing House, 1992).
[26] Wilkins, "The Use of 'Disciple' in the New Testament" (Unpublished Master's Thesis product, Talbot Seminary), 1977, cited in *Following the Master*, n. 19.
[27] Wilkins, *Following the Master*, 342.

context. He extends his study on disciple-making and discipleship from each Gospel account and the book of Acts to demonstrate the subtle contextual differences of meaning and emphasis during Jesus' earthly ministry and in the life of the early church. The information on the use of the term "disciple" in the Gospels and the book of Acts is vital to understand the accurate biblical teaching about the nature and process involved in the of making disciples of Christ. Wilkins also presents the major views concerning why the words "disciple" or "disciples" do not occur in the New Testament after the book of Acts. This information supports the place of disciple-making movements in the planting of local churches.

Wilkins emphasizes three critical qualities that characterize the life of an obedient and maturing disciple: [1] abiding in Jesus' words, [2] loving other disciples, and [3] bearing fruit. A disciple grows into Christ's likeness by pursuing and prioritizing these essential characteristics and ministries. This concept supports the nature of a holistic disciple who lives like Christ for the sake of others.

One of the strongest points of the book is the author's obvious conviction that discipleship and growth into Christ-likeness is a life-long journey involving effort, sacrifice and commitment. Wilkins highlights the obligations and responsibilities of a faithful disciple who obeys the Lord.

Organic Disciplemaking[28]

The authors of this book write from years of experience ministering at Xenos Christian Fellowship, a church and movement made of dozens of house churches with a total membership of more than 5,000 in Columbus, Ohio. The book presents the basic philosophy of the Xenos house church ministry that emphasizes "organic disciple-making." The concept of organic disciple-making is built upon personal relationships in the community and individual discipleship towards spiritual growth and service to others. Organic disciple-making goes beyond the practice of basic spiritual disciplines to the intentional development of mature character and ministry skill.

The authors do not promote a specific program for discipleship. Instead, they focus on nine areas of personal and corporate growth. They advocate a multi-year personalized discipleship process that focuses on grounding disciples in the faith and development of godly character and ministry skills to effectively minister to others.[29] The authors also present practical instruction to the disciple maker on how to both coach and mentor their disciples to pursue Christ-likeness.

Organic Disciplemaking reinforces the idea that a biblical disciple is personally involved in a lifelong pursuit of spiritual growth while also seeking to mentor others in their own spiritual

---

[28] Dennis McCallum and Jessica Lowery, *Organic Disciplemaking* (Houston: Touch Publications, 2006).
[29] McCallum and Lowery, 43-44.

growth. The authors emphasize the need for pursuing growth and maturity as a disciple through serving and ministering to others.

A Biblical View of Discipleship[30]

James Samra seeks to answer the following questions through the study of several key Scriptures: "What is discipleship? How is discipleship accomplished? What is involved in promoting discipleship?"[31] He begins the article by delineating the reasons he believes Christians are often confused by the concept of discipleship. He provides a basic definition of discipleship as the process of becoming like Christ, which supports the basic premise in this thesis about the character of a holistic disciple. Samra writes, "Since a holistic sense of 'disciple' seems to be intended as the ideal in the Gospels, so that Jesus' disciples were becoming so much like him that they were identified with Him, a holistic sense of discipleship is necessary to encompass all the New Testament material on discipleship. Discipleship involves both becoming a disciple and being a disciple."[32]

Through a survey of key New Testament passages, Samra demonstrates the need for a disciple to pursue a lifelong process and intentional striving to become like Christ as one grows spiritually through spiritual transformation into Christ-likeness. He includes valuable information, particularly from the writings of the

---

[30] James G. Samra, "A Biblical View of Discipleship," *Bibliotheca Sacra* 160: 638 (April—June 2003), 219-234.
[31] Samra, 219.
[32] Samra, 220.

Apostle Paul, to help disciples understand and to apply the practical ways that Paul modeled and taught discipleship.

Samra provides solid analysis on how the biblical nature of discipleship is the will of Christ for all believers. His analysis of how both Jesus and Paul sought to make disciples provides needed information for this study to strengthen the basic understanding on discipleship. He claims that the central purpose of discipleship is to become like Christ in a holistic or whole-person sense, based upon the lifelong quest for spiritual maturity and life transformation. He asserts that spiritual growth and maturity are developed through service and good works.

Primary Resources on the Mission of Christ

The written resources reviewed that address the mission of Christ are briefly described below:

Reaching and Teaching[33]

David Sills presents a needed perspective and call to return to a biblically balanced practice regarding the fulfillment of Jesus' mission in the world. Sills' exhortation to the church and mission agency is that Christ's mission priority is not to concentrate solely on the "reaching" of people for Christ (evangelism), but on "teaching them to observe all that I have commanded you" (Matthew 28:19). The disciple-making mandate forms the primary objective of Christ's mission in the world.

---

[33] M. David Sills, *Reaching and Teaching: A Call to Great Commission Obedience* (Chicago: Moody Press, 2010).

Sills calls the church and mission agency back to the core of Christ's commission as presented in Matthew 28:18-20. He claims that the call to teach disciples to obey (verse 19) has become "the great omission of the great commission" for many missional ministries today.[34] Sills is critical of the emphasis that presents the mission of Christ almost exclusively with reduced evangelistic goals ("reaching").

Sills explains how Christ's mission has been reduced to mean simply "reaching" people for Christ through evangelistic efforts. He believes that this reduction of Christ's mission has resulted in the creation of arbitrary measures of success illustrated with stories of numerical success to attract financial supporters and new missionary candidates. These factors, among others, have contributed to redirect and truncate the core priority of making disciples and teaching believers to obey all that Christ has commanded.

As Sills states, "The task of international missions is not just to reach and leave, but rather to reach and disciple and teach the nations" to live like and for Christ by obeying all that he has commanded.[35] This message applies both to cross-cultural ministry as well as to the ministry of every local church. This biblical focus is central to the creation of disciple-making movements and to the priority of making holistic disciples who live, look, and love like Jesus.

---

[34] Sills, 15—19.
[35] Sills, 219.

The Mission of God[36]

Author Christopher Wright has written one of the most comprehensive and influential theologies on the mission of God. The author describes what he believes God has revealed as the overriding "grand narrative" of the Scriptures. He then develops a missional hermeneutic from a historical-grammatical, contextual approach to discover the biblical author's intended meaning.

The author divides his work into four sections: [1] "The Bible and Mission," [2] "The God of Mission," [3] "The People of Mission," and [4] "The Arena of Mission." The thesis of this study is most directly supported in Chapter 15 of the fourth section entitled, "God and the Nations in the New Testament Mission."[37] Wright believes that the mission of God as presented in the New Testament completes the theology and emphasis on the mission of God from the Old Testament. The goal of Jesus' life and ministry was to gather the nations to Himself as the new messianic people of God.[38]

Wright's survey of the mission of God in the Bible is based upon the premise that God's universal and central purpose is to bless all of the families or nations of the earth. He believes that the great commission account in Matthew and the Christ-centered priority of making disciples and teaching them to obey all that Christ has commanded are part of, but not the central focus of,

---

[36] Christopher J. H. Wright, *The Mission of God: Unlocking the Bible's Grand Narrative* (Downers Grove, IL: IVP Academic, 2010).
[37] Wright, 501-530.
[38] Wright, 506.

God's overall mission. Wright does not highlight the making of disciples and the task that all believers have to make disciples of all peoples as the priority and unique mission of God through the Person of Christ in the world today. Wright shares the perspective of other contemporary authors who do not make a distinction between the work and mission of God as revealed in the Old Testament and the authoritative declaration of Christ's mission for his followers during the church age. Wright defines God's general activity in the world as being to bless humanity but does not plainly differentiate how the mission of Christ, as presented in Gospels and Acts, provides an exclusive and final mandate for the church.

Paradigms in Conflict[39]

In *Paradigms in Conflict*, Hesselgrave addresses ten crucial issues facing the church in its quest to fulfill the great commission. Three of these issues deal with some aspect of the thesis of this study regarding the mission of Christ in the world.

Chapter 4 is entitled, "Holism and Prioritism: For Whom is the Gospel Good News?" This chapter discusses the nature of the mission of Christ. Hesselgrave asks if the priority in Christ's mission to make obedient disciples should include an equal emphasis to promote justice and peace by meeting physical, material and social needs? Hesselgrave promotes "prioritism"

---

[39] David J. Hesselgrave, *Paradigms in Conflict: 10 Key Questions in Christian Missions* (Grand Rapids, MI: Kregel Publications), 2005.

which supports the emphasis of this study that making disciples is the central priority of the mission of Christ. Chapter 5, "Incarnationalism and Representationalism: Who Is Our Missionary Model—Jesus or Paul?" presents the nature and scope of Christ's mission. Is Jesus' earthly Messianic mission towards Israel the model believers are to prioritize today? Or did the Apostle Paul provide the pattern we are to follow in disciple-making, which is to faithfully fulfill the mission of Christ? Hesselgrave argues that the mission of Christ is distinct from his unique messianic ministry to Israel during his earthly ministry.

In Chapter 10, "The Kingdom of God and the Church of Christ: What on Earth is God Building—Here and Now?", Hesselgrave analyzes how an ecumenical and liberal theological emphasis in missions today has broadened the purpose and scope of Christ's mission to focus upon the establishment of God's kingdom. This position holds that every activity that the church does in the world is part of its mission to advance and build God's kingdom. Hesselgrave believes that this influential perspective can contradict or weaken the great commission mandate of making disciples that the Lord commanded his followers to accomplish.

Primary Resources on the Making of Holistic Disciples

Introduction

Throughout the literature review the precise phrase "holistic disciples," referring to the complete and mature character of a disciple, was not found. A few references to the phrases "holistic disciple-making" and "holistic discipleship" were discovered in the literature reviewed. It is important to understand that the use of the adjective "holistic," when combined with "disciple-making" and "discipleship" in this study, does not carry the same meaning commonly attributed to the contemporary concept of "holistic" ministry. The term "holistic" when used regarding Christian ministry, almost always refers to efforts involved in meeting *needs in* all aspects of a person's whole being—their physical, social, and spiritual needs. Authors who used the term "holistic" in this way describe the scope or nature of one's ministry focus to meet physical and social needs, *not* to refer to the character transformation involved in making a complete or mature disciple. In this study the reference to "holistic disciples" is used consistently to refer to a disciple's Christ-like spiritual character. The literature referred to below includes primary sources that support and help to define the concept of "holistic disciples."

Transforming Discipleship[40]

Ogden is concerned that disciples are made who are not just spiritually mature but also live intentionally to reproduce other mature disciples. Ogden presents a model for transformational discipleship built on spiritual growth in the Scriptures and the practice of effective disciple-making principles. He believes that

---

[40] Greg Ogden, *Transforming Discipleship* (Downers Grove, IL: InterVarsity Press, 2003).

the "missing tool in the arsenal of disciple making" is the triad of commitments involving: [1] relational transparency, [2] the truth of God's Word, and [3] life-changing accountability based upon covenants and dependence upon the Holy Spirit.[41] This triad of commitments is central to his disciple-making philosophy.

Ogden provides helpful information on the values and priorities that keep churches from seriously pursuing the making of transformational disciples. After examining the discipleship practices of Jesus and the Apostle Paul, Ogden describes how principles on spiritual growth should be realized in the church through small disciple-making units that provide the atmosphere to grow people into mature disciples.

Ogden emphasizes the fact that Jesus invested himself in a few individuals to make disciples through personal training based on their relationship and ministry with Him so that they would multiply. Ogden explains how Jesus' example and role towards his disciples changed as they grew in their knowledge and understanding of his mission.

He also describes how the Apostle Paul's primary passion and ministry goal was to help others grow into maturity in Christ. He describes how the Apostle worked with believers as a parent works with their developing child by leading them through the process of spiritual development from infancy to maturity.

This book contributes to the thesis of this study by emphasizing how Paul's goals support the holistic disciple concept.

---

[41] Ogden, 17-18.

Ogden's emphasis on purposeful multiplication of disciples through practicing his model of the triad of commitments helps to support this thesis.

The Kingdom Life: A Practical Theology of Discipleship and Spiritual Formation[42]

The authors that contribute to the development of the thesis of this study are Keith Matthews, Bill Hull, and Keith Meyer. Matthews emphasizes that a disciple makes a personal and public intentional commitment to learn and obey all of Christ's commands.[43] Hull emphasizes that transformation of character underlines the fact that spiritual formation into the likeness of Christ is a lifelong pursuit and is therefore not achieved through external practices or activities in and of themselves.[44] Meyer stresses that spiritual formation is not a simple technique or program but the ongoing process of transformation of the whole person through God's power.[45] Meyer's chapter emphasizes whole-life transformation which supports the holistic nature of spiritual disciples as defined by the thesis of this study.

---

[42] Alan Andrews, ed., *The Kingdom Life: A Practical Theology of Discipleship and Spiritual Formation* (Colorado Springs: NavPress, 2010).
[43] Keith J. Matthews, "The Transformational Process," in *The Kingdom Life*, ed. Alan Andrews (Colorado Springs: NavPress, 2010), 83-104.
[44] Bill Hull, "Spiritual Formation from the Inside Out," in *The Kingdom Life*, ed. Alan Andrews (Colorado Springs: NavPress, 2010), 105-136.
[45] Keith Meyer, "Whole-Life Transformation," in *The Kingdom Life*, ed. Alan Andrews (Colorado Springs: NavPress, 2010), 137-162.

The arguments presented in these chapters support this study's thesis on the "holistic" character and process for developing a godly disciple. Each of these authors also affirms the intentional nature and process inherent in disciple-making. The authors cited above agree that this process is not automatic but involves a lifelong pursuit of spiritual transformation.

The τελειος as a Goal of Pauline Spiritual Formation[46]

Lin, in his Master of Theology thesis, presents how the Apostle Paul used the Greek term, "τελειος" (meaning "perfect", "whole", "complete"), to describe the concepts of spiritual growth, maturity and Christ-likeness. Lin provides an overview of the Hebrew Old Testament concept of "wholeness" or "perfection" (τελειος). He examines how Matthew uses the term τελειος in Matthew 5:48, and how both James and the Apostle Paul used τελειος. Lin notes that Paul uses the term τελειος to define an intentional process. τελειος is a synonym for a believer who is "spiritual" and is "closely tied to the behavior of the believer."[47] Lin also notes from Ephesians 4:13 that τελειος refers to spiritual maturity that is achieved through both personal and corporate effort.

A τελειος disciple is a whole, mature, and complete disciple. Lin describes how the use and meaning of the word

---

[46] Tony Lin, *The τελειος as a Goal of Pauline Spiritual Formation* (Masters Product, Dallas Theological Seminary, 2005).
[47] Lin, 71.

τελειος illustrates the manner in which the Apostle Paul understood and prioritized the intentional pursuit of spiritual maturity and growth into Christ-likeness.

Choose the Life: Exploring a Faith that Embraces Discipleship[48]

Bill Hull appeals to his readers to choose the life of true discipleship. "A transformed life is needed, a life of depth of true disciples who have chosen to follow the life that Jesus lived."[49] Hull identifies five dimensions of discipleship: [1] believe what Jesus believed (a transformed mind), [2] live as Jesus lived (transformed character), [3] love as Jesus loved (transformed relationships), [4] minister as Jesus ministered (transformed service), and [5] lead as Jesus led (transformed influence).[50] Hull laments a "nondiscipleship Christianity" that separates obedience from pursuing Christ's likeness and has produced people who have faith but are not being transformed by Christ.[51]

Hull states that the making of disciples and the forming of believers into Christ-likeness is the obligation and ministry goal of every church. He believes that disciples are made, in part, through

---

[48] Bill Hull, *Choose the Life: Exploring a Faith that Embraces Discipleship* (Grand Rapids, MI: Baker Books, 2004).
[49] Hull, *Choose the Life*, 215.
[50] Hull, *Choose the Life*, 14.
[51] Hull uses the term "nondiscipleship Christianity" as a type of Christianity that divorces Christ's mandate to make disciples who obey his commandments from the spiritual reality of the believer's justification. He sees it as the practice of promoting salvation from judgment without teaching the necessary goal of transformation in the believer's life. See *Choose the Life*, 23-34.

mentoring relationships that promote personal interaction, submissive relationships, and self-denial. It is through this process that the "teaching them to obey all ..." aspect of Christ's mandate to make obedient disciples is achieved.

For Hull, the regular practices of various spiritual disciplines are needed to intentionally pursue transformation of character and growth for maturity to become a reality in the disciple's life. Hull emphasizes that the disciple must pursue a transformed mind through the study and practice of God's word. His emphasis on the characteristics of humility and others-centeredness supports the concept of a holistic disciple who grows into Christ-likeness and lives for others. Hull's emphasis on service, good works, and submission to others is a core part of what it means to be a holistic disciple. He aptly describes in a tangible way the unique calling to make holistic disciples as central to the mission of Christ.

The Externally Focused Church[52]

Rusaw and Swanson have written a practical and useful book that relates both to the making of holistic disciples and to the creating of disciple-making movements. The authors provide a solid biblical rationale for ministry to those outside the walls of a church as well as varied practical examples of how a church can focus on the needs of people through good deeds.

---

[52] Rick Rusaw and Eric Swanson, *The Externally Focused Church* (Loveland, CO: Group Publishing, 2004).

The authors describe the power of service in both the lives of the served and the life of the servant. They carefully tie the concept of God's love from the life and teaching of Christ to the idea that disciples are made through service to others. They state that ministry to others can be as beneficial as, or even more beneficial to one's growth into Christ-likeness than a focus on personal spiritual disciplines alone.

The authors note that Ephesians 2:10 states that every believer is born with a purpose—to do good works that God has prepared beforehand.[53] They present a balanced perspective on how the proclamation of the gospel can and must go hand in hand with good deeds. The authors' emphasis on pursuing good works is central to the making of holistic disciples and the creation of disciple-making movements.

Primary Resources on the Mission of Christ from Selected Examples in Church History

Introduction

To determine which periods or people throughout Christian church history contribute in some way to the thesis of this study, four church history scholars were asked for their input. From the recommendations received from these scholars, four people and periods from church history that relate in some way to the thesis of this study were chosen. The people or movements studied are: [1] Irish piety from the sixth and seventh century; [2] Cistercian piety,

---

[53] Rusaw and Swanson, 87.

particularly the influence of Bernard of Clairvaux in the twelfth century; [3] German Pietists in the seventeenth and eighteenth centuries; and [4] Dietrich Bonhoeffer, German pastor and author, put to death in a Nazi concentration camp in 1945. The literature review focuses on two or three of the most useful resources concerning the people or periods mentioned above, as they relate to the thesis of this study.

Primary Resources on Sixth to Seventh Century Irish Piety

Early Irish Monasticism[54]

Thom provides a thorough study on the formation and character of early Irish monasticism during the sixth through the eighth centuries that positively affected the growth of Christianity in Europe for centuries. Early Christian missionaries developed monastic rules and adapted their efforts to evangelize and make disciples of the native people. Thom describes how several select missionaries, namely Patrick, Columba and Columbanus, contributed to the rise of "The Golden Age of Monasticism" in Europe.[55] Thom identifies several practices that missionaries and monastic leaders pursued that demonstrated a systematic emphasis on an individual's growth in Christ-likeness and a movement to establish new churches through the making of disciples.

---

[54] Catherine Thom, *Early Irish Monasticism: An Understanding of its Cultural Roots* (New York, NY: T&T Clark, 2006).
[55] Thom, 34-35.

Irish Spirituality[56]

In this volume, the authors describe the uniqueness of Irish Christianity in the seventh and eighth centuries as the monastic movement spread through Ireland and elsewhere. The author describes how the Irish monastic system served as a social and educational center that improved the quality of life and developed many "disciples" from the teaching of the monastic founders and spiritual guides.[57] The important place of the monastic schools and in-depth Bible study are emphasized. The lives of Patrick and Columbanus are highlighted to describe their commitment to spread the gospel, train others, and grow the body of Christ. The authors record how Patrick and Columbanus systematically evangelized, trained new believers, and promoted spiritual growth and disciple-making movements through the commitment of the monastic community.

The Celtic Way of Evangelism[58]

In this book, Hunter explains how Celtic Christians ministered effectively to advance Christ's mission in their world and how the Western church today can emulate their methods. The author explains how early Irish monasticism did not follow the

---

[56] Michael Maher, ed., *Irish Spirituality* (Dublin, Ireland: Veritas Publications, 1981).
[57] Michael Curran, "Early Irish Monasticism," in *Irish Spirituality,* ed. Michael Maher (Dublin, Ireland: Veritas Publication, 1981), 20-21.
[58] George G. Hunter III, *The Celtic Way of Evangelism: How Christianity Can Reach the West . . . Again* (Nashville, TN: Abingdon Press, 2000).

Roman Church model but rather sought to evangelize the indigenous people of Ireland and beyond by making disciples and establishing local churches in culturally appropriate ways. Early missionary pioneers communicated Christianity in culturally appropriate ways to the Druids and affected many lives through their consistent and sacrificial examples of godliness. The message they brought was supported by the personal commitment, relationships and contextualized ministry modeled by the early missionaries. These characteristics of early Irish monasticism demonstrate the power of disciple making movements and the impact of committed disciples to enhance the spread of the gospel.

Primary Resources on Twelfth Century Cistercian Piety and Bernard of Clairvaux

The Cistercians[59]

Pennington describes how Cistercian monasticism grew from a few isolated monasteries to more than 360 at the death of Bernard of Clairvaux in 1153. The author claims that it was the school of spirituality, though mystical, that allowed Cistercian monasticism to gain an immense following and ongoing impact on Christian spirituality throughout the centuries.[60]

Pennington describes how personal mystical experience was central to Cistercian spirituality along with a prescribed

---

[59] M. Basil Pennington, "The Cistercians," in *Christian Spirituality,* eds. Bernard McGinn and John Meyendorff (New York, NY: The Crossroad Publishing Company, 1985).
[60] Pennington, 206.

regimen of ascetical living. The author focused on the monasteries founded by Bernard in Clairvaux and how Bernard and three other key Cistercian fathers developed the inner life and character of their disciples. Bernard's emphasis on systematic training, and on the person of Christ and his love, supports the important characteristics in the process of the making of holistic disciples.

Finding the Monk Within[61]

The author of this book supports the belief that Christians should draw upon the rich heritage of monastic spirituality. Sellner concentrates on the contribution of Cistercian monasticism and particularly of Bernard of Clairvaux in Chapter Ten, "Valley of Light—Bernard of Clairvaux." He describes how Bernard developed a Christ-centered focus on love and taught that the most important aspect of a Christian's life was their response to God's love. Bernard felt that the Christian's love for souls resulted in their desire to serve them and one's love for God was evidenced through the desire to cultivate the inner life through silence, solitude, and prayer. This focus on love is essential to the development and motivation involved in making holistic disciples and disciple-making movements.

---

[61] Edward C. Sellner, *Finding the Monk Within: Great Monastic Values for Today* (Mahwah, NJ: HiddenSpring, 2008).

The Spiritual Teaching of Bernard of Clairvaux[62]

In this volume, Sommerfeldt presents the major facets of Bernard's teaching based upon his original writings. Although the author's focus is to present the intellectual, philosophical, and mystical nature of Bernard's writings, the emphasis throughout is clearly on the Person of Christ and the development of the spiritual life of his followers. Bernard sought to stimulate his readers to actively contemplate key truths from God's Word to grow into Christ-likeness.

Two key themes characteristic of Bernard's writings are the development of humility and love. Bernard clearly looked to Jesus as the model and goal for all spiritual growth. Sommerfeldt demonstrates that Bernard taught that the type of spiritual life that Christ requires is an active life to be chosen and pursued. This is a life that lives out the love of Christ for others' benefit. He reveals how Bernard emphasized the need for a spiritual mentor to instruct and rebuke younger Christians. Significant to the thesis of this study is Bernard's teaching that loving service brings growth and joy in one's life. Spiritual growth and maturity is developed through sacrificial service to others, an essential emphasis in the development and character of holistic disciples.

---

[62] John R. Sommerfeldt, *The Spiritual Teaching of Bernard of Clairvaux: An Intellectual History of the Early Cistercian Order* (Kalamazoo, MI: Cistercian Publications, 1991).

Primary Resources on Seventeenth and Eighteenth Century German Pietists

Understanding Pietism[63]

In this book, the author seeks to describe the origins and legacy of Pietism from the seventeenth century to the present. Brown highlights the emphasis Pietist leaders placed on individual regeneration and sanctification, spiritual growth in community, biblical authority in daily life, godliness, and the believer's relationship with the Holy Spirit.

Brown highlights how Jacob Spener taught that the inward work of God in the life of the believer manifests itself in an outward pursuit of good works. He explains how the Pietists addressed the weakness in contemporary Lutheranism and promoted spiritual transformation and service to others.

German Pietism During the Eighteenth Century[64]

This book focuses on the teaching and legacy of August Hermann Francke, the influence of the Spener-Halle Pietist's center, and Zinzendorf's role in renewing the Moravian Church and spreading Pietism through a priority on world missions.

Francke was a primary and powerful voice in the development and spread of Pietism. Stoeffler delineates how the

---

[63] Dale W. Brown, *Understanding Pietism* (Nappanee, IN: Evangel Publishing House, 1996).
[64] F. Ernest Stoeffler, *German Pietism During the Eighteenth Century* (Leiden, Netherlands: E.J. Brill, 1973).

influence of Pietism grew through Francke's pulpit ministry, as a professor at the Pietist's university in Halle, and his advocacy for the educational, physical, and social needs of the downtrodden in society. Stoeffler describes Francke's understanding of the spiritual life and the practical and measurable outcomes that he felt should characterize a believer's "active" and intentional pursuit of maturity in Christ.[65] Francke's passion was to develop Christ-like character in the lives of believers.

Stoeffler also describes the innovative ways that Francke focused on the needs of individuals and society. Francke visited parishioners in their homes, hosted small group Bible studies, established innovative private schools and orphanages, and sent out missionaries to the East Indies through the cooperation of the King of Denmark. The author describes how the Moravian Church became part of the Pietist movement and how, led by Von Zinzendorf, they promoted a "Christocentric" faith that promoted the sending of missionaries to reach the marginalized and persecuted peoples of the known world.[66]

The Value of Theology[67]

In this master's thesis, Scott Way describes how the central difference between the teaching of Lutheranism and Pietism in the seventeenth and eighteenth centuries in Germany was related to the

---

[65] Stoeffler, 20-21.
[66] Stoeffler, 146.
[67] Scott W. Way, *The Value of Theology: Philipp Jakob Spener's Doctrine of Sanctification* (Master's Thesis product, Dallas Theological Seminary, 2006).

doctrine of sanctification. Way describes the common struggle believers face in striking a balance between "head" knowledge and "heart" obedient faith, between a theology based upon scholasticism and one based upon pietism. He delineates how Pietism developed in Germany as an effort to renew the Lutheran church from an exclusive focus on strict intellectual orthodoxy to a life-changing faith.[68]

The author explains how Spener's Pietism presented a "holistic approach" that prioritized both knowledge (head) and obedience (heart) to grow in a biblically balanced way into Christ-likeness.[69] He traces the development of orthodox faith and scholasticism that resulted from the Protestant Reformation and the drive for doctrinal fidelity. Way describes the influence of Francke and Von Zinzendorf in promoting good works, social involvement and missions, and their influence on John Wesley's ministry and American Protestantism.

The main focus of this book is on Spener's life, ministry and theological distinctive. Way analyzes Spener's development of the *Collegia Pietatis* and his influential work, *Pia Desideria.* Way's primary purpose is to explain Spener's core teaching in the areas of soteriology and sanctification. He emphasizes that Spener taught and lived what can be described as a holistic view of theology and practice which many evangelicals share today. This analysis helps to support the thesis of this study.

---

[68] Way, 3.
[69] Way, 12ff.

Primary Resources on Dietrich Bonheoffer's Legacy

The Cost of Discipleship[70]

The Cost of Discipleship, written by Bonhoeffer in 1937, is his classic treatise on the nature of discipleship. In the first section of the book, Bonhoeffer describes how God's grace in salvation is related to discipleship. The author is known for his strong criticism of "cheap grace." He states that, "Cheap grace is the preaching of forgiveness without requiring repentance, baptism without church discipline, communion without confession, absolution without personal confession. Cheap grace is grace without discipleship, grace without the cross, and grace without Jesus Christ, living and incarnate."[71] Bonhoeffer defines the biblical nature of a disciple in terms of "costly" grace through obedience, sacrifice and life-long commitment.

In the first section of his book, Bonhoeffer examines the "Sermon on the Mount" (Matthew 5-7). He takes the reader through each section of the Sermon, focusing on the teaching of Christ related to the life of his disciples and the nature of discipleship. Both (1) the character qualities—the "being" of a disciple and (2) the life priorities—the "doing" of a disciple, are described in this section.

---

[70] Dietrich Bonhoeffer, *The Cost of Discipleship* (New York, NY: Macmillan Publishing Company, 1963).
[71] Bonhoeffer, 47.

In the last two sections of the book, Bonhoeffer describes the disciple of Jesus as a "messenger" (based on Matthew 9:35—10:42), and describes the role of the church in the life and growth of a disciple. He identifies several characteristics of a disciple from the account of Jesus sending out the Twelve to minister to the lost sheep of Israel. He also describes the disciple's life as intricately related to the church. Bonhoeffer makes a clear emphasis on the visible acts of obedience of a disciple to witness to the truth, serve others, and obey the will of God. A disciple functions in community as he or she follows Christ and lives out the likeness of their model, the incarnate Christ. Much of Bonhoeffer's thoughts on "costly" grace, discipleship, and living for the benefit of others support the concepts of the making of holistic disciples and the place of disciple-making movements.

Bonhoeffer for the Missional Church[72]

Patrick Franklin, in his master's thesis, presents an extensive comparison between the ecclesiology of the missional church and that of Dietrich Bonhoeffer. In evaluating Bonhoeffer's views on ecclesiology, the author also presents Bonhoeffer's beliefs on the doctrines of sanctification, discipleship, and Christology.

---

[72] Patrick S. Franklin, *Bonhoeffer for the Missional Church: An Exposition and Critique of the Missional Church Movement's Ecclesiology in Light of the Ecclesiology of Dietrich Bonhoeffer* (Master Thesis, Regent College, 2004).

Franklin highlights Bonheoffer's views on the church and Jesus' desire that his followers function as witnesses and lights of Jesus Christ to the world. He notes that Bonhoeffer believed that the church as Christ's corporate community should proclaim God's word through both verbal witness and good deeds. Bonhoeffer taught that Christ is "incarnated" into the lives of believers who proclaim his word through both their words and good deeds. The central aspect of Bonhoeffer's theological perspective was the importance of understanding Christology and how it informed and influenced his teaching on discipleship and ecclesiology.[73]

Bonhoeffer emphasized the need for disciples to live responsibly in the midst of the world. Ministries of loving service characterize the activity of the church as it presents an active witness of God's love with the gospel message. A significant emphasis in Bonhoeffer's ecclesiology is that the church exists for others. He believed that genuine discipleship occurs when disciples are actively engaged in the world and willing to experience suffering and rejection like Christ in his crucifixion. Genuine discipleship is not detached spirituality but following Christ in the way of the cross.[74]

---

[73] Franklin, 132-35.
[74] Franklin, 197.

Anxious Souls Will Ask[75]

In this book, the author presents Bonhoeffer's emphasis that the spiritual life was centered on the Person and work of Christ. Matthews emphasizes Bonhoeffer's belief that "the church is the church only when it exists for others."[76] He notes that Bonhoeffer believed that Christ is present in the world through his church and that he is known in the world through both prayer and action. Bonhoeffer believed that spiritual life and maturity should result in personal fulfillment and a deeper meaning in life. Bonhoeffer claimed that a disciple's fulfillment and meaning in life is a result of his love for his neighbor and sacrificial service to others. Bonhoeffer taught that the church should share in the problems and challenges of modern society and life, not dominating or controlling, but providing loving service in the likeness of Christ.

Literature Review on Resources Related to the Mission of Christ

Introduction

Two important movements in American evangelical Christianity directly address, in some way, the nature and fulfillment of the mission of Christ in the world. One popular and growing area of literature and local church practice is the concept of the "missional church." Another emphasis primarily advocated

---

[75] John W. Matthews, *Anxious Souls Will Ask: The Christ-Centered Spirituality of Dietrich Bonheoffer* (Grand Rapids, MI: William B. Eerdmans Publishing Company, 2005).

[76] Matthews, *Anxious Souls Will Ask*, 21.

through cross-cultural mission strategy is the concept outlined in "Church Planting Movements."

**Primary Resources on the
Missional Church**

Church Between Gospel & Culture[77]

George Hunsberger and Craig Van Gelder are two key scholars in the "missional church movement" (MCM) and were key founders of the Gospel and Our Culture Network (GOCN).[78] Hunsberger and Van Gelder serve as editors of this book. The authors assert that there is a crisis in the American church that has caused it to be disconnected from the changing culture and *to be* ineffective in communicating with and ministering to the world. Based upon this conclusion, the authors promote the need for the development of a missionary or missional church for the gospel to impact the culture in relevant ways. The authors believe that the

---

[77] George R. Hunsberger and Craig Van Gelder, eds., *Church Between Gospel & Culture: The Emerging Mission in North America (*Grand Rapids, MI: William B. Eerdmans Publishing Company, 1996).

[78] "The Gospel and Our Culture. A network to provide *useful research* regarding the encounter between the gospel and our culture, and to encourage *local action* for transformation in the life and witness of the church. What faithful action is required of us in this kind of world? The question compels three kinds of activity which give shape to the missionary way the church is called to live: 1) *Social and cultural analysis.* What kind of setting are we in and how do we understand its importance in light of God's mission in the world? 2) *Biblical and theological reflection.* As we take this setting seriously, how are we ourselves faced with the meaning of the gospel in new ways? 3) *Vision for the church and its mission.* What kind of church do we need to be to show what it means to believe the gospel, and to live and speak as though it is true?" http://www.gocn.org/network/about.html (accessed July 28, 2010).

local church by nature and design is missional and should emulate the priorities and activities of foreign missionaries. They challenge the North American church to pursue a missionary-like perspective as it seeks to meet the needs of people in its community.

In addition to Hunsberger and Van Gelder, several of the contributing authors (i.e. David Lowes Watson, Charles C. West, James V. Brownson, William A. Dyrness, and Alan Roxburgh) also believe that the holistic gospel has been weakened and needs to be restored to effectively communicate to a postmodern culture. The missionary nature and agenda of the church is discussed and a call is made for the church to study and adapt to the cultural realities of North American society. The authors call for a redefinition of what it means to be the church, a missional church that presents a relevant gospel to the world.

Missional Church: A Vision for the Sending of the Church in North America.[79]

Darrell Guder is the "project coordinator" and editor of this book and authored three of the nine chapters. GOCN research, along with the writings of Bishop Lesslie Newbigin, formed the basis for this volume. There is a strong emphasis on the missionary nature of God as expressed in the Trinity. It teaches that each

---

[79] Darrell L. Guder, Project Coordinator and Editor, *Missional Church: A Theological Vision for the Sending of the Church in North America* (Grand Rapids, MI: William B. Eerdmans Publishing Company, 1998).

member of the Trinity is active in sending the church into the world as God's missionary witness.

Guder and the other five authors present in this volume the findings of a research project they were involved in "to explore the possible shape and themes of a missiological ecclesiology for North America."[80] A central focus to the developing missional ecclesiology was on Jesus' teaching on the reign of God. The missional church participates with Christ in advancing the reign of God as it is sent into the world.

Throughout the book, the emphasis is given to the nature of the church as community, the body of Christ, led by the Spirit. The church is defined as the people of God sent to announce the gospel and represent the reign of God, which is both present through the church and fully expressed in the future. The church is sent out as an apostle or missionary to the world, sent by God to defeat the enemy and complete Jesus' ministry.

The Essence of the Church: A Community Created by the Spirit[81]

In this book, the author examines the biblical definition of a church with the goal of defining how it can improve in fulfilling God's redemptive purposes in the world. The author writes to help

---

[80] Guder, 8.
[81] Craig Van Gelder, *The Essence of the Church: A Community Created by the Spirit* (Grand Rapids, MI: Baker Books, 2000).

the church become relevant in the North American context as it serves to accomplish God's mission in the world.

Van Gelder advocates for viewing the church as intrinsically missionary, the Spirit led body of Christ in the world. Mission is not something that the church does but is something that the church is. Van Gelder believes this new understanding of a missiological ecclesiology defines the nature of all of theology. From this missional ecclesiology, Van Gelder elaborates on the *missio Dei* ("mission of God") and the reign of God in the world to redeem all of creation.[82]

Van Gelder asserts the kingdom of God as the reality that enacts the redemptive reign of God throughout all of creation. The church demonstrates the character of God's kingdom as it participates with God in his redemptive purpose in the world.

Primary Resources on Church Planting Movements

The phrase, *disciple-making movements*, refers to the process of reproducing obedient disciples of Christ who faithfully repeat the process among all peoples resulting in the formation of local churches. Much of the literature reviewed demonstrated an understanding that Christ's great commission command to make disciples should result in an ongoing practice to reproduce disciples. The term *disciple-making movements* in this study refers to Christ's divinely ordained process to make disciples who

---

[82]Van Gelder, 33.

reproduce more disciples among all people groups. Disciples who are taught to obey all that Christ has commanded will engage in a self-replicating movement that forms the foundation of Christ's promise to build his church. As disciples are made—local churches are established; as local churches are established—more disciples are made, and the disciple-making movement continues.

At this point in the study, references to *disciple-making movements* were discovered only on various Internet web sites, the majority of which were created in 2010 and 2011.[83] The phrase, *disciple-making movements*, was not found in any of the printed literature reviewed. However, the governing principle that disciples are made to grow and to reproduce or multiply other disciples is clearly the mandated strategy taught by Christ and reinforced by teaching and examples throughout the New Testament (Matthew 28:19; 2 Timothy 2:2, etc.). As demonstrated in the Internet search, there is a growing emphasis on building *church planting movements* (typically in reference to cross-cultural

---

[83] Data results for Google search of "disciple-making movements," (accessed August 23, 2011). Of the over 9,000 results from the Google search for the phrase *disciple-making movements,* the majority of these references equate *disciple-making movements* with the *church-planting movements* (C.P.M.) concept, making no distinction between the two. Most of these web sites are influenced by the perspective of David Garrison and the International Mission Board of the Southern Baptist Convention and their emphasis on *church planting movements* (see Chapter 5). Most of these sites limit their understanding on the importance of disciple-making movements and see biblical discipleship only as *one of several* necessary elements of the church planting process. The majority of these sites did not support the perspective that the heart of Christ's mission is the making of holistic disciples who form disciple-making movements as the divinely ordained process to build his church (Matthew 16:18; 28:19).

missions), and *missional church movements* (usually in reference to churches within the United States). The conclusion of this study is that the biblical mandate and divine plan of Christ to build his church and make disciples of the nations is best accomplished through pursuing *disciple-making movements*.

Most of the literature mentioned previously in this chapter that deals with the topics of disciple-making and discipleship refers to reproducing disciples, the concept referred to as *disciple-making movements*. Several of the works listed in this review are examples of literature that, although not using the term *disciple-making movement*, do describe the priority and process involved.

Conclusion

The purpose of this literature review was to survey and synthesize the pertinent literature available that supports the thesis of this study. The literature review focused on the three major areas of this study: [1] disciple-making movements, [2] the making of holistic disciples, and [3] both concepts as they relate to the mission of Christ. The literature reviewed focused on the general topics of missions, discipleship and the missional church. This study included the review of published and unpublished material as well as numerous journal articles, master's theses and doctoral dissertations. Numerous web sites were also reviewed that included helpful articles and resources primarily on the missional church.

The literature review was written to present the best four or five examples of pertinent literature in five specific areas of the study. These areas of study include the biblical nature of a disciple and the mission of Christ; disciple-making and discipleship; the examples and lessons from four periods and individuals of church history; information on the missional church; and emphasis on the subject of church planting and development. The significant amount of literature reviewed supports and strengthens the thesis of this study. It is interesting to note that there was no direct reference to the phrases "holistic disciples" or "disciple-making movements" in any of the literature reviewed. However, the essence of these concepts was referred to with other terms and phrases in some of the literature, and there was sufficient material reviewed that can be used to support the major components of the study's thesis.

CHAPTER 3
THE MISSION OF CHRIST IN THE WORLD

Introduction

From Genesis to Revelation the Scriptures reveal the mission of the triune God to actively engage and redeem mankind for his glory. This redemptive record has been referred to in Latin as the "*missio Dei*," or the "mission of God." In evangelical Christianity today, there is a growing emphasis for believers to become "missional" by aligning themselves with the triune God and his mission in the world. Although many believers desire to join God in his mission, there are a wide variety of options on what precisely constitutes God's mission. If believers are to join God meaningfully and obediently in his mission, an accurate understanding of what the Bible reveals about God's mission and the role of Christ is paramount.

The thesis of this study is that the making of holistic disciples and the creation of disciple-making movements constitute the biblical teaching on the mission of God as revealed in the New Testament. Understanding the basis and significance of God's mission is dependent on a correct understanding of Scripture. An accurate biblical hermeneutic will enable believers to discover God's mission and align their lives to accomplish his purposes. In this chapter, the author defines the mission of Christ. After an overview of the author's hermeneutic, the nature and scope of the mission of Christ based on his post-resurrection authority and Lordship will be examined. Finally, the priority of the mission of Christ to make disciples of all peoples will be explored along with its implications for believers today.

Theological Framework for Understanding the Mission of Christ

Introduction

The mission of Christ presents a divine picture of reality as defined by God. It presents a compelling motivation for believers to align their lives with Christ's priorities as revealed in his word. As Hesselgrave states, "the primary question in missions, then, is not 'What in the world is God doing?' but 'What in the Word is God doing?' What He is doing in the world is what we find him doing first in the Word."[84]

There are a diversity of opinions, perspectives, and positions about what constitutes the mission of God in the world. Some contemporary writers believe that any activity pursued in the name of God qualifies as a legitimate candidate for mission. This study suggests that the mission of God is the central and foundational message of the Bible. In the New Testament, God's mission is revealed in the person and work of Christ so that all believers can obediently live for his purposes.

---

[84] David J. Hesselgrave, "Challenging the Church to World Mission," *International Journal of Frontier Mission* 13:1 (January-March 1996), 29-30.

The Theological Importance of Understanding Salvation History

The term "salvation history" (or "redemption history") refers to the progressive revelation of God's plan to offer salvation to mankind[85] as recorded throughout the Scriptures. It is important to understand the unique ways God has interacted with different groups of people throughout biblical history. Salvation history traces how God has initiated a relationship with people since creation to offer salvation to human beings.[86] Through an understanding of God's progressive revelation, the interpreter of Scripture can identify how God sovereignly administered and applied salvation to mankind based upon the message God chose to reveal to mankind at a certain age or time.[87]

The distinct period of salvation history centered upon the death, burial, resurrection and ascension of Christ is called the "church age." This age was initiated through the baptism of the Holy Spirit at the feast of Pentecost (Acts 2) following Christ's ascension to heaven. It is in this current age of salvation history

---

[85] For the sake of clarity concerning references to females or males as a collective group, the author of this study has chosen to use the terms mankind or man. Although other terms such as humankind or humans could also be used, the terms mankind or man are intended to refer to all people and all ethnic groups of people in a way that is as concise as possible. The same principle holds true for the use of male pronouns to refer to individuals, regardless of gender.
[86] Craig A. Blaising and Darrell L. Bock, *Progressive Dispensationalism* (Wheaton, IL: A BridgePoint Book, 1993), 112-13.
[87] Ryrie, *Dispensationalism Today*, 131.

that God has chosen to manifest his salvation for mankind only through faith in Christ.[88]

Hermeneutical Principles for Identifying the Mission of Christ

The mission of Christ is not a mystery but a clearly revealed commandment for Christ's followers. It is the conviction of this author that an accurate process for interpreting Scripture is found through a literal, grammatical, contextual, historical, and progressive revelation hermeneutic.[89] This literal hermeneutic enables the believer to accurately understand and apply God's revelation to his life.[90]

Many experts in eschatology believe that the theological framework known as "dispensationalism" best presents a consistent understanding of salvation history, based on a literal hermeneutic.[91] Dispensationalism teaches that God revealed his message in Scripture through a planned "succession of different dispensations throughout history."[92] Dispensationalism teaches that God has worked in different periods of history in specific and observable ways toward mankind to achieve his *missio Dei*. Dispensationalists believe that in the current dispensation or period,

---

[88] Blaising and Bock, 112.
[89] It is acknowledged that some biblical scholars within evangelicalism uphold a high view of Scripture and its literal, grammatical, contextual, and historic hermeneutic, and may arrive at a different view that does not support the dispensational interpretation of salvation history and the mission of Christ.
[90] Ryrie, *Dispensationalism Today*, 97.
[91] Ryrie, *Dispensationalism Today*, 97.
[92] Blaising and Bock, 14.

God's revealed will for mankind's salvation is uniquely provided through the person and mission of Christ.

Dispensationalism identifies the Church as a new work of God in salvation history and distinct from national Israel. This work of God is referred to as a "mystery." The term "mystery" does not refer to something that cannot be understood or discovered, but to something kept hidden or secret and later revealed. Jesus referred to the "mysteries of the kingdom of heaven" (Matthew 13:11) that were "given" by him to his disciples while being kept from the nation of Israel ("them").[93] Referring to this mystery, Derickson notes from Matthew 13,

> When Jesus said that "many prophets and righteous men desired to see what you see, and did not see it, and to hear what you hear, and did not hear it" (v. 17), He indicated that the Old Testament prophets were not recipients of the truths He was revealing to his disciples at that time. What Jesus was describing in the parables the Old Testament prophets would like to have seen and heard, but they had not and could not.[94]

The Apostle Paul later described how Christ's followers were heirs of that mystery as members of Christ's Body, the church. Dickerson continues,

> Paul described "mystery" in this same sense ["here"]. In other generations [it] was not made known to the sons of men, as it has now been revealed to his holy apostles and prophets in the Spirit" (Eph. 3:5). Further it was also kept "hidden" in past ages and generations and only in Paul's

---

[93] Gary W. Derickson, "The New Testament Church as a Mystery," *Bibliotheca Sacra* 166: 664 (October-December 2009), 436-45.
[94] Derickson, 437.

day was it "manifested to his saints," the church (Col. 1:26). Remaining unrevealed "for ages," it had "been hidden in God" (Eph. 3:9). This mystery was something He did not want his prophets or people to know before its outworking in history. It was unknowable, not because it could not be understood, but because its information was unavailable for analysis. [95]

The reality of the church as God's unique mission in salvation history was kept hidden in the mind and plan of God until he was ready to reveal it.[96] In this new reality, the church, Jesus began to describe God's new and unique program (mission) for this age without detailing specific information concerning its precise nature and function (Matthew 16:17-18).[97] The mystery is that Jews and Gentiles are now the focus of God's mission and are equal members of his church through faith in Jesus. This constitutes the new and supreme aspect of God's mission that was never a reality for the Old Testament saints or the nation of Israel."[98]

---

[95] Derickson, 437.

[96] Derickson, 442.

[97] Derickson, 443. Matthew presented God's kingdom program "in three aspects. First, the earthly literal kingdom was offered to Israel in the person of Jesus, the Messiah, at his first coming. Second, the kingdom was postponed because Israel rejected its Messiah. This postponed kingdom will be established at Christ's second coming. Third, Christ Jesus is now engaged in building his church, composed of those who in this age are the heirs of the kingdom, p. 443.

[98] Ryrie, *Dispensationalism Today*, 135.

The Mission of Christ in Relationship to the Kingdom of God

There are clear differences of interpretation on how the kingdom of God is related to the mission of Christ and his church. After being rejected by Israel, Christ promised that he would "build his church," (Matthew 16:18). Before ascending to heaven, he told his disciples that the Father alone established a future time for the kingdom based on the Father's authority and timetable. Their place in Christ's mission was to be his witnesses in all the world through the coming power of the Holy Spirit (Acts 1:6-8). Christ's new mission is consequently a future work to his earthly life and ministry and is not the same work of God as the kingdom about which he had just been teaching them. Christ's mission is different from God the Father's future promised reign over Israel as promised in Scripture. Christ's mission is to be characterized by a worldwide witness about him, not on the restoration of the kingdom determined by God the Father[99] Hesselgrave notes,

> Though God is always building his kingdom, he is in this age building his church as an expression of that kingdom. Nowhere in Scripture are we specifically called upon to obey "kingdom mission" in the way we are called upon to obey the great commission. "Kingdom mission" was and remains uniquely the mission of Christ, though we are to witness to it in very practical ways. "Great Commission mission" is uniquely ours and requires us to make disciples by preaching, baptizing, and teaching the peoples of the earth. Christ will bring his kingdom and so he teaches believers to pray that God's kingdom will come *on earth as*

---

[99] Ryrie, *Basic Theology*, 397-98.

it is now in heaven. Christ is *building* his church so he commands believers to witness and work for its completion now and in this age.[100]

The Kingdom is a reality of God's work and represents the universal reign of God, throughout the history through which his blessings on all mankind are experienced. The church is the assembly of those who have been purchased by the blood of Christ through faith. Believers in Christ live under the reign of God through the lordship of Christ. In Christ, believers have entered into the spiritual reality, blessings, and divinely ordained plan for their lives as members of his body.[101] The King, who as Lord has all authority to build his church and makes disciples who proclaim salvation in God's Kingdom, has been given all authority over the lives of his followers. Ladd observes, "There can be no spiritual reign of God in this age without a church, and there can be no church without God's Kingdom but they remain two distinguishable concepts: the rule of God and the redemption and fellowship of men and women."[102]

A majority of dispensational scholars make a further distinction between the promised future messianic kingdom and Israel's role in that kingdom with the mission of Christ in the world during this age. Toussaint clarifies this point by stating:

> In the Gospels and Acts, the Lord Jesus is offered to Israel as Messiah. The coming of the kingdom was contingent

---

[100] David J. Hesselgrave, *Paradigms in Conflict*, 347-48.
[101] George Eldon Ladd, *Theology of the New Testament* (Grand Rapids, MI: William B Eerdmans Publishing House, 1993), 117.
[102] Ladd, 117.

upon their response. Because of Israel's negative response, God is now working with the church distinct from Israel (Rom. 9-11; Eph. 2:11-22, 3:1-12). The church, therefore, is a mystery, never prophesied in the Old Testament (Eph. 3:4-6). It is neither a 'new Israel' nor a new form of the kingdom.[103]

The truth that the church is a work of God, distinct and different from God's future kingdom plan for Israel, does not mean that Christ's church is unrelated to other purposes of God. Although the unique mission of God in this age is characterized by the post-resurrection authority and lordship of Christ, it is incorporated into God's overall plan for mankind and Christ's universal reign in the world.[104]

The Unique Nature, Purpose and Task of the Mission of Christ in the World

Introduction

The mission of Christ is the unique work of God, distinct in nature, purpose, and task from Christ's promised kingdom. Christ's mission, as revealed in the New Testament, is now the singular focus of God's work in the world based upon Christ's death, burial, resurrection and ascension (Matthew 16:17-18; 28:18-20). His purpose is to establish communities of disciples, congregations of followers, from all nations.

---

[103] Stanley D. Toussaint, "Israel and the Church of a Traditional Dispensationalist," in *Three Central Issues in Contemporary Dispensationalism*, ed. Herbert W. Bateman IV (Grand Rapids, MI: Kregel Publications, 1999), 249.
[104] Charles C. Ryrie, *Dispensationalism Today*, 144.

From the Gospel accounts, the Gospel of Matthew presents the most comprehensive summary of the promises and commands that define the mission of Christ. From Matthew's account, we see that Christ based his mission on his promise to build his church (Matthew 16:18) on his sacrificial death for mankind and on his commandment to his followers to make obedient disciples of all people (Matthew 28:19). Therefore, this study understands the essence of Christ's mission as the spreading of the Gospel and the making of disciples from all peoples, resulting in disciple-making churches among all peoples. The following material explains in greater depth the unique mission of Christ, based on the person of Christ and his plan for mankind during this age.

The Authority, Lordship, and Christ-Centered Mission in the World

Through Christ's mission, God is glorified and the Lord Jesus receives honor, blessing and praise from multitudes composed of all ethnic peoples, nations and tongues, rescued through faith in Christ at the end of the age (Revelation 5:9-14). In Matthew 28:18 Jesus states, "All authority has been given to Me in heaven and on earth." The word "authority" denotes Jesus' divinely bestowed and unlimited power, authority and right, as God's Son and mankind's savior to freely act. Christ's right to rule was mutually invested in him in perfect agreement between the Father, the Son, and the Holy Spirit.[105]

Jesus was given all authority over all of creation. The aorist form of the verb "to give" (εδοθη) in Matthew 28:18 denotes sovereign power and authority that had already been given to him. Plummer notes that it is "not mere power or might (δυναμις), but *'authority'* as something which is his by right, conferred upon him by one who has the right to bestow it (Revelation 2:27)."[106] It is the authority of the King of kings and the Lord of lords. With this authority, Jesus is declared as the sovereign Ruler who initiates a new age and exercises universal dominion through his followers for the making of disciples of all people (Revelation 5:12-14; 19:6). In Matthew's gospel Christ is presented as the "the King of the Jews" (2:2; 21:4-5; 27:37), fulfilling the messianic promises. Based on his sacrificial death and resurrection, he is presented as God's appointed and empowered Lord over all created beings, his followers and all nations (c.f. Philippians 2:6-11).[107]

Wilkins highlights the "all-inclusive" scope of Christ's authority from Matthew 28:18-20 as the declaration of his missional purpose for this age. The repetition of the adjective "all" (πασ—"all authority," "all nations," "all things," and "all days"), provides a comprehensive declaration of Christ's Lordship over

---

[105] D. Edmond Hiebert, "An Expository Study of Matthew 28:16-20," *Bibliotheca Sacra* 149: 595 (July- September, 1992), 346.
[106] Alfred Plummer, *An Exegetical Commentary on the Gospel According to S. Matthew* (Grand Rapids, MI: Wm. B. Eerdmans Publishing Company, 1953), 428-29.
[107] Hiebert, 345.

every aspect of his followers' lives.[108] Christ's authority is focused in his right to rule over the lives of all believers so that they obediently carry the gospel and make holistic disciples of the nations.[109]

Christ's universal post-resurrection authority forms the basis of his mission. Heibert states that, "Because of this authority, Jesus has the right to issue his followers their 'marching orders,' but he also has the ability to help them carry out those orders."[110] The mandate to "make disciples" given by Christ to his followers is a divine command, given by the One who possesses and has gained the right to rule over the universe.

Wilkins provides a summary of Jesus' declaration of authority in Matthew 28:18:

> 1) Jesus now possesses all authority. In his earthly ministry Jesus declared his authority as the Son of Man to forgive sin (9:6) and to reveal the Father (11:27). Now as the risen Messiah he clearly alludes to his fulfillment of Daniel's prophecy of the Son of Man who has been given all authority, glory and power, who is rightly worshipped by all nations, and whose dominion and kingdom last forever (Dan. 7:13-14). Jesus can make this claim only if he is fully God, because the entire universe is contained in the authority delegated to him.
> 2) This authority, as emphasized by the (divine) passive voice, 'has been given' to him by the Father. The Son of God is the mediatorial King through whom all of God's

---

[108] Michael J. Wilkins "Matthew," in *The NIV Application Commentary: From Biblical Text to Contemporary Life*, ed. Terry Muck (Grand Rapids, MI: Zondervan, 2004), 951.

[109] Hiebert, 347.

[110] Craig L. Blomberg. *Matthew*. The New American Commentary, vol. 22 (Nashville, Tennessee: Broadman Press, 1992), 431.

authority is mediated. The resurrected Jesus appears before the disciples to initiate a new order to existence that anticipates his future glorious exaltation and enthronement at God's right hand (Luke 24:51; Acts 1:9; Phil. 2:9-11). 3) As the One with all authority, Jesus rules the plan of establishing God's kingdom throughout the earth. The particularism of the gospel message restricted to Israel during the earthly mission is fulfilled and lifted, as he now authoritatively directs his disciples to a universal mission.[111]

Christ Is the Lord of His Church

The title that appropriately describes Jesus' authority and mission in this age is "Lord." The title "Lord" comes from the Greek term "κυρίος" with the basic meaning of supremacy. Jesus used the title "Lord" to delineate an important characteristic of his relationship to his followers in Mark 2:28, 11:3, and 12:37. In Mark 12:36-37, Jesus refers to King David's use of the term "Lord" in Psalm 110:1 where David's "son," the promised coming all-powerful Messiah, is called the "κμρίος" ("Lord") in the Greek version of the Old Testament (The Septuagint). This is one of several Scriptures that Jesus used referring to himself during his earthly ministry that led believers to think of Jesus as their coming Messiah, the divine κμρίος.[112]

With the coming of the Holy Spirit recorded in Acts 2, Christ's promised church becomes a reality and believers begin to refer to Jesus as their "Lord." Authors Blaising and Bock

---

[111] Wilkins, "Matthew," 950-51.
[112] Ladd, 169.

emphasize that as the source of salvation for all mankind Christ is now recognized as the divine Lord who saves:

> On the basis of Jesus' current authority over all, Peter makes his emphatic call to the crowd to repent and be baptized in the name of Jesus Christ (Acts 2:38). Salvation's benefits are so totally in Jesus' hands that sacred rites are now carried out in his name. Those who would come to God must come through Jesus. The Lord on whom one must call to be saved (Joel 2 and Acts 2:21) is Jesus, the Lord at God's right hand (Psalm 110 and Acts 2:34-46). Jesus' ascension elevates him to the point where what was said of Yahweh in the Old Testament can now be said just as easily about Jesus! The vindication is complete, and the rule of the Lord Christ over salvation benefits is absolute.[113]

The title "Lord" is a clear and direct reference to Jesus' deity. Peter, citing Joel 2:32, accentuates the power of the Lord Jesus to save in his sermon in Acts 2:21-36. Those who call on the Lord are to be baptized in the name of Jesus (Acts 2:38) in order to be saved (Acts 2:40). Only Christ can save sinners and salvation is available to all who "call upon the name of Lord Christ" (Acts, 22:16; 1 Corinthians 1:2; Romans 10:13; 2 Timothy 2:22). Christ died for the sins of humanity "so every knee should bow, in heaven and on earth and under the earth, and every tongue confess that Jesus Christ is Lord, to the glory of God the Father" (Philippians 2:10-

---

[113] Craig A Blaising and Darrell L. Bock, editors, *Dispensationalism, Israel and the Church: A Search for Definition* (Grand Rapids, MI: Zondervan Publishing House, 1992), 54.

11).[114] Because of his sacrificial death, all authority is his and all people and nations are subject to his Lordship and rule.

Christ's lordship is a key factor in motivating obedient disciples to submit humbly to him. Jesus stated that the greatest commandment of the Law is to "love the Lord your God with all your heart and with all your soul and with all your mind" (Matthew 22:23-40; Mark 12:28-34). Bietenhard observes that, "In reply to the Jewish teacher's question about the great commandment Jesus declares that their *kyrios* is to be given complete and undivided attention."[115]

Wilkins summarizes what Jesus meant when he announced that all authority in heaven and earth had been given to him. Wilkins rightfully understands that Christ's universal authority is demonstrated through his right to rule in the life of every believer:

> A new authority or regime is established in the hearts of Jesus' followers. That authority affects all that we are, in all that we do, in all spheres of life. The motif of the kingdom means that there is not a scintilla of life that does not come under the authority of Jesus Christ. Fundamentally we are kingdom people, which means that Jesus is Lord in our hearts, homes and workplace; our attitudes, thoughts, and desires; our relationships and moral decisions; our political convictions and social conscience. In every area of our interior life, personal relationships or social involvement, we seek to know and live the mind and will of God.[116]

---

[114] Blaising and Bock, *Progressive Dispensationalism*, 244.

[115] H. Bietenhard, "Lord" in *The New Testament Dictionary of New Testament Theology*, General Editor Colin Brown, vol. 2 (Grand Rapids, MI: The Zondervan Corporation, 1976), 516.

[116] Ogden, 28.

Frost and Hirsch declare, "Here lies the interface between the disciple and God. It is through the redeeming lordship of Jesus. And when we talk of lordship, we are talking about God's redemptive claim on our lives and our existential response to this claim."[117]

Defining the Mission of Christ in the Church Age

Contemporary evangelical literature delineates a variety of definitions of Christ's mission. Christopher Wright provides a description of "mission" on which a biblical definition of mission could be understood. Wright's basic definition of mission is "a long-term purpose or goal that is to be achieved through proximate objectives and planned actions."[118]

To understand the nature of Christ's mission, it is vital to recognize that the purpose and fulfillment of his mission is centered solely on the person and redemptive work of Christ. Through Jesus' obedience and sacrificial death, God's theocentric purpose and work in salvation is fulfilled in that "God was reconciling the world to himself in Christ" (2 Corinthians 5:19).[119] Peters states,

> While Christianity is God-centered, it is so only as God is known in and through Jesus Christ. Therefore, it can be stated that Christianity is Christocentric. Christianity is God-centered in orientation and purpose and Christ-

---

[117] Michael Frost and Alan Hirsch, *ReJesus: A Wild Messiah for the Missional Church* (Peabody, MA: Hendrickson Publishers, Inc., 2009), 135.
[118] Wright, *The Mission of God*, 23.
[119] Wright, *The Mission of God*, 66.

centered in revelation and salvation. Christ in revelation and mediation becomes the foundation for Christian mission.[120]

The Christ-centered nature of Jesus' mission is essential to the thesis of this study. Christ alone defines and determines the goals of his mission. Jesus' mission is clear, strategic and quantifiable only because it is founded on the person, work and word of Christ.[121] Ott and Strauss underscore the importance of Christ's great commission.

> The intimate connection between Christ's life and work and the Great Commission makes inescapable the conclusion that the missionary mandate is not simply one among many good things that the church should do . . . . This mandate is the climax of Jesus' teaching, a logical consequence of his redemptive work, his marching orders for the church, and his parting words as the threshold of a new era in salvation history.[122]

Some scholars promote a broader understanding of the mission of Christ than the making and reproducing of obedient disciples and the building of his church. Some appeal to other scriptural passages, rather than the great commission passages, to define the nature of the mission of Christ and his church. Other scholars assert that the mission of the church is to emulate the Messiah's pre-crucifixion ministry by prioritizing the meeting of

---

[120] George Peters, *A Biblical Theology of Missions* (Chicago: Moody Press, 1972), 30-31.

[121] Craig Ott and Stephen J. Strauss, *Encountering Theology of Mission: Biblical Foundations, Historical Developments, and Contemporary Issues* (Grand Rapids, MI: Baker Academic, 2010), 40-41.

[122] Ott and Strauss, 41.

physical and social needs of people, citing passages like Luke 4:18-19 and Luke 7:22. Still other scholars claim that the great commission account in John 20:21 provides a more complete understanding of Christ's mission—to bring peace (*shalom*) between God and mankind, and between people themselves. Hesselgrave, referring to the perspective of John Stott, states:

> It has been argued that the traditional understanding of the Great Commission is faulty. According to this line of reasoning the "crucial form" of the Great Commission is the Johannine. "As the Father hath sent me, even so send I you" (John 20:21). In this statement, it is maintained, Jesus made his own mission a model of ours ("as the Father hath sent me, so send I you'). This does not mean that we become *saviors*. But it does mean that we become *servants* . . . The mission encompasses all that the church is sent into the world to do, including humanitarian service and the quest for better social structures. In short, according to this view, social and political activities are *partners* of evangelism and church growth in the Christian mission.[123]

Some scholars believe that the heart of the mission of Christ is founded upon addressing mankind's material, social, political and religious needs.[124] Hesselgrave counters this understanding of mission:

> As evangelicals, we agree that the Great Commission applies to us today. We also agree that the great commission constitutes an authoritative command and is not to be interpreted according to the vagaries of the contemporary agendas of either the world or the churches. But if we do not exercise care, confusion growing out of

---

[123] David J. Hesselgrave, "Confusion Concerning the Great Commission," *Evangelical Missions Quarterly* 15:4 (October 1979): 201.
[124] Moreau, Corwin and McGee, 74.

> unwarranted exegesis and prioritizing will first distract and then deter us from fulfillment of the great commission . . . . Often lulled into quiescence by spiritual exercises and numbed by overwhelming world-wide physical, social and political needs, all Christians need to respond in obedience to the Great Commandment to love God and neighbor. But, united in our commitment to the great commission, it is imperative that we examine our marching orders carefully and respond to them obediently.[125]

A concern for the physical and social needs of people is an important part of what it means to live and love like Jesus, in obedience to his word. The greatest commandment calls all Christians to love their neighbors as they love themselves (Luke 10:27). The parable of the "Good Samaritan," teaches that mercy and compassion for the abused and marginalized demonstrates our love for neighbor. According to Matthew 28:18-20, when disciples are taught to obey all that Christ has commanded, they will follow his example of showing love and compassionate service to the marginalized and needy. Disciples are to live like Christ in the world—living in a way that consistently demonstrates the love, grace and others-centered compassion of Jesus. Throughout the New Testament, disciples are called to do good deeds eagerly.

The Priority of Matthew 28:18-20 in Defining the Mission of Christ

The nature and scope of Christ's mission is defined by two central priorities—the building of his church and the making of

---

[125] Hesselgrave, "Confusion," 203.

Christ's disciples among all peoples. The four Gospels and the Book of Acts include post-resurrection accounts of Jesus' final instructions and commands to his disciples (Matthew 28:18-20; Mark 16:15; Luke 24:44-47; John 20:20-21; and Acts 1:6-8). When these great commission statements are combined with Christ's promise to build his church (Matthew 16:18), they present a full-orbed understanding of the mission of Christ in the world.

Many scholars agree that Matthew 28:18-20 presents the most precise, comprehensive and measurable statement of Christ's mission in the Gospels. Since the time of William Carey (1792), Matthew 28:18-20 is the most widely cited great commission passage to describe Christ's global mission. Carey used Matthew 28:18-20 to challenge the apathetic Christian leaders of his day.[126]

Wilkins notes the significance of Matthew 28:18-20 in the entire gospel account:

> As Matthew comes to the final three verses of his Gospel, he encapsulates the primary thrust of the whole book . . . . In this famous "great commission," Jesus declares that his disciples are to make more of what he has made of them. In that sense, the commission encapsulates Jesus' purpose for coming to earth, and its placement at the conclusion of this Gospel indicates Matthew's overall purpose for writing. Jesus has come to inaugurate the kingdom of God on earth by bringing men and women into a saving relationship with himself, which heretofore is called "discipleship to Jesus."[127]

---

[126] Moreau, Corwin, and McGee, 43.
[127] Michael J. Wilkins, "*Matthew*," 950.

Ott and Strauss stress the importance of Matthew's great commission account:

> Here the gospel mandate is made the foundation of the missionary task. Preaching the gospel, making disciples, and gathering these believers into communities whose members are committed to one another and to God is foundational to all else. This reflects the Great Commission according to Matthew 28:19-20. This is the gospel mandate. Missions must begin here, or it does not begin.[128]

Bosch observes that, "In Matthew's view, Christians find their true identity when they are involved in his mission, in communicating a new way of life, a new interpretation of reality and of God, and in committing themselves to the liberation and salvation of others."[129] Pentecost states, "The missionary message is a message that is now unmistakable. God's progressive revelation has come to its ultimate, and did so in the words of Christ Himself when He said, 'Go therefore and make disciples of all the nations . . .' accompanied by His promise: '. . . and lo, I am with you always, even to the end of the age' (Matt. 28:19,20)." Hesselgrave claims that Matthew 28:16-20 should exercise special authority over the life of an obedient disciple. "Theologians should pay special attention to Matthew 28:16-20. First, the precedence traditionally accorded to the Matthean statement is hermeneutically correct since, as far as the Gospels are concerned, it is Jesus' final and most complete statement on the subject. Second, it highlights

---

[128] Ott and Strauss 158
[129] David J. Bosch, *Transforming Mission: Paradigm Shifts in Theology of Mission* (Maryknoll, NY: Orbis Books, 2002), 83.

priorities that bode well for mission in the new millennium."[130] Hesselgrave sees the holistic nature of Matthew 28:18-20 and claims that, "we are called upon to disciple the nations by teaching them to observe <u>all</u> that Christ has commanded. There is inclusivity—a wholeness—in the Matthean statement of the great commission whether one interprets the object of 'teach' to be 'observing/obeying' or 'all things Christ commanded.'"[131] Regarding the exact nature and clarity of Matthew 28:18-20, Hesselgrave continues, "If we take our Lord seriously our task is indeed an encompassing and exacting one—much more than many of us have thought it to be."[132]

Hesselgrave declares,

> The Great Commandment neither completes the Great Commission, nor competes with it. It was a summation of the Law and, as one of Christ's commands, complements the Great Commission . . . . Teaching people to obey it is essential to disciple-making and part of the Great Commission mission. Actually obeying it is an important aspect of discipleship, and part of our Christian duty.[133]

From a literal hermeneutic and based on the progressive revelation of salvation history, the great commission as revealed in Matthew 28:18-20, is the most clear, precise, and comprehensive statement of his mission for his followers during this age.

---

[130] David J. Hesselgrave *"Redefining Holism," Evangelical Missions Quarterly* 35: 3 (July 1999), 281.
[131] David J. Hesselgrave "Great Commission Contextualization," *International Journal of Frontier Missions*, 12: 3 (Jul-Sep. 1995), 139.
[132] Hesselgrave, *"Great Commission Contextualization,"* 139.
[133] Hesselgrave, *Redefining Holism*, 283.

Christ-Saturated Mission—
From *Missio Dei* to *Missio Christi*

Christopher Wright, in analyzing salvation history, states that "*Jesus himself* [emphasis added] provided the hermeneutical coherence within which all disciples must read these texts, that is, in the light of the story that leads *up* to Christ (messianic reading) and the story that leads on *from* Christ (missional reading)."[134] Mitchell also claims that Christ's ministry fulfills both a messianic role regarding Old Testament prophecy and an ongoing missional role in the New Testament. He states,

> Jesus himself asserts that the Law of Moses, the Prophets and the Psalms are all fulfilled in himself, and here he obviously has more in mind than what are ordinarily considered messianic passages—Jesus is speaking of the whole of the Old Testament. The Old Testament is part of one story, and that story ultimately is about Jesus Christ and his mission, continued in the New Testament.[135]

The redemptive work of Christ and his post-resurrection authority form the core of his great commission. The *missio Dei* has once and for all been focused upon the *missio Christi*. God's mission in the world is now defined solely by Christ's mission to make disciples and establish his church among all peoples (2 Corinthians 5:18-20).

Blaising and Bock clarify how Jesus' post-resurrection mission focused on him:

---

[134] Wright, *The Mission of God,* 41.
[135] Robinson W. Mitchell, *Mission: A Mark of the Church? Toward a Missional Ecclesiology* (Master's Thesis, Reformed Theological Seminary, 2008), 26.

> He (Christ) inaugurates the present dispensation, that of the eschatological Spirit, through his atonement, resurrection, and enthronement. He is the one who will come to complete the restoration of all things. The dispensationalism of this book . . . is Christo-logically centered. The movement from the past to the present and then to future dispensations is . . . due to the history of Christ's fulfilling the plan of holistic redemption in progressive phases (dispensations). The previous dispensation anticipated and then witnessed him. After his ascension to the father's right hand, Christ inaugurated the present dispensation of his earnest, the gift of the Holy Spirit.[136]

Hirsch describes how the *missio Christi* is a continuation of larger concept of the *missio Dei*. The different persons of the Godhead are involved in particular ways to fulfill the *missio Dei* in this age. He sees in Scripture a "biblical monotheism" that focuses the missional activity of a distinct Person of the Godhead in salvation history. In the Old Testament, the monotheistic missional focus of the Trinity centered on God the Father and his relationship to Israel. In the New Testament, the monotheistic missional focus is on the Christ and his redemption of mankind. This "Christo-centric monotheism" has a missional focus based on Jesus' authority and mission to build his church and make disciples of all peoples. God the Father and the Holy Spirit support the advancement of the mission of Christ in the world.[137] In salvation history, the *missio Dei* has become in Jesus the *missio Christi*. All that the triune God intends and plans to do in salvation history

---

[136] Blaising and Bock, *Dispensationalism, Israel and the Church*, 382-83.
[137] Frost and Hirsch, *ReJesus*, 133.

during this age is defined by and characterized by the mission of Christ.

The Dual Objectives of Christ's Mission in the World

Introduction

The mission of God in Christ is based on God's gracious provision of salvation through Christ for the world (John 3:16-17; 2 Corinthians 5:18-19). Christ's mission is divinely composed of a twofold objective, involving the promised work of Christ to build his church and his commandment to his disciples to make disciples of all peoples.

Much has been written on these two aspects of the mission of Christ. In this section of the study, this first aspect of Christ's mission—to build his church—is presented. The remainder of the chapter focuses on the second aspect of Christ's mission, the making of holistic disciples.

The Mission of Building Christ's Church

In Matthew 16:18 Jesus announced his plan to build his church. In response to Christ's question about the peoples' opinion of his identity, Peter reveals Jesus' identity as the promised Messiah, the Son of the living God. Christ confirms Peter's declaration as a true statement of his deity and identity as the Messiah.

Toussaint underscores the significance of Peter's declaration in Matthew 16:18:

By *Messiah,* Peter identified Jesus as the One in whom all of the Old Testament hopes had been placed. He was the fulfillment of their Scriptures. More specifically, Jesus was the Son of the living God. Before (Matthew 14:33) they had acknowledged that He was a son of God, now Peter identifies Him as *the* Son of the only genuine God. The fact that Christ was the Son of God was proof that He was the Messiah of Israel and the King of the future kingdom."[138]

Jesus uses Peter's declaration to reveal his mission to build his church on "this rock."[139] "There are three main interpretive positions to explain the meaning of the word 'rock' in this passage—the rock is Peter, the rock is Christ; and/or the rock is the truth contained in Peter's confession about Jesus' deity."[140] Christ's statement, "on this rock," refers to the truth that he is both God and Israel's messiah. This understanding is supported by the statements of Paul and Peter concerning the person of Christ and the foundation of his church (Romans 9:33; Ephesians 2:20; 1 Peter 2:5-8).[141]

Jesus redefined the term "church" to refer to an entirely new and unique reality that never before existed nor was ever conceived of in the way that Jesus defines it. Toussaint notes the significance of the title "church" in Matthew 16:18:

> The fact that Christ calls it *my* church distinguishes it from all else. The Lord certainly could not say of Israel "My church." A further proof that *ecclesia* does not allude to

---

[138] Stanley D. Toussaint, *Behold the King: A Study of Matthew* (Portland, OR: Multnomah Press, 1981), 200-201.
[139] Toussaint, *Behold the King*, 201.
[140] Toussaint, *Behold the King*, 201-02.
[141] Toussaint, *Behold the King*, 202.

anything then in existence is the future tense of the verb "to build" (*oikodoumeo*). He was yet to build the church. The term is an explanation of that which will transpire on the earth from Pentecost until the seventieth week of Daniel preceding the establishment of the kingdom.[142]

The word "build" implies missional planning and a definite design. The building is completed as obedient disciples are made of all nations.

The Mission of Making Christ-like Disciples

The process of making disciples involves both evangelism—helping unbelievers to trust Christ alone for their salvation—and discipleship—the life pursuit of growing into Jesus' likeness. Hull correctly understands the nature and scope of Christ's mission and disciple-making when he states, "The mission of the great commission is more about depth than strategy. Taking on the mission requires a revolution of character transformation."[143]

The main governing imperative and heart Christ's mission in Matthew 28:19 is to "make disciples" (μαθητεύσατε). The grammatical form of μαθητεύσατε is imperative aorist active, 2nd person plural. The words, "make disciples" are therefore a 2nd person plural command in the Greek language.[144] Many scholars emphasize the participles, "go," " baptizing," and "teaching," in Matthew 28:18-20, that delineate the essential activities involved

---

[142] Toussaint, *Behold the King,* 203.
[143] Hull, *The Complete Book of Discipleship*, 202.
[144] Hiebert, 348.

in making disciples. Heibert describes the nature of these three participles:

> The other three terms (go, baptizing, teaching) are nominative plural participles, all directly related to the plural subject of the main verb. The construction thus stresses the focal point in this commission, namely, the assignment to "make disciples of all the nations." The three participles, grammatically dependent on the main verb, denote activities related to the accomplishment of the central assignment.[145]

The aorist participle translated "go" in Matthew 28:18 can be translated in English, "as you go" or "while you go." The aorist tense of the participle translated "go" (πορευθέντες) can accurately be translated, "having gone," which demonstrates that the missionary activity involved making disciples. The responsibility to "go" with the gospel belongs to every believer so that whether they go near or far, they are necessarily involved in reaching others for Christ.[146] Rogers notes that the aorist participle "go," is "vitally related" to the command to "make disciples." The participle "go" points to a specific activity to be fulfilled and carries the weight of a command. Therefore, "The aorist makes the command definite and urgent," for "without the going, the making of disciples is not possible, and especially when 'all nations' is the object."[147]

Jesus' authoritative commission to make disciples who obey all that He has commanded demonstrates that there is a

---

[145] Hiebert, 348.
[146] Hiebert, 348.
[147] Cleon Rogers, "The Great Commission," *Bibliotheca Sacra* 130: 519 (July-September 1973), 262.

product (disciple) and a process (make) central to the great commission. The main verb indicates that it is essential to develop disciples of Christ who learn to live like Jesus by seeking to obey all that Jesus commanded. The three participles in Matthew 29:18-20 (going, baptizing, teaching) are dependent on the command to make disciples and describe how that central activity is to be accomplished. "Any activity unrelated to or inconsistent with this assignment is, in terms of Jesus' commission, a failure to carry it out."[148]

Hiebert observes that the participle "teaching" is closely related to the commandment to make disciples and could be translated as "discipling all nations." The word "disciple" (μαθητεύσαντε) in its noun form means "a learner, adherent." The command form to "make disciples" involves causing someone, who does not know Christ, to become a follower, adherent, or apprentice of another, accepting him as his/her authoritative teacher, master, and model.[149]

> Hendrickson, in his commentary on this passage states: The term "make disciples" places somewhat more stress on the fact that the mind, as well as the heart and the will, must be won for God. A disciple is a *pupil, a learner* . . . . Mere mental understanding does not as yet make one a disciple. It is a part of the picture, in fact an important part, but only a part. The truth learned must be practiced. It must be appropriated by heart, mind and will, so that one

---

[148] Hiebert, 348.
[149] Hiebert, 349.

> *remains* or *abides* in the truth. Only then is one truly Christ's "disciple" (John 8:31).[150]

Disciples of Christ, whether new or growing in maturity, must be committed to the continuous transformational process of learning and living-out the Word of God in their pursuit of Christ-like transformation.

The task of "making disciples" for all disciples, whether they have been saved two days or twenty years, involves specific and ongoing instruction in the foundational and deep truths of God's word. The ministry of the Holy Spirit, in and through the life of the disciple, is essential for all who seek to be obedient to the teaching and life of Christ. However, since spiritual growth never occurs in a vacuum, the fellowship, ministry, and relational growth with other disciples in the local church promotes individual and corporate spiritual growth and mutual edification (Ephesians 4:11-18).

The intended divine result of ongoing teaching is the transformed life of a disciple who is equipped "to observe all that I (Christ) commanded you" (Matthew 28:19). The scope of this teaching is comprehensive, "all that I commanded you." The words, *panta ousa* meaning "all things, as many things as," underscores the thorough and authoritative nature of his teaching and the comprehensive commitment of the disciple to learn from and obey his Lord. The present tense participle, "to observe," ("to be

---

[150] William Hendriksen, "Exposition of the Gospel According to Matthew," *A New Testament Commentary* (Grand Rapids, MI: Baker, 1973), 999-1000.

keeping, observing, fulfilling"), indicates that the process of instruction aims not only at providing vital information but an ongoing application of biblical truth in one's life characterized by obedience to the word. [151] The teaching from God's Word is to powerfully work in the life of the disciples to transform, control and mold their entire life and character to obey Christ. Christ's word is the source, the disciple's obedience is the means, and transformation into Christ's likeness is the goal of every disciple of Jesus.

The expression "all that I commanded you", does not denote that Jesus rejected or intended his disciples to ignore all other inspired revelation. Jesus fulfilled the Law of Moses in its entirety. Plummer rightfully points out, "It is not the O.T. which Christ gives to the Apostles as the source of the instruction which they are to give to the new disciples; the basis of their teaching is to be 'all things whatsoever I commanded you.'"[152] Plummer goes on to state,

> What was "said to them of old time" is not enough; it is what "I say unto *you*" . . . expanding, deepening, spiritualizing what has been taught by the Law and the Prophets, that is to be the Apostles' guide in teaching all the nations. And, lest they should fear that they would forget much of what He had enjoined, He had already promised them that the Holy Spirit would "bring to their remembrance all that He said to them."[153]

---

[151] Hiebert, 352.
[152] Plummer, 435.
[153] Plummer, 435.

The lessons from Old Testament truth made up much of what Jesus taught and served as a basis for the teaching in the Gospels. Christ's teaching also includes the Gospel accounts, Acts, the Epistles and the Revelation. All inspired Scripture in included in the phrase, "all I have commanded you."

The great commission command of Christ does not end with the words "make disciples." The disciple-making process is a lifelong obligation all believers share to choose to know, obey and submit to Christ and his word for his sake. A disciple is to be radically transformed from the inside out—from Christ-like character to others'-centered service. The maturing disciple will pursue Christ-like transformation by intentionally observing all that Christ commanded. Spiritual transformation and growth brings discernment that motivates obedience, service and the making of other disciples. As Hiebert states, "As each believer faithfully carries out his duty to reach out to others, he has an active share in furthering Christ's self-perpetuating program for world evangelization."[154]

The reference to "all nations" refers to all ethnic peoples, including both Jews and Gentiles, showing that the commandment of Christ to make disciples is supra cultural and focused on all people. Jesus commands his disciples to obediently "cross boundaries of all types (geographic, political, ethnic, linguistic) to make disciples."[155]

---

[154] Hiebert, 353.
[155] Moreau, Corwin, McGee, 45.

The Mission of Christ Is Measurable and Clear

When Christ gave his "great commission", he expected it to be fulfilled by his disciples. Christ's mission to make disciples of all peoples parallels his own promised mission to build his church. The building of his Church and the making of disciples of all peoples are codependent. The mission to make disciples among all ethnic groups will continue to the end of the age when salvation history is fulfilled and all the earth's tribes, tongues, nations and peoples worship the Lamb who was slain forever (Revelation 5:9-10 and 7:9-10).

Christ's great commission strategy delineates both an essential *process* to be obeyed and the creation of a specific *product* that is *made*. The product is the creation of Christ-like disciples of all peoples. This process involves intentional effort toward the goal of Christ's likeness by training obedient disciples (Matthew 29:19b). The people tasked with making disciples (all believers) and the people targeted to become disciples (all ethnic groups) are clearly delineated. The divine power and presence to make Christ's mission a continual success is promised when he said, "I am with you always to the end of the age," Matthew 28:20. It is therefore appropriate to note that all aspects of the disciple-making process, as given by Christ to his disciples, involve tangible and measurable results based on the promises and presence of Christ. Christ, in his mission to his followers, presents a practical, reasonable and achievable goal to pursue. No aspect of culture, education, ethnicity, or social development should stand in the way of making obedient, holistic disciples of all peoples.

Hull emphasizes both the product and process of disciple-making when he states, "In answer to the age-old question, 'Are disciples born or made?' I contend they are born to be made. The vision Jesus set into motion meant finding and training more people like the Eleven, a lifelong experience where imperfect people would be shaped into his likeness—marked by progress, not perfection."[156]

Progress towards Christ-likeness is demonstrated to the degree that disciples *learn to obey all* that Christ has commanded, are transformed into Christ's character, and live a life of others-centered service. They seek to love and obey the Lord with their entire being so that they long to be like Jesus and choose to live sacrificially for the sake of others in their quest to reproduce more Christ-like disciples. Adsit underscores the process involved in spiritual transformation into Christ-likeness:

> A disciple is a person-in-process who is eager to learn and apply the truths that Jesus Christ teaches him, which will result in ever-deepening commitments to a Christ-like lifestyle.
> The concept of disciple represents an attitude of commitment. If the learning attitude is there, the character qualities and disciplines will eventually show up; but not

---

[156] Hull, *The Complete Book of Discipleship*, 33.

all at once, and not in any highly predictable sequence or at any prescribed rate. [157]

Christ's mission is essentially "people-centric" as presented in Matthew 28:18-20. As Dr. Ron Blue often says, the great commission simply involves "People, loving people, to reach people."[158] Centered on growing into the likeness of the person of Christ, the people of Christ (his disciples) are to pursue the evangelization of people everywhere who are then taught to grow in obedience to Christ and his word.

Conclusion

A vital question to answer is, "What does the New Testament clearly teach to be the guiding theme and ultimate purpose of Christ's mission in the world?" In divinely ordained salvation history, the mission of God in this age is founded upon the post-resurrection authority, promises and commands of Christ. The *missio Dei* is during this age focused on the *missio Christi*. As Horton notes, "The mission statement that Jesus delivered to his church is an urgent imperative to proclaim the gospel to *everyone*,

---

[157] Christopher B. Adsit, *Personal Disciple-Making: A Step-by-Step Guide for Leading a Christian from New Birth to Maturity* (San Bernardino, CA: Here's Life Publishers, Inc., 1989), 35.

[158] Information from personal interaction and classes with Dr. Blue over the past two decades. Dr. Blue was a world mission professor at Dallas Theological Seminary for 17 years and then the President of CAM International for 10 years. The author was both a student of Dr. Blue, a missionary with CAM International during his Presidency, and a companion on several international trips.

to make disciples of all nations."[159] The mission of Christ is to build his church by making disciples of all peoples. Christ's two missional objectives are clear, measurable, and achievable through the obedience of his followers and the ministry of the Holy Spirit. The building of his church is interdependent on the making of obedient disciples.

---

[159] Michael Horton, *The Gospel Commission: Recovering God's Strategy for Making Disciples* (Grand Rapids, MI: Baker Books, 2011), 84.

CHAPTER 4
THE NATURE OF
HOLISTIC DISCIPLES

Introduction

The mission of God, during this period of salvation history, is assigned by Christ to his followers who, through their obedience, make disciples of all peoples. The *missio Dei* in this age is defined by the *missio Christi*—the promised building of his church and the command to make disciples of all nations.

The purpose of this chapter is to describe the type of disciple in terms of nature and character, which Jesus desired and envisioned when he commanded his followers to make disciples. That is, what is the essence and attributes of a Christ-like disciple.

Defining the Nature and Character of a Holistic Disciple of Jesus Christ

Introduction

The greatest motivation and most satisfying pursuit in life involve obedience to what Jesus referred to as the "greatest commandment." Matthews writes,

> Teacher, which is the great commandment in the Law?" And he said to him, 'You shall love the Lord your God with all your heart and with all your soul and with your entire mind. This is the great and first commandment. And a second is like it: You shall love your neighbor as yourself.

On these two commandments depends all the Law and the Prophets (Matthew 22:36-40).

These commandments describe a holistic disciple—a believer who loves God completely with their entire being and lives to serve others. A holistic disciple learns to obey Christ wholeheartedly and lives to make disciples of others for God's glory.

The Contemporary Understanding for Making Disciples and Discipleship

A great challenge facing evangelical ministries is the implementation of a biblical disciple-making process that transforms believers into Christ's likeness. Regrettably, many church leaders and believers do not pursue biblical discipleship. Many seem more comfortable with what Matthews refers to as a "conversion-centered" Christianity:

> [A] conversion-centered approach to the gospel has for many people been interpreted as a finish line or an ending, instead of a starting line or new beginning. This understanding has *huge* [emphasis added] implications for how we live life now! If being forgiven and now having heaven assured is what it means to become a Christian, anything I do from then on is an add-on. "Why talk to me about discipleship? Why do I need that?" I've been forgiven. I'm already going to heaven. What more do I need to do? But without foreseeing the consequences, this conversion-centered gospel has created a two-tiered reality for those in the evangelical church. Most people see themselves as Christians at the point of conversion, but the call to be a disciple is for many a second-level option, often

reserved for the more serious Christian and notably absent from the conversion-centered gospel appeal.[160]

The sad reality is seen in churches and ministries where success is not measured by Christ-transformed lives, but by the numbers of attendees, diversity of programs, the acquisition of more property and buildings, or the size of the pastoral staff. Things like stirring worship experiences, relevant preaching, and attractive, age-graded programs for the entire family are often the measure of a successful ministry. In this context, many believers are never taught how to grow as a disciple and reproduce other holistic disciples of Christ. Sadly, few pastors and ministry leaders are trained biblically and expected to prioritize the development of a holistic disciple-making ministry.[161]

The type of commitment and obedience that Jesus calls for in the "Sermon on the Mount" (Matthew 5-7), is rarely expected to characterize the lives of believers. Many believers are comfortable with a "babes in Christ" entry level of Christianity focused on the basic truths of salvation and are never instructed or challenged to pursue a dynamic, Christ-centered life. Jesus taught that his followers are characterized by a commitment that leaves sin and self behind and leads them to follow him obediently as his disciple.[162]

---

[160] Matthews, "The Transformational Process," 86.
[161] Rick Wood, ed. "A Discipleship Revolution: The Key to Discipling All Peoples" *Mission Frontiers* (January-February, 2011), 4.
[162] Keith Meyer, "Whole-Life Transformation," in *The Kingdom Life* (Colorado Springs: NavPress, 2010), 142-143.

Christian syndicated columnist and author, Cal Thomas writes, "The problem in our culture . . . isn't the abortionists. It isn't the pornographers or drug dealers or criminals. It is the undisciplined, undiscipled, disobedient, and biblically ignorant Church of Jesus Christ."[163] Thomas' words hit hard against the church that does not purposefully make disciples of its members. A weak and ineffective church, producing immature disciples rather than obedient ones, is sadly more the norm than the exception. That is not what Christ envisioned as he called his followers to make disciples of the nations.

Hull believes that the key problem facing the church is the teaching that promotes a personal faith that does not transform believers into Christ's likeness. He describes a "non-discipleship Christianity," centered on personal conversion but does not prioritize the biblical teaching of pursuing a disciple's transformed life. He notes that both Jesus and Paul taught that the evidence that one believes in and belongs to Him is through a life aligned to Jesus' life (Luke 9:23-25; Philippians 2:1-8).[164] Hull contends that, "The trouble with our evangelism is that we have made it so easy to enter the Christian life that we have missed the repentance, commitment, and regeneration that provide the power to live the Christian life."[165]

---

[163] Interview with Cal Thomas, *Christianity Today*, April 25, 1994, quoted by Greg Ogden, *Transforming Discipleship: Making a Few Disciples at a Time* (Downers Grove, IL: InterVarsity Press, 2003), 23.
[164] Hull, *Choose the Life*, 23.
[165] Hull, *Choose the Life*, 24.

Hull believes that real faith produces inner transformation and a life of obedience:

> The whole point of the gospel is to be transformed into the image of Christ . . . (Gal. 4:19-20) . . . The English word *formed* in this passage is from the Greek *morphe*, a word familiar to us largely because of computerized videos and graphic design. Romans 12:2 uses the same root word in "be *transformed* by the renewing of your mind." Another example is found in Romans 8:29: "For those God foreknew he also predestined to be *conformed* to the likeness of his Son." Transformation is the goal, but it is not always easy to achieve due to our default setting.[166]

Because the church has essentially taught a "non-discipleship Christianity" based on agreement to biblical truth, Hull asserts that it should not surprise us that in his estimation, over fifty percent of professing Christians have not chosen to make a serious commitment to follow Jesus. A faith that focuses on agreement with biblical truth has been taught instead of a faith that results in wholehearted commitment to follow Jesus.[167] Spiritual maturity and the normal Christian life, for many, is equated with the goal of understanding and accepting biblical truth, not with a commitment of personal spiritual transformation resulting in a Christ-like disciple who lives for the sake of others.

Hull addressed the state of non-discipleship Christianity in the church he pastored by challenging the congregation to choose the life of discipleship and following Jesus:

---

[166] Hull, *Choose the Life*, 24-25.
[167] Hull, *Choose the Life*, 29.

> I told them discipleship was not optional: being spiritually transformed is the primary and exclusive work of the church. I told them the evidence of being a follower of Jesus is following Jesus. I told them believing the right things was not enough: the faith Jesus taught and lived included behavioral evidence. . . . I told them discipleship is a choice; we don't drift into it or amble our way halfheartedly down the path of obedience. . . . I was going to ask them to *choose the life*—the life of following Jesus, the life that is the answer to the weakness of the church and the boring ineffectiveness of our lives.[168]

Christ's will and goal for all believers is their sanctification. The biblical goal of holistic disciple-making is rarely understood or taught as *mandatory* for believers. Ogden reiterates the problem found in many churches and ministries:

> A close examination of biblical discipleship does not allow for two classes of followers: the ordinary and extraordinary. There are Christians who have not lived up to the expectations of a disciple yet can still be called Christians who have not progressed as babes in Christ who are still drinking milk, when they should be taking solid food (1 Cor. 3:1-3).[169]

Platt summarizes the fundamental error that many believers make:

> We take Jesus' command in Matthew 28 to make disciples of all nations, and we say, "That means other people." But we look at Jesus' command in Matthew 11:28, "Come to me, all you who are weary and burdened, and I will give you rest," and we say, "Now, that means me." We take Jesus' promise in Acts 1:8 that the Spirit will lead us to the ends of the earth , and we say, "That means some people."

---

[168] Hull, *Choose the Life*, 18.
[169] Ogden, 48-49.

> But we take Jesus' promise in John 10:10 that we will have abundant life, and we say, "That means me."
> In the process we have unnecessarily (and unbiblically) drawn a line of distinction, assigning the *obligations* of Christianity to a few while keeping the *privileges* of Christianity for us all . . . .
> . . . each follower of Christ in the New Testament, regardless of his or her calling, was intended to take up the mantle of proclaiming the gospel to the ends of the earth. That's the reason why he gave each of them his Spirit and why he gave them all the same plan: make disciples of all nations.[170]

A solemn conviction that holistic disciple-making is Christ's mandate for all believers is lost when believers prioritize comfort and conformity over Christ-likeness. Agreement to biblical truth not put into practice through obedience deceives the believer into believing that they are living in accordance with Christ's intended purpose and will.

Understanding the Two-Faceted Nature of Salvation

In order to understand why the making of disciples is central to the mission of Christ, it is vital to understand the two-faceted nature of one's salvation as taught in the New Testament. There is more than one divine purpose in mankind's salvation. Christ died *not only to save* people so they could be forgiven of their sins and inherit heaven. He also saves people *to shape them* into his likeness to accomplish his purposes through their lives.

---

[170] David Platt, *Radical* (Colorado Springs, CO: Multnomah Books, 2011), 73.

Theologians have identified three applications for the words "saved," and "salvation" in the New Testament. The most frequent use of "salvation" refers to a believer's justification before God because of faith in Christ resulting in being declared righteous, indwelled with the Holy Spirit and the gift of eternal life (John 3:16). The Greek terms translated into English as "saved," "salvation," can also refer to the believer's saved life after being justified, as they progressively grow (are shaped) into Christ-likeness. This aspect of salvation involves Christ's intended transformation of a believer through the ministry of the Holy Spirit into spiritual maturity (Philippians 2:12-13; Galatians 5:16-23). It is known as sanctification. Finally, the terms "saved" or "salvation" can refer to the eternal reality when a believer is present with Christ in Heaven (Acts 15:11), also known as "glorification."

Many believers do not understand the divinely ordained process of sanctification in the life of the believer. The biblical teaching that faith in Christ makes a believer righteous before God (justification) is clearly taught by many. However, a serious lack of teaching and accompanying practice that promotes obedience and submission to Christ's word and lordship is largely absent. Ogden notes how Jesus responded to people who had expressed their desire to follow him: "When Jesus says, 'If anyone would come after me, let him deny himself and take up his cross daily and follow me' (Luke 9:23), is he intending this to be the standard for all who name him as Savior? The empirical answer to that is apparently no. Many people have clearly made a distinction between being a Christian and being a disciple."[171]

For many believers, there is a serious lack of understanding on the divine mandate to pursue continuously Christ's likeness (sanctification) throughout life. Atkinson and Roesel make this point:

> Positionally, Christians are set apart or sanctified by God at the moment of their salvation. However . . . God wants us to be sanctified experientially. Paul expressed this dimension of sanctification when he prayed for his friends at Thessalonica: (1 Thess. 5:23). Being sanctified "through and through" describes ongoing action. The Christian has been sanctified and is being sanctified as an ongoing experience. This ongoing sanctification occurs in discipleship. Discipleship refers to the human side of this process; sanctification, to the divine side. A Christian follows Jesus in discipleship. As the disciple follows the Lord, the Holy Spirit carries out the process of sanctification. Sanctification, like discipleship, is an ongoing process, never finished on this side of heaven.[172]

The evangelical tradition has largely failed to teach consistently the necessity of obedience to Christ, leading to transformation of one's will and character. As Hull observes,

> The problem is that separating these two theological terms [justification from sanctification] gives the impression that being a Christian means obtaining a protected status before God. We've taught that this act of justification settles the issue—"Come in where it's safe and secure"—rather than teaching that a call to believe in Christ should also compel

---

[171] Ogden, 48-49.
[172] Donald A. Atkinson & Charles L. Roesel, *Meeting Needs Sharing Christ: Ministry Evangelism in Today's New Testament Church* (Nashville: LifeWay Press, 1995), 55.

following him. In other words, the point of salvation (justification) isn't the finish line; instead it's the starting line for a lifelong journey (sanctification).[173]

A.W. Tozer long ago noted the great need to teach obedience in evangelical Christianity:

> I must be frank in my feeling that a notable heresy has come into being throughout evangelical Christian circles—the widely accepted concept that we humans can choose to accept Christ only because we need him as Savior and that we have the right to postpone our obedience to him as Lord as long as we want to!
> This concept has sprung naturally from a misunderstanding of what the Bible actually says about Christian discipleship and obedience . . . . The truth is that salvation apart from obedience is unknown in the sacred Scriptures.[174]

Many contemporary scholars believe the problem mentioned above is rooted in a misunderstanding and reduction of the gospel message itself. Many believe there has been an inadequate communication of a full-orbed gospel, focusing exclusively on the justification of a sinner by God and not the implications of that salvation. Hull states,

> The problem we face is that we have created and taught a faith that doesn't transform people . . . .
> Both Jesus and Paul taught that following Jesus is proof of being a Christian. The gospel of the kingdom Jesus delivered in the Sermon on the Mount is the same gospel preached in Acts and the same gospel Paul presented in Romans, Ephesians, Philippians, and Colossians. When

---

[173] Hull, *The Complete Book of Discipleship*, 42-43.
[174] A.W. Tozer, *I Call it Heresy And Other Timely Topics From First Peter* (Camp Hill, PA: Christian Publications, 1991), 1-2.

Jesus commanded, "Make disciples," he wasn't simply referring to converts. He wants followers who follow—people who submit to his teachings and his ways.[175]

However, the problem does not lie precisely in the *message* of the gospel that saves (justifies), but its implication in an understanding of the spiritual life (sanctification) of the believer. Lovelace has described what others claim to be a "reduction" or a "hole" in the gospel as actually a "gap" in the doctrine of sanctification.

> There seemed to be a sanctification gap among Evangelicals, a peculiar conspiracy somehow to mislay the Protestant tradition of spiritual growth and to concentrate instead on frantic witnessing activity, sermons on John 3:16 and theological arguments over eschatological subtleties. Other sectors in the church argued over issues of real substance, but with such rancor and exaggeration that one wished that some attention had first been given to sanctification.[176]

Ogden refers to the same spiritual malaise as a "discipleship gap" or a "discipleship deficit" between the biblical standards of spiritual life and the reality in Christian experience.[177]

A reduction or gap has occurred in the mission of Christ to make disciples of all peoples. It is a disciple-making gap, an obedience gap, that has less to do with the essence of the Gospel's message than a proper understanding and application of the

---

[175] Hull, *The Complete Book of Discipleship*, 43.
[176] Richard Lovelace, *Dynamics of the Spiritual Life: An Evangelical Theology of Renewal* (Downers Grove, IL: InterVarsity Academic, 1979), 232. His overall discussion on this topic is found on pages 229-237.
[177] Ogden, 21-38

obedient spiritual life intended for all believers. Hull clarifies the problem:

> There is widespread confusion about the nature of salvation because of the separation of justification from sanctification. The gospel we preach must make whole again the unity of justification and sanctification. Bonhoeffer does this with his statement that "only the believer is obedient—only the obedient believe." Justification and sanctification can be unified within the single concept of discipleship.[178]

Returning to a biblical understanding and practice of disciple-making will remove any reduction in disciple-making and an inactive and passive response to God's grace. The process of sanctification revolves around the consistent efforts of believers to "work out their own salvation" (Philippians 2:16). The believer's saved life is centered and defined by spiritual transformation into Christ-likeness.

Along with a practical reduction in the understanding and pursuit of sanctification, there is a serious lack of biblical teaching about the authority and Lordship of Christ. What is at issue can be referred to as a problem of "lordship sanctification." Believers are to live under the authority of Christ so that they submit to and obey all that Jesus has commanded. By living under Jesus as Lord, a believer demonstrates love for him and grows into his likeness. Willard declares, "To present his Lordship as an option leaves it squarely in the category of the special wheels, tires, and stereo equipment. You can do without it. And it is—alas!—far from clear

---

[178] Hull, *Choose the Life*, 11.

what you would do with it. Obedience and training in obedience form no intelligible doctrinal or practical unity with 'salvation' presented in recent versions of the gospel."[179] Spiritual transformation into Christ-likeness results from an unreserved submission and obedience to the Lordship of Christ. Taken together, an inadequate understanding of sanctification and the lack of submission to the Lordship of Christ have created a non-disciple-making version of Christianity. Sanctification under the lordship of Christ results in holistic disciple-making.

Understanding the Nature of a Holistic Disciple

To obey Christ's mission, it is essential to understand what the New Testament reveals about the nature and essence of a holistic disciple of Christ. Christ's design for his disciples is his own likeness and character. Romans 8:28-29 states that all believers are predestined ("pre-designed") by God to become like Christ. God's ultimate goal for all believers during their life on earth before heaven is spiritual transformation into Christ-likeness.[180] It is the will and plan of the Father for Christ's followers to become like their Lord and make other disciples like him.

---

[179] Dallas Willard, *The Great Omission: Reclaiming Jesus' Essential Teachings on Discipleship* (San Francisco: HarperCollins, 2006), 5.
[180] Wilkins, *Following*, 42.

Defining Discipleship and Disciple-Making Biblically

"Disciple" (μαθητής) is used over 265 times in the New Testament as the normal title given to those who followed Jesus. Words like apprentice, student, follower or learner of a master teacher are synonymous with the biblical concept of a disciple.[181]

The making of disciples by influential leaders was a common practice in the Roman Empire and in Judaism during Jesus' day.[182] Individuals committed themselves to thoroughly learn the teaching, philosophy and life-practice of a master teacher. The teacher invited his chosen disciple into a relationship where he imparted not only valuable information but also a philosophy of life. Jesus essentially called his disciples to participate in this same discipleship process. A faithful disciple of Christ sought to consistently teach, represent, and model a life dedicated to Christ's teaching and example.[183] Christ's ultimate goal, both during his earthly ministry and today, involves the making and reproducing of holistic disciples who are transformed into his likeness (Matthew 28:18-20; Acts 14:21; Romans 8:29).

The making of Christ-like disciples is an *intentional process* involving a serious commitment to transformation into his likeness *and* training others to do the same. Holistic disciples are believers who pursue the process of growing into Christ-likeness

---

[181] Matthews, *The Transformational Process*, 87.
[182] Wilkins, *Following*, 78-79, 92-94.
[183] Wilkins, *Following,* 78.

and are divinely called to pursue others by training them to become his faithful disciples.[184]

The greatest need in ultimately fulfilling the mission of Christ is the training of believers to pursue transformation into Christ-like, holistic maturity. Ogden identifies the basis of the problem that limits disciple-making: "We have not called people into an apprentice relationship with Jesus. Jesus is not looked to as our discipler, teacher and Lord. We do not see him as the compelling figure who is our trainer in this life."[185]

Willard believes there is a lack of commitment to disciple-making in the church:

> One is not required to be, or to intend to be, a disciple in order to become a Christian, and one may remain a Christian without any signs of progress toward or in discipleship. Contemporary Western churches do not require following Christ in his example, spirit, and teachings as a condition of membership—either of entering into or continuing in fellowship of a denomination of a local church . . . so far as the visible Christian institutions of our day are concerned, *discipleship clearly is optional*. . . .
> Most problems in contemporary churches can be explained by the fact that members have not yet decided to follow Christ.[186]

---

[184] Robert E. Coleman, "The Master's Plan" in *Perspectives on the World Christian Movement: A Reader*, Fourth Edition, eds. Ralph D. Winter and Steven C. Hawthorne (San Bernardino, CA William Carey Library, 2009), 125.
[185] Ogden, 47.
[186] Willard, *The Great Omission*, 4-5.

Unfortunately, the biblical concepts of making disciples and of discipleship are seldom prioritized or practiced in much of evangelical Christianity today.

The clear biblical and divinely intended goal in disciple-making is the formation of his moral character in Jesus' followers. In Luke 6:40, Jesus taught that the trained disciple learns to live like his teacher. The disciple who replicates the character, teaching, and practice of his teacher is a faithful disciple, trained to carry on the unique teaching and priorities of his teacher. Garrison notes that a disciple "is someone who has an ongoing personal relationship with a teacher, whose life is a pattern to be imitated. The habits, speech, personality, behavior, reactions, and attitudes of the disciple are patterned after those of the teacher (Luke 6:40). As a result of this life-oriented following, the student then gladly shares that learning with others."[187]

The promise given in Luke 6:40 describes the same process inherent in teaching to obey all that Christ has commanded in Matthew 28:19, involving obedience and faithfulness to the master's teaching and lifestyle. The central feature that develops a disciple is their quest to continue learning and obeying Christ's Word (Matthew 28:19). Thayer identifies the close relationship that exists between the Greek terms μανθάνο (to learn) and μαθητής (learner, disciple) in verse 19. These words indicate that disciples are taught in such a way that they put into use and

---

[187] Alton Garrison, *The 360° Disciple: Discipleship Going Full Circle* (Springfield, Missouri: Gospel Publishing House, 2009), 8.

practice the knowledge they acquire.[188] Moulton believed that μανθάνο, used here with the term "disciple," means "to learn by practice or experience, acquire a custom or habit."[189] Arndt and Gingrich note that the term for learning in verse 19 (μανθάνο) refers to learning that comes through life and practice, not just through intellectual study.[190] A disciple is taught to be like Christ through a lifelong learning process that involves learning God's word and through life in a way that demonstrates obedience to Christ's will.

It is essential to understand the life-long nature of discipleship. Hirsch and Frost emphasize this process of becoming like Jesus through discipleship:

> Focusing our discipleship on Jesus forces us to take seriously the implications of following him, of becoming like him. It sets the agenda for our spirituality. It acknowledges that Jesus as our model, our teacher, and our guide is normative for the Christian life. He is the standard by which we measure ourselves, the quality of our discipleship, and therefore our spirituality.
> If the heart of Christian spirituality is to increasingly become like our founder, then an authentic comprehension of Jesus becomes critical. All too often the focal point of our corporate and individual life shifts from its true center in Jesus, resulting in various anomalies in our spirituality. A true Christian expression models itself on Jesus, and it is God's unambiguous aim to make us to be more like his Son.

---

[188] Joseph Henry Thayer, *Greek-English Lexicon of the New Testament* (New York: Harper Brothers Publishers, 1899), 389.
[189] Harold K. Moulton, ed., *The Analytical Greek Lexicon Revised* (Grand Rapids: Zondervan1981), 257.
[190] William F. Arndt and F. Wilbur Gingrich, *Greek-English Lexicon of the New Testament* (Chicago: University of Chicago Press, 1957), 490.

In fact, this is our eternal destiny: "to be conformed to the likeness of his son" (Rom. 8:29).[191]

Wilkins underscores the growth process in all aspects of one's character, involved in discipleship. It is a process of holistic change of one entire being into Christ-likeness.

> *Discipleship* is the ongoing process of growth as a disciple. *Discipling* implies the responsibility of disciples to help one another to grow as disciples . . . . Thus, when we speak of Christian discipleship and discipling we are speaking of what it means to grow as a Christian in every area of life. Since *disciple* is a common referent for *Christian*, discipleship and discipling imply the process of becoming like Jesus Christ. Discipleship and discipling mean living a fully human life in this world in union with Jesus Christ and growing in conformity to his image.[192]

Hull notes that spiritual growth through "discipleship is a lifelong process, and I will be extremely needy until that wonderful moment we are completely and eternally changed. In fact the more we become like Jesus, the more we are dependent on him."[193]

Spiritual maturity does not only occur through the study of Christ's word but through relationship with other believers in the church and non-believers in the community. Hull emphasizes the role of the body of Christ in the making of disciples as involving "the intentional training of disciples, with accountability, on the basis of loving relationships."[194] Ogden continues to emphasize the place of relationships in the growth of a disciple. "My working

---

[191] Frost and Hirsch, *Re-Jesus*, 13.
[192] Wilkins, *Following*, 41-42.
[193] Hull, *Choose the Life*, 180.
[194] Bill Hull, *The Disciple Making Church* (Grand Rapids, MI: Revell, 1988), 32.

definition of discipling . . . (is) . . . 'Discipling is an intentional relationship in which we walk alongside other disciples in order to encourage, equip, and challenge one another in love to grow toward maturity in Christ. This includes equipping the disciple to teach others well.'"[195]

Once a person places their faith in Christ, they begin a lifelong quest (mission) of transformation into his holiness. As a disciple grows into Christ-likeness, their missional character grows to emulate his Person and character. The participle "go" and the focus on the "nations" in Matthew 28:18-20 presents the divine call for all disciples to live and work among lost people and make Christ-like disciples as a natural consequence of the relationships they pursue in obedience to Christ.[196]

Making Holistic Disciples:
The Product and the Process

This study uses the word "holistic" to refer to the entire, complete, whole life of a believer including the immaterial aspects of a person (mind, heart, soul, spirit, will) as well as their outward behavior. A holistic disciple's worldview, beliefs, values, and affections are in the process of transformation into Christ's likeness as the maturing believer aligns his life with Christ's will (Romans 12:2). A holistic disciple is a spiritually healthy disciple. Hull notes how obedient faith forms a holistic disciple:

---

[195] Ogden, 129.
[196] Hull, *The Complete Book of Discipleship*, 34.

> The most basic issue confronting us is restoring the gospel message of Scripture that will create healthy followers of Jesus. For many, this will require the redefining of the very nature of faith as a faith that follows, a faith that forms the inner person, a faith consistent with the call of Christ to "follow me . . . and I will make you fishers of men" (Matthew 4:19).[197]

A Holistic Disciple Pursues Holistic Transformation into Christ's Likeness

Transformation into Christ's likeness begins with a renewed mind (Romans 12:2) and results in a reformed will and life orientation. This is the way Jesus formed his disciples, as they "acted in a new way of thinking".[198] The Greek root word μορφή, in English "form," refers to the "inward and real formation of the essential nature of a person or living being."[199] It describes a process of complete and unchangeable transformation that originates at the core of one's being. This concept contrasts with the similar Greek term σχήμα, also translated "form." However, *schema* describes the outward and changeable form of an object, while μορφή refers to a new, permanent change of one's immaterial nature. The Apostle Paul contrasts the concept of μορφή with *schema*, when he exclaims, "Do not be conformed [συσχήματιζομαί] to this world. But be transformed (μεταμορφομαί) by the renewal of your mind" (Romans 12:2).

---

[197] Hull, *The Complete Book of Discipleship*, 44.
[198] Alan Hirsch, *The Forgotten Ways: Reactivating the Missional Church* (Grand Rapids, MI: Brazos Press, 2006), 123.
[199] Ogden, 104

Holistic and lasting transformation into Christ-likeness affects one's nature and originates on the inside while simple conformity of behavior originates on the outside through change that reflects one's surrounding culture.[200]

The Apostle Paul describes the process of transformation as removing the old and replacing it with the new. Ogden describes this process of transformation:

> A true transformation would have meant removal of the rubbish, to be replaced by clean soil. This is why Paul constantly connects transformation with the image of "putting off" the old nature and "putting on" the new nature (Eph. 4:17-32).
>
> For Paul, the fully devoted, reproducing disciple is one who has grown to reflect the character of Jesus is his or her life. The process of transformation removes all that reflects the old, sinful self, while the scent of Christ permeates the whole being from the inside out. Maturity for Paul is our readiness to have Jesus reflect his nature through every aspect of our being.[201]

Hull declares that holistic transformation into Christ-likeness involves, "Believing what he (Christ) believed (transformed mind), . . . living the way he lived (transformed character), . . . loving the way he loved (transformed relationships), . . . ministering the way he ministered (transformed service), . . . leading the way he led (transformed influence)."[202]

During his earthly ministry, Jesus addressed people's spiritual, physical, and social needs. Jesus' work of sanctification

---

[200] Ogden, 104
[201] Ogden, 104-105.
[202] Hull, *Choose the Life*, 19-20.

begins with one's immaterial nature and moves out into all aspects of one's life. Disciple-making is the process mandated by Christ to transform the whole person to bring holistic change into Christ-likeness.Allen states, "Through an examination of Christ's earthly ministry, we see that the 'whole' is glorifying God and advancing his kingdom through the discipling of the nations (Matt. 24:14; 28:18-20). This is God's 'big agenda'—the principal task that he works through his church to accomplish."[203]

A Holistic Disciple Obeys All That Christ Has Commanded

When Christ commanded his followers to make disciples by teaching them to "obey all that I have commanded you" (Matthew 28:19), he provided a working model of a holistic disciple whose character and will are focused to accomplish his purpose. Blomberg notes that, "Teaching obedience to all of Jesus' commands forms the heart of disciple-making. Evangelism must be holistic . . . the testimony of the Gospels and the commands Jesus issued . . . must comprise the central core of Christian faith and proclamation."[204] The growth of a disciple is not static. Christ did not die *just to* make disciples. He died to make *obedient* disciples who *learn to obey* all that he has commanded. Hull states, "The gospel requires us to make disciples who learn to obey

---

[203] Scott Allen, "William Carey: A Missionary Who Transformed a Nation," *Mission Frontiers* 33, no. 5 (September-October 2011): 16.
[204] Blomberg, "Matthew," 433.

everything Christ taught. The evidence of salvation is living a life of transformation."[205] It is a divine principle—the believer who pursues obedience to the Word is transformed into Christ's likeness. Willard declares, "What transforms us is the will to obey Jesus Christ from a life that is one with his resurrected reality day by day, learning obedience through inward transformation."[206] Obedience is the required pathway in the making of holistic disciples.

Willard underscores the need for obedience in spiritual transformation:

> I can tell you that the transformation of character comes through learning how to act in concert with Jesus Christ. *Character is formed through action, and it is transformed through action,* including carefully planned and grace-sustained disciplines. To enter the path of obedience to Jesus Christ—intending to obey him and intending to learn whatever I have to learn in order to obey him—is the true path of spiritual formation or transformation.[207]

Obedience does not come without effort. Willard makes a clear distinction between grace and work. "Grace is not opposed to effort, it is opposed to earning. Earning is an attitude. Effort is an action. Grace, you know, does not just have to do with forgiveness of sins alone. Many people don't know this, and that is one major result of the cutting down of the gospel to a theory of

---

[205] Hull, *The Complete Book of Discipleship*, 44.
[206] Willard, *Omission*, 65-66.
[207] Willard, *Omission*, 65.

justification."[208] Hull affirms the need for work and effort in spiritual growth:

> The Scriptures extol its benefits (1 Cor. 9:24-27; Galatians 6:7-9; Colossians 1:28-29; 1 Timothy 4:7; Hebrews 5:14) . . . God's grace is a gift and is not for sale or given to the hardest worker. But grace gives one the endowment of power and resources to give a full effort (see Ephesians 2:8-10). The mystical relationship of grace and effort is given credence by Paul's autobiographical teaching: (Col. 1:28-29). Paul worked hard; he struggled—but it was with God's power that he does so.[209]

Living in obedience comes from a life of learning through obedience. Obedience breeds more obedience. When believers understand that God saved them to not only go to heaven but also to align their lives under his Lordship to accomplish his mission, they can understand the key role and importance obedience plays in their lives.

Unfortunately, for many, agreement with orthodox doctrine and biblical familiarity are equated with spiritual maturity, part of the sanctification gap mentioned above. Agreement with the ministry and teaching in a church are often considered evidence of a growing spiritual life. Yet, Scripture is consistent—the only route to please and honor God is obedience. Only submission and obedience to God pleases him and displays spiritual maturity (1 Samuel 15:22). As Hirsch and Frost note, "As followers of Jesus, we have to start obeying long before we know and understand

---

[208] Willard, *Omission*, 61.
[209] Hull, *"Spiritual Formation from the Inside Out,"* 126.

much of him whom we obey. More than that, if we take obedience out of the equation, we cannot even hope to truly understand the Bible."[210] The disciple's model is Jesus, who "humbled himself by becoming obedient to the point of death" (Philippians 2:8). Faith only becomes the power that can transform lives *through* obedience. Willard succinctly states,

> The missing note in evangelical life today is not in the first instance spirituality but rather obedience. We have generated a variety of religion to which obedience is not regarded as essential . . . .
>
> But I don't understand how anyone can look ingenuously at the contents of the scripture and say that Jesus intends anything else for us but obedience. So my first point is simple, life in Christ has to do with obedience to his teaching. If we don't start there, we may as well forget about any distinctively *Christian* spirituality.[211]

New Testament Terms Supporting the Holistic Disciple Concept

Although the term *disciple* does not occur after Acts, the concept of disciple-making and discipleship is clearly taught throughout the New Testament. Every believer is called to become fully developed spiritually in keeping with God's predestined purpose to conform every disciple into Christ's likeness (Romans 8:29). In other passages (1 Peter 2:2; 1 Corinthians 3:2-3; 13:11; Hebrews 5:11-14), becoming like Christ is compared to the natural and expected process of physical growth and maturation. Spiritual

---

[210] Frost and Hirsch, *Re-Jesus*, 155.
[211] Willard, *Omission*, 44-45.

maturity is consistently presented as an intentional process (Philippians 3:12-15; 1 Timothy 4:7; James 1:2-4; 2 Peter 3:18), to be pursued by all believers (1 Corinthians 13:12).[212]

The Apostle Paul described his labor and constant effort to make complete, mature and whole (holistic) disciples (Colossians 1:28-29). Ogden observes,

> If you listen carefully to Colossians 1:28-29, you will hear the echo of Jesus' command to "go and make disciples." Paul articulates the call upon his life: (Col. 1:28-29). One purpose demands all of Paul's effort and energy—to bring everyone to maturity in Christ . . . . In Colossians 1:29 Paul tells us that he puts his energy into bringing people to adulthood in Christ. Paul begins, "For this I toil." The root of the Greek word for "toil" means beatings or the weariness that comes from being struck. As this term evolved, it became an analogy for the weariness that comes from hard work, labor or striving.
> This image is coupled with "struggle." "For this I toil and struggle." A literal transliteration from the Greek would be "agonize." On another occasion Paul used this same word to compare the Christian life with that of an athlete "Athletes exercise (agonize) self-control in all things; they do it to receive a perishable wreath, but we an imperishable one" (1 Corinthians 9:25). In articulating his personal mission statement, Paul says that his singular focus is to assist everyone he encounters toward maturity in Christ.[213]

A synonym for biblical *maturity* is the term *perfect* (ἄρτιος) which describes someone who is in fit shape or condition, complete and proficient. This term is used generally to describe a

---

[212] Garrison, *The 360° Disciple*, 17-20.
[213] Ogden, 101-02.

person's character. In 2 Timothy 3:17, God's inspired word, after shaping believers into Christ-likeness (reproof, correction, etc.) is to have its powerful effect in their lives "that the man of God may be competent (perfect), for every good work." The word translated "competent" or "fully equipped" comes from the Greek verb εξαρτιζο. When the verb εξαρτιζο is combined with the adjective άρτιος (perfect, complete). it signifies that God has given us his word to completely and fully outfit, furnish, equip, and supply the obedient disciple for "all good works."[214] A holistic disciple is a "man of God" who is "competent, equipped for every good work" (2 Timothy 2:16-17). Hull notes that, "training to be godly is very different from trying to be godly. Trying to be godly doesn't work, training does."[215] It is vital to understand that the divine goal of training in righteousness (spiritual formation) is the equipping necessary to serve others through every good work.

Essentially the terms "spiritual formation" and "transformation" refer to the same process of change towards Christ-likeness. Hull describes the process of formation:

> Spiritual formation involves a radical internal change in which the spiritual heart directs the transformation of the entire person to reflect Jesus Christ (see Matthew 5:20; 15:18-20; Romans 6:17-19).This means developing congruency between inward transformation and external activity so that the entire person is obedient to Jesus (see Galatians 4:19; Ephesians 4:22-24).[216]

---

[214] Ralph Earle, "2 Timothy," *The Expositor's Bible Commentary,* ed. by Frank E. Gaebelein (Grand Rapids, MI: Zondervan Publishing House, 1978), 410.
[215] Hull, *Choose the Life,* 78.
[216] Hull, *"Spiritual Formation from the Inside Out,"* 105.

The word *transformation* is made from a combination of two Greek terms, *trans* (μετα) and *formation* (μορφή). *Trans* signifies moving something from one place to another place. *Formation* means to change into a new reality (Romans 12:2; Galatians 4:19). In spiritual transformation, a believer's mind is transformed around the reality found in Christ. They no longer depend on the flesh but on the Spirit to accomplish the will of Christ (Romans 12:2; 2 Corinthians 3:16-18).[217] Character transformation is learned, created through a process of obedience and faithfulness over time.[218] Matthews notes,

> Our growth into Christlikeness does not occur through osmosis. Of course, when we talk about effort, we are not saying to grit your teeth and just act more Christian . . . .
> What must be understood about intentionality is that the work of transformation is God's work in us, but we are not passive in the process. The apostle Paul knew full well this synergistic participation between God and us. (Phil. 2:12-13; Colossians 1:29) Both of these verses affirm the action of humanity and the action of God working simultaneously. This is not about works righteousness but about wisdom-filled living.[219]

A synonym for Christ-likeness is the term *godliness*. In 1 Timothy 4:7-8, the Apostle Paul instructed Timothy to give diligent attention to train himself for godliness. The verb *train* in Greek is γύμναζε, from which we get the English word *gymnasium*. Godliness is declared to provide training in life that is far superior

---

[217] Hull, *The Complete Book on Discipleship*, 188.
[218] Matthews, *"The Transformational Process,"* 94-95.
[219] Matthews, *"The Transformational Process,"* 91.

to physical exercise because God rewards the godly person it the present life and the life to come.[220]

Peter exhorts his readers to "prepare their minds for action" in their pursuit of holiness (1 Peter 1:13-16). Spiritual maturity begins in the mind because obedience originates as an act of the will. Pursuing holiness begins by "being sober-minded" not controlled by other desires that come from within. Being holy means not being conformed to evil desires and passions of the flesh but through obedience, disciples are called to reflect the pure nature of God in their lives.[221] "Though absolute holiness can never be achieved in this life, all areas of life should be in the process of becoming completely conformed to God's perfect and holy will."[222]

The author of Hebrews also commends training in the pursuit of spiritual maturity. In Hebrews 5:12-14 the writer decries how his readers have not pursued holistic discipleship. Spiritual maturity and a related obligation to teach others is understood for those who are not new converts to Christ. Bruce notes that

> ... the immaturity of the people ... was due to a disinclination to press on in the Christian way .... The "milk" corresponds to ... some of the "first principles" ... in Ch. 6:1f. Those who have not proceeded beyond this stage are still infants, "without experience of the word or righteousness." It is ethically mature men, those "who by

---

[220] Ralph Earle, "1 Timothy," *The Expositor's Bible Commentary,* ed. by Frank E. Gaebelein (Grand Rapids, MI: Zondervan Publishing House, 1978), 373.
[221] Roger M. Raymer, "1 Peter," *The Bible Knowledge Commentary: New Testament*, eds. John F. Walvoord and Roy B. Zook (Wheaton: IL Victor Books, 1983), 842-843.
[222] Raymer, 843.

reason of use have their senses exercised to discern good and evil," who have built up in the course of experience a principle or standard of righteousness by which they can pass discriminating judgment on moral situations as they arise.[223]

Training through in-depth doctrine prepares a holistic disciple so that his senses are transformed and he can thus discern how to live in an obedient and righteous manner.

Becoming a Holistic Disciple is a Choice

Holistic disciples grow through a sustained life of obedience to Christ's word and submission to his lordship. The holistic disciple increasingly does what pleases the Lord (Romans 12:2), because all aspects of his person are being substantially transformed into Christ's likeness.[224] Willard states, *"The redemptive process of forming the inner human world so that it takes on the character of the inner being of Christ himself.* In the degree to which it is successful, the outer life of the individual becomes a natural expression or outflow of the character and teaching of Jesus.[225]

Every believer must choose to pursue transformation through love and obedience to Christ. Believers must be taught

---

[223] F. F. Bruce, *The Epistle to the Hebrews*, The New International Commentary on the New Testament (Grand Rapids, MI: Wm. B. Eerdmans Publishing Co. 1964), 108-09.
[224] Dallas Willard and Don Simpson, *Revolution of Character: Discovering Christ's Pattern for Spiritual Transformation* (Colorado Springs: NavPress Publishing Group, 2005), 182.
[225] Willard, *Omission*, 105.

about the nature of the spiritual life and reject any teaching that does not promote consistent effort and obedience towards Christ's likeness. As Platt states, "Making disciples by going, baptizing, and teaching people the Word of Christ and then enabling them to do the same thing in other people's loves—this is the plan God has for each of us to impact the nations for the glory of Christ."[226]

The Motivation and Reproduction of Holistic Disciples of Jesus Christ

Introduction

Obedience ignites greater faith that results in acts of service for the benefit of others. It is the love of Christ that motivates believers to obey him and not live for their own benefit, but for Christ and his purposes (John 14:23-24; 2 Corinthians 5:14-15). The disciple who loves Christ seeks to be like him and help other disciples do the same.

Love of God and Others—
The Motivation of a Holistic Disciple

The *Shema* of Israel (Deuteronomy 6:4-9) was the basis of Jewish faith in the Old Testament. Faithful Jews daily lived under the authority of God and responded in obedience and worship to display their love for Him. The act of worship called *yichud* ("unification") involved offering all of one's life and being to God. As the *Shema* was recited daily, all other loyalties that restricted

---

[226] Platt, *Radical*, 103

God's active control of one's life were renounced and all motivations were directed to honor, obey and worship God alone. The *Shema* was the discipleship process to promote true holiness and obedience.[227]

Christ declared that his followers should pursue this same obligation as well as loving their neighbor as themselves: "You shall love the Lord your God with all your heart and with all your soul and with all your mind. This is the greatest and first commandment. And a second is like it, You shall love your neighbor as yourself. On these two commandments depend all the Law and the Prophets" (Matthew 22:37-40). The *Shema* and the second greatest command (Leviticus 19:18) together form the principal motivation for Jesus' disciples as well. Holistic disciples love God with their entire being, expressed in obedience to Christ, and lives given to serve others and reproduce disciples. Thompson notes, "The Great Commandment calls the church to love God and as an outworking of this to love neighbor—the two cannot be separated (Matt. 22:37-39; 1 John 4:20). Love is the mark of discipleship (John 13:35). Love is the fulfillment of the law of God (Rom. 13:10; Gal. 5:14). Love reflects the very character of God (1 John 4:8)."[228] Thompson continues describing the place of love in the life of the disciple:

> One cannot fully comprehend the significance of this commission (the Great Commission) without first understanding the implication of the Great Commandment

---

[227] Frost and Hirsch, *ReJesus*, 124.
[228] Ott and Strauss, 159.

to love our God (Matthew 22:35-38), and to love our neighbor (Matthew 22:39-40). Thus, when an individual accepts Christ as their personal Lord and Savior, they are also accepting their commitment to grow in an on-going love relationship with their God; to be Christ-like to others in love and service; and to actively seek ways to lead others to be disciples.[229]

In John 13:34-35 Christ gave a *new* commandment to his disciples to love one another as he has loved them. Hull notes that, "He commands us to love others until it shatters defenses, brings down strongholds, tears apart barriers, and even slips through the firewalls of culture. This is the revolution that Jesus calls his disciples to, and it requires sacrificial living."[230] Kincaid observes, "In John 13:34, Jesus says, 'As I have loved you, so you must love one another.' Jesus is our example. He who came to us, took the form of a man, and gave his life for us is the standard for our love for others. Like Jesus, we just sacrifice our rights, serve others, and give up our lives for the sake of others."[231]

In 2 Corinthians 5:14-17 the Apostle Paul declares that what compels and drives the believer to obedience and action is the *love of Christ*. The remaining verses in this chapter relate to the marvelous reconciling work of God in Christ (vv. 14b, 18-19). The *love of Christ*, refers to the love Christ displayed through life and in his substitutionary death for mankind through which salvation is

---

[229] Michelle Sung-Mee Thompson, *Disciple-Making Congregations* (Doctoral Dissertation, Anderson University School of Theology, Anderson Indiana, 2004), 54.
[230] Hull, *The Complete Book of Discipleship*, 141.
[231] Ron Kincaid, *A Celebration of Disciplemaking* (Wheaton, IL: Victor Books, 1990), 88.

made available to all. His love should control believers to "no longer live for themselves but for him who for their sake died and was raised" (2 Corinthians 5:15b). The core motivation of the holistic disciple is to live for the benefit, pleasure, honor and glory of Christ and not for one's own sake. Living for Christ should result in living for others' benefit. Hull adds, "For our discussion of disciples and disciple-making, (we can) define love in its boldest form: an action designed for the benefit of another."[232] The believer's will to obey all that Christ has commanded comes from a desire to love Christ in every aspect of our life and being.

The Importance of Godly Examples in Making Holistic Disciples

The root word for *complete* or *mature* in the Greek language is the term τέλειοω (noun form τέλειος) meaning, *having reached its end* or *goal, finished, complete,* or *perfect*.[233] In 1 Corinthians 14:20, the Apostle Paul contrasted being like a child in one's thinking with being mature (τέλειος). In Ephesians 4:13-14, Paul taught that the mature (τέλειος) grow into the measure of the full stature of Christ. Immature childlike faith and spiritual immaturity causes a believer to be unstable and susceptible to deceitful schemes (Ephesians 4:13-14). In James, the believer is exhorted to grow spiritually through trials so that they can exercise endurance and become τέλειος, not lacking anything necessary for

---

[232] Hull, *The Complete Book of Discipleship*, 154.
[233] W. E. Vine, *The Expanded Vine's Expository Dictionary of New Testament Words* (Minneapolis, MN: Bethany House Publishers, 1984), 845-46.

pleasing God. For James, spiritual maturity (τέλειος) comes through perseverance through trials and obedience to Christ resulting in wise living.[234] Clearly, completeness, perfection, or spiritual maturity is a goal that can be realized as one becomes like Christ.

Several New Testament passages convey the idea of imitation and modeling to emulate the life of Christ. Meyer asserts that "The power of an exemplary life is probably the most important teaching of Jesus, Paul, and the other writers of the New Testament as well as the early church fathers. Imitation and mimicry abound in their writings and testimonies. There is a passed down living tradition of life that we are missing."[235] Paul instructed the Corinthian believers to "Be imitators of me, as I am of Christ" (1 Corinthians 11:1). Striving to imitate Jesus promotes growth in his likeness and allows the believer to grow in obedience and dependence on him (Galatians 2:20). Observing a believer's Christ-like life and example provides a motivation and pattern for one's pursuit of his character in their lives.[236]

The Apostle Paul includes similar instruction in 1 Corinthians 4:16, "I urge you, then, be imitators of me." The word for *imitate* in the Greek is μιμέομαι, from which is translated the English word *mimic*. Μιμέομαι often accompanies the Greek word τύπος, which means *example*, *model* or *pattern* (1 Corinthians 11:1; Philippians 3:17; 1 Thessalonians 1:6-7; 2 Thessalonians 3:7, 9).

---

[234] Lin, 101.
[235] Meyer, 159.
[236] Hull, *The Complete Book of Discipleship*, 114-115.

Imitation signifies patterning one's lifestyle after the example of another. The Apostle Paul frequently used these synonyms to promote how Christ's life should serve as the pattern for the disciple's own life and as an example of their efforts to make disciples of others (ex. Philippians 3:17).[237]

In 1 Timothy 4:11-16, the Apostle Paul exhorted Timothy to carefully train Ephesian believers both through his own teaching and godly example. Apart from authoritative instruction, Timothy was to "set the believers an example (τύπος) in speech, in conduct, in love, in faith, in purity (1 Timothy 2:12). Meyer comments on the significance of the word translated *example* found in 1 Timothy 4:11-12, 15-16:

> The Greek word *tupos* has four different meanings. First, it can mean "to mark from pressure or to strike" or "to leave a mark." You might call to mind the popular expression, "That'll leave a mark." Second, it means making a "copy" or an "icon" and is used to describe the similar look of a child's facial features to a parent. Third, it means "a pattern or form of life" or "a common way of life." Fourth, it means something like a "type" or similar kind.[238]

Paul and Timothy used their words, life examples, priorities and Christ-like character in their mentoring of others to promote an example and pattern for believers to follow.

---

[237] Ogden, 106.
[238] Meyer, 160.

The Challenge of Reproducing Holistic Disciples

When the eleven disciples heard Jesus' command to *make disciples* (Matthew 28:19), they would have naturally remembered all that he had done to make them his disciples. Jesus' example of making disciples forms the pattern for others to follow. Reproducing holistic disciples is central to the formation of disciple-making movements. Platt notes,

> Jesus was anything but casual about his mission. He was initiating a revolution, but his revolution would not revolve around the masses or the multitudes . . . it would revolve around choosing a few people . . . . All he wanted was a few men who would think as he did, love as he did, see as he did, teach as he did, and serve as he did. All he needed was to revolutionize the hearts of a few, and they would impact the world.[239]

The New Testament Church grew throughout the Roman Empire through the intentional effort of believers to make disciples of all people. The Apostle Paul demonstrated his concern for making disciples when he wrote to Timothy, "and what you have heard from me in the presence of many witnesses, entrust to faithful men who will be able to teach others also" (2 Timothy 2:2). For Christ's disciples, the making of holistic disciples who were mature and faithful was a serious concern and commitment if other disciples of similar character were to be reproduced.[240] McCallum and Lowery observe that

---

[239] Platt, 88.
[240] Hull, *Choose the Life*, 31.

> . . . Paul was concerned with duplicating disciples down through four generations: 1) himself, 2) Timothy, 3) 'reliable men," and 4) "others." From this single verse, we clearly see that Paul used personal discipleship as a conscious strategy for developing leadership in the early church. He also urged women to disciple other women (Titus 2:3), a practice unknown in Judaism.[241]

Hull notes how Paul instructed Timothy that the task of making holistic disciples would not be easy. It would require the personal discipline of a soldier, the focus of a winning athlete, and the patience of a farmer to reproduce faithful disciples (2 Timothy 2:3-7).[242] The training necessary to make disciples who are faithful and equipped to make other disciples of godly character is intense, exhausting, and grueling—but worth every drop of sweat for God's glory." Some of the greatest passages in the New Testament extol effort (see 1 Cor. 9:24-27; 2 Cor. 11:23-29; Gal. 4:19; Phil. 3:9-16; Col. 1:28-30; 2 Tim. 2:1-11; Heb. 5:11-13)."[243] Reproducing disciples involves effort, commitment, and continual labor to develop mature, holistic disciples of others (Philippians 2:12-13; 1 Timothy 4:13-16; 1 Peter 1:14-16; 2 Peter 1:4-11).

Platt states the clear challenge involved in making disciples:

> Making disciples is not an easy process. It is trying. It is messy. It is slow, tedious, even painful at times. It is all these things because it is relational. Jesus has not given us an effortless step-by-step formula for impacting nations for his glory. He has given us people and he has said, "Live for them. Love them, serve them, and lead them. Lead them to

---

[241] McCallum and Lowery, 27.
[242] Hull, *The Complete Book of Discipleship*, 283.
[243] Hull, *Choose the Life*, 68-69.

follow me, and lead them to lead others to follow me. In the process you will multiply the gospel to the ends of the earth."[244]

The Necessity of Others-Centered Service in the Making of Holistic Disciples

Perhaps the most overlooked component in developing spiritual maturity is others-centered service. God has designed, as an integral part of maturity and spiritual transformation, that disciples learn and grow to deeper levels of Christ's character through investing their lives in serving others.[245] Others-centered service, focused on making disciples and deeds of service, is an essential quality of a holistic disciple's life that develops Christ's likeness and continued faithfulness to the Lord.

In Mark 10:45 (Matthew 20:28), Jesus declares, "For even the Son of Man came not to be served but to serve, and to give his life as a ransom for many." Wilkins understands that, "This passage is important for us to examine because it is the key to understanding Jesus' perspective of discipleship. By comprehending the essence of Jesus' ministry as servant-hood, the disciples will comprehend the essence of discipleship as servant-hood, including their motivation, position, ambition, expectations and example . . . ."[246] McManus observes, "There is something wonderful and uniquely powerful about servant-hood because God

---

[244] Platt, 93.
[245] Wood, 4.
[246] Wilkins, *Following*, 197.

is a servant. When we serve others, we more fully reflect the image of God, and our hearts begin to resonate with the heart of God. We may never be more like God than when we're serving from a purely selfless motivation."[247] Christ taught that a life that influences others occurs when his disciples seek to live for the benefit of others. Christ's disciples need to develop an others-centered perspective, realizing that others-centered service presents the greatest platform and influence for the making of disciples and the fulfillment of Christ's mission.

Others-centered living is focused on helping others become holistic disciples. The disciple-maker who leads other disciples in their spiritual growth is referred to by some as a spiritual *mentor* or *coach*. Wilkins notes how mentoring in the Old and New Testaments was characterized by mentoring and others-centered service:

> The goal of these mentoring relationships was to prepare individuals to serve God's people, either within the nation or within the church. Individuals were equipped for service through these relationships. When we hear the words "discipleship" and "mentoring" we often think of personal growth or some such thing. Growth is important, but the goal of growth is service.[248]

Others-centered service reveals a divine principle inherent in disciple-making. When disciple-making believers are committed to making disciples of others, they are intrinsically propelled to

---

[247] Erwin Raphael McManus, *An Unstoppable Force: Daring to Become the Church God Had in Mind* (Loveland, CO: Group, 2001), 175-76.
[248] Wilkins, *Following*, 68.

greater levels of personal spiritual growth and Christ-likeness in the process. As Hull claims, "Discipleship—the effort both to be a disciple and to make other disciples—is about the immense value of God at work in one individual's life and the resulting impact on other lives."[249] In fact, holistic spiritual maturity cannot be experienced in any other way but through disciple-making and investing in the lives of others. The Lord has so designed life that spiritual growth toward godliness is the divinely ordained outcome of service as believers invest themselves in the lives of others. Believers who do not offer themselves in service to God and others, begin to stagnate spiritually and stunt their personal growth and understanding of Christ. Kincaid states, "when we commit to making disciples, we are instantly spurred on to growth in our spiritual pilgrimage. God designed life so that spiritual growth would come as an outgrowth of service to Him"[250] Kincaid continues,

> With few exceptions a living cell either reproduces or it dies: the principle is so simple that no one has bothered to call it a principle. A cell is born in the division of a partner cell. It then doubles in every respect: in every part, in every kind of molecule, even in the amount of water it contains. What is true in the biological sphere is true in the spiritual realm. We either reproduce or die. We commit ourselves to making disciples and spend ourselves in service to others, or we cease to grow toward Christian maturity.[251]

---

[249] Hull, *The Complete Book of Discipleship*, 28.
[250] Kincaid, 20.
[251] Kincaid, 21.

It is an amazing spiritual truth that when disciples commit themselves to serving others they experience greater growth in Christ-likeness, a deeper personal knowledge of God and increased strength and faith to continue serving Him.

A Holistic Disciple Is Created
for a Life of Good Works

The great Christological hymn in Philippians 2:5-11 begins in verse 5, "Have this mind among yourselves, which is yours in Christ Jesus." The Greek word translated mind (φρονος) translates in English as *attitude*, *mind-set*, or *frame of mind*. Since this verse contains a command, the worldview, mindset and attitude that Jesus models, as presented in verses 6-8, is obligatory for his disciples as well.[252]

A humble and submissive mindset leads the holistic disciple to obey and sacrificially serve for the benefit of others. The Apostle Paul highlights the others-centered, service-oriented life of Timothy and Epaphroditus in Philippians 2:20-30. Timothy was unique because he emulated the others-centered mindset of Christ by not seeking his own interest but rather the spiritual well-being and benefit of others. The Apostle Paul called Epaphroditus "my brother and fellow worker and fellow soldier, and your messenger and minister to my need" (verse 25). Epaphroditus was to be honored because "he nearly died for the work of Christ, risking his life to complete what was lacking in your service to me"

---

[252] Hull, *Choose the Life*, 160-61.

(Philippians 2:25-30). Timothy and Epaphroditus were highlighted by the Apostle Paul as normative examples of men who chose an others-centered and service-focused life, the life of a holistic disciple transformed by Christ.

Rusaw and Swanson describe how service opens doors for the gospel:

> Good deeds form a great bridge over which the good news can travel! The doors to salvation have opened through service. People from the community have asked our churches to start churches in nursing homes, to mentor juvenile offenders, to serve as chaplains in nonprofit agencies, to work with the homeless, to work in schools, and to serve in many other environments into which we never could have forced our way.[253]

The ministry of service and sacrifice inherent in the making of disciples also uniquely affects the disciple-maker. Others-centered living strengthens the spirit and motivates the believer to pursue Christ's likeness. This is why a disciple can only grow to full maturity in Christ through sacrificial service to others. Kincaid notes how holistic disciple-making is the key to spiritual maturity:

> Christians grow toward spiritual maturity only when they give themselves to some aspect of the missionary mandate. We grow tremendously when we spend ourselves in service to Christ. When we refuse to reach out to others, failing to use our gifts in service to Christ, our spiritual growth is halted. Giving ourselves to disciple-making is essential to growing toward maturity.[254]

---

[253] Rusaw & Swanson, 61.
[254] Kincaid, 76.

A remarkable truth concerning the divinely ordained identity and purpose of a disciple is found in Ephesians 2:10, "For we are his workmanship, created in Christ Jesus for good works, which God prepared beforehand, that we should walk in them." Every disciple is God's work of art (ποίημα).[255] Before time, God had purposefully equipped every disciple to live a life characterized by good works uniquely designed to accomplish Christ's purposes. United with the mission of Christ these good works are designed to accomplish his disciple-making purpose. Rusaw and Swanson note,

> We are not saved *by* good works but we are saved *for* good works that "God [has] prepared in advance for us to do." Our job is not to invent those good works but to discover what they are. How we are made (our skills and desires) is probably an indication of the type of good works we will be passionate about—where our desires and skills intersect with the needs of the world around us.[256]

Waggoner observes, "Every Christian is created to produce good works. Service to God and others is not an a la carte offering of a spiritual menu; it's part of the main course."[257]

The holistic disciple responds to God's great grace by zealously pursuing good works. Titus was to teach disciples to live for others and be zealous for good works (Titus 2:11-15). Titus was to teach the believers that their salvation served as the

---

[255] R. Kent Hughes, *Ephesians: The Mystery of the Body of Christ* (Wheaton, IL: Crossway Books, 1990), 81.
[256] Rusaw & Swanson, 86-87.
[257] Brad J. Waggoner, *The Shape of Faith to Come: Spiritual Formation and the Future of Discipleship* (Nashville, TN: B&H Publishing Group, 2008), 111.

platform from which they zealously served others. Titus was to insist on others-centered service, so that believers would be careful to devote themselves to good works, which are profitable for others (Titus 3:8). Titus was to help disciples "learn to devote themselves to good works, so as to help cases of urgent need, and not be unfruitful (Titus 3:14). The Apostle Paul emphasized that training in godly character (holistic discipleship) is inextricably linked with doing good works. Disciples need training to live an others-centered life of service and good work. Others-centered living does not come naturally but through transformation into Christ-likeness.

Conclusion

Christ commanded his disciples to make disciples who are taught to obey all that He had commanded. In doing so, he commanded them to make holistic disciples transformed into his likeness. For the mission of Christ to be accomplished, the making of holistic disciples and disciple-making movements must be prioritized and pursued by all believers. As Kincaid states

> . . . to serve others and seek to touch them with Christ's love. Our own resources simply will not suffice . . . .
> An involvement in disciple-making is essential to Christian maturity. Go and make disciples. Give yourselves to the church's calling to make disciples and you will be ushered into a whole new experience of Christ's presence, power, joy, and promises."[258]

---

[258] Kincaid, 28.

Many churches and believers have not been taught about the two-faceted nature of their salvation. Few believers understand their responsibility to actively pursue maturity into the likeness of Christ. Many believers are never taught how to live under the authority and lordship of Christ. Few understand the believer's lifelong obligation to work out their salvation and discipline themselves to be godly. Many do not understand the purpose of their salvation as the transformation of their whole person into his likeness (Romans 8:29). What is needed is an understanding and solemn commitment to the mission of Christ—to make holistic disciples of all peoples.

Holistic disciples are trained to live for and to be like Christ. The love of Christ motivates obedient disciples to live for Jesus and his mission. MacDonald notes,

> Servanthood and stewardship from this perspective require a value shift of monumental proportions. I can no longer agree with my culture that my life is my own, that my time is a personal possession, and that others exist for my benefit. I cannot affirm the attitude of ads that declare, "It's worth it," "I deserve it," and "this I do for me."[259]

Believers who commit to holistic discipleship are transformed into Christ's likeness to serve his purposes obediently. As holistic disciples live to serve others, their lives of good works will result in the making of other holistic disciples for God's glory.

---

[259] Glenn MacDonald, *The Disciple Making Church: From Dry Bones to Spiritual Vitality* (Grand Haven, MI: FaithWalk Publishers, 2004), 230.

CHAPTER 5
THE NATURE OF DISCIPLE-MAKING MOVEMENTS

Introduction

McCallum and Lowery describe the incredible growth of the church during the first century:

> The period from the death of Christ until the end of the first century was the most fruitful in the history of the church. During these few decades, Christianity spread clear across the Roman Empire and even penetrated deeper into Africa, the Parthian Empire, and India. The best estimates put the number of Christians at the end of the first century at around 1 million. That's an increase of 2000 times the number of Christians before Pentecost (perhaps 500). And all of this growth was facilitated by the process of discipleship. Without mass media, advertising, church buildings or seminaries, the primitive church expanded at a rate never equaled in the nineteen centuries since.[260]

The reason the first century church experienced this phenomenal growth can be attributed to the all-out commitment of the church to obediently make disciples of all peoples. Christ left his followers with one method, one strategy, and one goal.

This Chapter advances the concept that the mission of Christ (the making of obedient disciples) is carried out most biblically, thoroughly, and efficiently through disciple-making movements. The author's purpose here is not to minimize the

---

[260] McCallum and Lowery, 28.

significance and ministry Christ has designed for his Church. The healthy and reproducing church is the intended outcome of the disciple making activity. Christ's mission, based upon his redemption and post-resurrection authority, is centered on the making of holistic disciples of all peoples. It is through disciple-making movements that his mandate and his promise are divinely achieved. His promise to build his church is accomplished as disciples are made. Christ's mission can be understood as containing a divine "cause and effect." The cause is the making of obedient disciples. The effect is the building of his universal church (Matthew 16:18).

The Growth of a Movement—
Great Commission Best Practices

Before ascending to heaven, Christ declared to his followers that the central priority of the mission was the making of holistic disciples. Ogden explains, "Jesus had already provided the mission statement for every church. It is popularly called the great commission (Matthew 28:18-20). Instead of coming up with a new mission as if it must be unique for each church, we should redirect our energy to making a fresh statement of Jesus' original marching orders."[261]

A growing number of Biblical scholars claim that the root problem in evangelicalism is its abandonment of discipleship. Hirsch defines the nature of the problem:

---

[261] Ogden, 101.

> By not intentionally focusing on making disciples, we had inadvertently cultivated the already immanent (religious) consumerism. I found out the hard way that if we don't disciple people, the culture sure will. This was a moment of truth for me as a leader of the movement and I vowed that from then on my practice must change and that somehow disciple making must become the central activity of whatever I would do through Christian community in the future.[262]

For holistic disciple-making to become the heart of every believer and church, there must be a practical and reproducible plan. Ogden agrees,

> A major reason we have not been producing fully devoted followers of Christ is that people have not been intentionally discipled in a manner that is reproducible. Can you imagine the kingdom impact if every believer had the . . . expressed purpose . . . to grow to become a reproducing disciple of Jesus? Church life would shift from the ministry of professionals to a mobilized body of multipliers.
> . . . If the goal is to grow self-initiating reproducing, fully devoted followers of Christ, then this means that we need contexts in which the metamorphosis into Christ-likeness can become a lifelong quest.[263]

Christ designed his mission to be accomplished through the process of reproduction—one disciple teaching, leading and modeling Christ to make other disciples who in turn make other

---

[262] Hirsch, *The Forgotten Ways*, 111.
[263] Ogden, 152.

obedient disciples. As Kuhne observes, "A multiplier is a disciple who is training his spiritual children to reproduce themselves."[264]

As spiritual reproduction of disciples occurs and groups of disciples are formed (church planting), they must be individually and corporately trained to grow together as Christ's body. As Hull declares,

> The principle behind discipleship does involve one person influencing another, which does result in a change in heart and mind. The success of discipleship doesn't depend on soldiering forward in a mechanical strategy of reproduction and multiplication. And discipleship doesn't involve developing a well-trained, elite sales force. Rather discipleship occurs when a transformed person radiates Christ to those around her. It happens when people so deeply experience God's love and they can do nothing other than affect those around them.[265]

The goal of Christ's mission for all believers and churches to pursue is the making of obedient disciples. We must view the disciple-making mission as biblically normative. To train a disciple is to train a faithful reproducer of other disciples. Kuhne makes the following definition of discipleship: "Discipleship training is the spiritual work of developing spiritual maturity and spiritual reproductiveness in the life of a Christian."[266]

---

[264] Gary W. Kuhne, "Follow-up—An Overview," in *Discipleship: The Best Writing from the Most Experienced Disciple Makers* (Grand Rapids, MI: Zondervan, 1981), 117.
[265] Hull, *The Complete Book of Discipleship*, 28.
[266] Kuhne, 117.

The Two Objectives of Christ's Global Mission

Christ promised to build his church (Matthew 16:16-18). Christ commanded his followers to "make disciples of the nations" (Matthew 28:19-20). Christ established these two global objectives to fulfill his mission (the *missio Christi*). Like two sides on a coin, there are two unifying, mutually supportive outcomes that define the one mission of Christ. It is essential to note that Christ himself promised to fulfill his first objective (build his church), but he entrusted the execution of his second objective (make disciples of all peoples) to his followers. One great missional outcome Christ promised to fulfill; the other great missional outcome he committed to his followers to accomplish.

An understanding of the two-fold nature of Christ's mission is important for several reasons. First, Christ has declared the successful founding of his church. Every local church is part of Christ's universal church. Each church is established when God blesses the efforts of faithful believers to make disciples. Churches are established when Christ's followers partner with him to accomplish his purposes. 1 Corinthians 3:5-9 demonstrates this divine/faithful disciple partnership:

> What then is Apollos? What is Paul? Servants through whom you believed, as the Lord assigned to each. I planted, Apollos watered, but God gave the growth. So neither he who plants nor he who waters is anything, but only God who gives the growth. He who plants and he who waters are one, and each will receive his wages according to his labor. For we are God's fellow workers. You are God's field, God's building.

Second, the process and responsible parties of his mission are defined. Christ established *rules* concerning how his mission was to be fulfilled. In the establishment of the church, Christ alone is the architect and builder. If Christ's disciples are to be made from all people, his disciples must be trained to obey and emulate Christ. An understanding of the two-fold nature of Christ's mission is significant for a third reason: it shows the reciprocal and interdependent relationship of Christ's two missional objectives. The building of Christ's church and the making of his disciples are interdependent activities. Without annulling his sovereignty, power, and perfect will, Christ made the fulfillment of his mission dependent on the obedience of his followers. This also implies that the success of the great commission is dependent upon the success of Christ's commitment to build his church. Hull understands the practical interdependency these two objectives have at a local church level. "Discipleship isn't just one of the things the church does; it is what the church does. It is not just part of the advancement of God's kingdom; the existence of serious disciples is the most important evidence of God's work on earth. Without enough of these workers, the task languishes and the work remains incomplete (see Matthew 9:35-38)."[267]

Christ's promise to build his church is central to his mission. In Acts 20:28, the church is declared to be purchased with his blood. The formation and biblical function of Christ's church are essential to fulfill Christ's mission. An amplified rendering of

---

[267] Hull, *The Complete Book of Discipleship*, 24.

Matthew 16:18 would read, "I will build my church by forming groups of obedient disciples all over the world who help others put their faith in Me and grow in My likeness, and reproduce other assemblies of disciples to do the same."

It is important to note that believers are not explicitly commanded to *build* Christ's church. The New Testament, carefully studied, teaches that a commitment to reproducing disciples through *disciple-making movements* is the heart of Christ's mission. When holistic disciples are made, the church is built. As the church is built, holistic disciples are reproduced. Both activities are equally important and interdependent. A divine partnership is the essence of Christ's mission. Ott and Strauss state,

> *The planting and healthy development of churches was central to Paul's mission.* He was not only concerned about evangelism. Recent New Testament studies have emphasized the importance of church planting and nurture in the ministry of Paul . . . . This is a key to understanding Romans 15:18-25. Paul could only consider his work in a region completed when reproducing churches had been planted and commended to local leaders. [268]

The Apostle's goal was to establish churches that developed holistic disciples who would faithfully train others. In order for churches to be planted and multiplied, disciple-making must be the ministry priority.

The inter-reliant relationship between disciple-making and the establishment of local churches must not be underemphasized. The priority of teaching believers to be obedient Christ-like

---

[268] Ott and Strauss, 119.

disciples is the *only* process Christ has ordained to build his church. The local church cannot become healthy and effective if its core growth ministry is not the making of holistic disciples.

The reason this point is extremely important in the fulfillment of Christ's mission is that a practical emphasis on disciple-making can readily drift into a lesser priority when the pressure of planning, forming strategy, and managing the ministry becomes the focus. Hirsch states,

> In so many churches, the mission of the church has actually become the maintenance of the institution itself. This was never Jesus' intention. Our goal in organizing as a people is not to set up, preserve, and maximize an institution over its life cycle, but to extend God's mission to the world. Our primary aim is not to perpetuate the church as an institution, but to follow Jesus into his mission to the world . . . . When we keep the mission in mind, the organic ideas about Christianity and church life will flow quite easily. When we have the institution of the church in mind, machinelike approaches are bound to follow, because its innate mechanism of responsiveness (mission) is effectively taken out of the equation. *Mission is, and must be, the organizing principle of the church.*[269]

When the disciple-making priority is the continuous focus of the church, disciple-making movements will be multiplied, holistic disciples will be made of all peoples, and healthy churches will be reproduced.

---

[269] Hirsch, *The Forgotten Ways*, 231-32.

Contemporary Approaches That Prioritize the Planting and Growth of Churches to Fulfill Christ's Mission

Throughout the world, godly and sincere servants of the Lord are seeking to advance Christ's great commission with the goal of establishing his church among all peoples. It is praiseworthy that many believers are pursuing creative strategies to evangelize, plant and develop new churches among the people with whom they work. However, while the Lord is worthy of all praise and glory for what is being accomplished, it is imperative that believers pursue the ministry strategy that Christ clearly commanded. All disciples are responsible before Christ, as his faithful stewards, to align their lives and ministries so that they make disciples of others and obey all that He has commanded.

One widely employed strategy to advance the building of Christ's church is what Garrison had called *Church Planting Movements* (CPM). Garrison states that, "A Church Planting Movement is a rapid multiplication of indigenous churches planting churches that sweeps through a people group or population segment."[270] Sills states that the emphasis on "CPM became one of the most prolific (strategies) because the largest mission agency mandated its use as the golden-key, single solution strategy for all of its missionaries worldwide."[271] Sills notes that advocates of CPM's, like Garrison, belief that the Great Commission if fulfilled through church planting:

---

[270] Garrison, *Church Planting Movements*, 21.
[271] Sills, 140.

> He (Garrison) believes that CPM is the way to finish the Great Commission task as fast as possible . . . . CPM seeks to multiply rapidly by planting churches that plant churches that plant churches. In order for this to happen, the old linear method of winning people to Christ one by one, then discipling them, then leading a Bible study, and them becoming a church, and so on, must be set aside as too slow. CPM emphasizes "wrinkling" the line and doing all the steps at once, rather than doing one step at a time, and then instilling this paradigm in the DNA of the new churches.[272]

CPM's seek to quickly identify and develop national leaders, putting them in charge of leading the growth of new churches with as little foreign missionary involvement as possible. The goal is to multiply the planting of local churches in the shortest time possible. However, Sills observes that some question if the desire to plant churches as fast as possible negatively affects the disciple-making priority and process of spiritual transformation of individual believers.

Sills continues to provide a helpful analysis of CPM methodology:

> Unquestioningly following the trends of popularity and having an uncritical embrace of the need for speed can lead missionaries to revere "whatever works" pragmatism. Many missions strategists are discouraging theological education among missionaries and nationals, saying that training them will slow down the work of Matthew 24:14 and their hopes for rapid advance that utilizes methods such as CPM.[273]

---

[272] Sills, 140-41.
[273] Sills, 148.

Another strategy is *Short-Cycle Church Planting* (SCCP). The mission agency, Avant Ministries, advocates SCCP's:[274]

> Short-Cycle Church Planting is a team-based approach to church planting. We aim to develop mature, reproducing churches led by nationals in as short of time as possible. With this approach, the elements of the church-planting process, from language learning to evangelism to leadership development, are undertaken simultaneously and accomplished as efficiently as possible . . . . Whatever the specific means, the goal is to establish and develop a church as quickly as possible so that, with whatever time God gives us in a field, lives are transformed by the power of Jesus Christ.[275]

Sills also provides this helpful analysis of Avant Ministries' SCCP church planting objective:

> The SCCP model calls for the team to "*sow the seed of the gospel early, often and directly* with a view to *finding key people* who will fully evangelize their community." Additionally, as CPM aims to avoid dependency and begins the race with the baton already in the hands of the nationals (rather than passing it off at some point in the future), so does SCCP:" "We strive to *eliminate dependence* by involving nationals *at all levels* of ministry." SCCP does not veil the need for speed. "The team will continuously look for leverage that will *accelerate* their efforts."[276]

It is crucial to note how this focus on evangelism does not fulfill the great commission. The objectives for SCCP's seem biblical since they focus on Christ's church. However, the question

---

[274] Avant Ministries, <http://www.avantministries.org> (accessed December 1, 2010).
[275] Avant Ministries, "Short-Cycle Church Planting" Avant Ministries, <http://www.avantministries.org/short-cycle.html> (accessed December 1, 2010).
[276] Sills, 141-42.

remains: "Is the heart of Christ's mission to make holistic disciples prioritized and intentionally pursued by this strategy?" Since the building of Christ's church is dependent on disciple-making, the question must be asked: "Is the church, as Christ defines it, established in such a way that its disciple-making mandate is achieved as a result of this strategy?"

One final model used to plant and multiply churches is promoted by the mission agency known as "DAWN" (Discipling a Whole Nation). Alan Johnson explains,

> DAWN works to mobilize the whole body of Christ in a country towards the goal of having an evangelical congregation for every village and neighborhood of every class, kind and condition of people in the whole country. It is concerned that Jesus Christ become incarnate . . . in the midst of every small group of people—400 or so to 1000 or more in number—in a whole country including all its people groups.[277]

Although their name includes the word *discipling*, DAWN's major ministry is to "plant enough congregations so that every person has access both geographically and culturally to a living body of believers also known as saturation church planting."[278] DAWN equates its focus on church planting with discipleship. Murray notes that, "The assumptions on which this strategy is based are that there are already many churches to be

---

[277] Alan Johnson, "Analyzing the Frontier Mission Movement and Unreached People Group Thinking, Part V: A Model for Understanding the Missionary Task," in *International Journal of Frontier Missions*, 18:3 (Fall 2001), 135.
[278] Johnson, 135.

mobilized . . . and that planting more churches will advance this cause and even bring the mission to completion."[279]

This author in no way seeks to criticize unduly the motivation and sincerity of those who pursue these CPM strategies. People are coming to Christ and churches are being established. Yet, it is paramount that the core mandate of Christ's commission remain the prioritized goal. Since Christ's command is to make holistic disciples, will that divine objective be most faithfully and strategically accomplished through prioritizing CPMs? Disciple-making is the product and the process Christ ordained to fulfill his mission and build his church.

The Problem With Prioritizing Church Planting and Growth Over Disciple-Making

Any strategy designed to fulfill the great commission that is not centered on the priority of making disciples does not perfectly achieve Christ's divine post-resurrection purpose. Church planting and growth that is not developed through disciple-making may make disciples (product of salvation) but not make holistic disciples who are trained to obey all that Christ has commanded. Advocates of CPM's assume that the making of holistic disciples will happen naturally over time through the ministry of a church. Yet, if the disciple-making priority is not pursued from the beginning and throughout the ministries of the church, obedience

---

[279] Stuart Murray, *Church Planting: Laying Foundations* (Scottdale, PA: Herald Press, 2001), 100.

to the mandate of Christ to make obedient disciples will likely never be fully realized.

Time, commitment, sacrifice, training, and obedience are required for a disciple-making movement that inherently establishes healthy churches. Sills highlights the place of training in healthy churches:

> . . . the church must also be faithful to God's Word and embrace sound evangelical theology if it is to please God and have his blessing. Only a theologically trained missionary can ensure that this process is faithful to God's Word and evangelical doctrine in the cultures where he works, and only discipled, trained, and equipped nationals can assist him in the process of critical contextualization. Trained missionaries must go forth and train trainers who can continue this process faithfully.[280]

The early church grew through a holistic disciple-making movement. Believers dedicated themselves to the Apostles' teaching and, "the Lord added to their number daily those who were being saved" (Acts 2:41, 47; 6:1, 7). New disciples in the church were taught to obey all that Christ had commanded. They committed themselves to reproduce other disciples. The New Testament Epistles provide practical instruction on how to grow and function as holistic disciples and how believers in the church should grow and minister to accomplish Christ's purposes. Biblically, the only measurement of accomplishing Christ's mission is the making of holistic disciples. Making holistic disciples always resulted in the planting of churches. The making

---

[280] Sills, 212.

of holistic disciples alone guarantees that a biblical church will be mobilized. This results in the creation of self-perpetuating disciple-making movements and the building of Christ's church.

Cole explains why the essence of a movement to fulfill the great commission must begin with disciple-making movements, not with church multiplication efforts. Cole supports the thesis of this study by affirming that it is through the multiplication of "healthy" (holistic) disciples, not churches in and of themselves, that fulfills the mission of Christ.

> Trying to multiply churches is starting at the wrong place. A church is a complex entity with multiple cells. We must go further down microscopically, to the smallest unit of Kingdom life if we want to start the multiplication process.
>
> If we cannot multiply churches, we will never see a movement. If we cannot multiply leaders, we will never multiply churches. If we cannot multiply disciples, we will never multiply leaders. The way to see a true church multiplication movement is to multiply healthy disciples, then leaders, then churches, and finally movements—in that order.
>
> As passionate as I am about church planting, I found it perplexing that the Bible never instructs us to start churches. There is not a single command in all of the Bible to initiate churches. The reason is quite clear: we are not to start churches, but instead to make disciples who make disciples. That is actually the way churches are started, at least in the New Testament. Jesus gave us instruction that is on the molecular level of Kingdom life, for a very good reason: it works. Trying to multiply large, highly complex organisms without multiplying on the micro level is impossible.[281]

---

[281] Neil Cole, *Organic Church: Growing Faith Where Life Happens* (San Francisco: Jossey-Bass, 2005), 98.

The two purposes of a disciple's salvation form both the *product and the process* of Christ mission—the making of disciples (salvation) who are transformed to live obediently like Christ (sanctification). Advocates of CPM's measure their success on the first aspect of Christ's mission—saving the lost. Narrowly defining the task of missions as success in gathering numbers and creating programs or in reaching and gathering believers misses the mark intended by Christ Jesus. This approach may actually impede the making and training of disciples of all peoples.[282] Sills reminds us that "Jesus did not command his church to go plant churches—even biblically sound ones; He commanded us to make disciples and teach them to observe all that He has commanded. Certainly, planting churches is a natural part of the process, but the emphasis is on making disciples and teaching them."[283]

A significant factor in differentiating between the making of holistic disciples and disciple-making movements is the vital nature of relationships and the process of spiritual transformation. Making holistic disciples and creating disciple-making movements will not happen without investing one's life into the life of another (Acts 20:18-21; 2 Timothy 2:2; 1 Thessalonians 1:4-6, 2:3-13). It is through in-depth relationships that believers grow (Romans 15:1; Galatians 6:2; Ephesians 4:26-29; 1 Thessalonians 5:14; 1 John 4:21; etc.). God works through his Word and through relationships. God's design for the sanctification process involves growing in

---

[282] Sills, 36.
[283] Sills, 149.

godliness through relationships. When time, energy and resources are directed towards church planting, programs and strategies as the means and priorities of the ministry, the focus on redemptive relationships and the growth process inherent in spiritual transformation is weakened.

McClung states,

> When personal discipleship is a way of life for a church or movement, it ensures that what they stand for is passed on. Discipleship helps create a culture . . . . But programs and strategies don't disciple people. Great ideas don't make disciples. There is no shortcut and there is not other way for a church or movement to reproduce itself and to have a transforming influence on a nation . . . . If you want to build a leadership culture, if you want to impart apostolic passion to your church or movement, and if you want to see the gospel have its desired transforming effect on people and nations, it will happen because you make disciples.[284]

The strategies to multiply as many churches in *unreached* areas as possible are considered by many as the most strategic and biblical. When the holistic disciple-making basis for church planting and development is bypassed or undervalued, the character of the church will be dominated by the prevailing and inherent worldview.[285] Sills makes this observation:

> The most frequent consequence is that churches left in the wake of such efforts either fall apart rapidly and disappear or degenerate into dysfunctional gatherings with unbiblical doctrine and practice. As a result, the new believers are often victims of aberrant doctrine, heresy, cult outreach, or

---

[284] Floyd McClung, "Disciple Making & Church Planting: God's Way to Transform Nations," *Mission Frontiers* 33: 5 (September—October 2011): 23.
[285] Sills, 12.

nominal Christianity for the rest of their lives. The church the missionaries leave behind is very often anemic at best and a syncretistic aberration at worst.[286]

Through prioritizing ongoing spiritual transformation into Christ-likeness, believers learn to live in obedience to Christ, his Word, and other believers. Transformation occurs over time through the renewing of the mind. Church planting and development are vital ministries, but their growth and success are necessarily anchored in the disciple-making mandate.

Sills records the account of a believer who survived the terrible ethnic-based civil war in Rwanda in 1994. He places the blame of this atrocity with the evangelical church planters who had not trained them to make holistic disciples:

> "I am from Rwanda"—the same country in which, in 1994, 600,000 Tutsis and 400,000 Hutus died, many of them slaughtered with machetes as they huddled in churches. "In all of your zeal for evangelism, you brought us Christ but never taught us how to live." If the end is in sight, how do we explain Rwanda, as well as other so-called Christian countries where unrestrained materialism, oppression of the underprivileged, and deterioration of moral values increase annually? Surely these are not the consequence envisioned by our Lord when he said, "Go and make disciples . . . (Matthew 28:18-20). Statistics from the same period of the genocide indicate that Rwanda was the most Christian nation in Africa, with over 90 percent of Rwandans having been baptized as Christians. Yet, over the course of just a few months, this very "reached" nation committed one of the most horrendous acts ever committed by humanity.[287]

---

[286] Sills, 12.
[287] Sills, 55.

It is not the percentage of *Christians*, the longevity, number or tradition of a particular church or denomination, the number of baptisms, members, prestige, ministry and reputation of key leaders, etc. that indicates faithfulness to Christ's mission. The popular strategy of multiplying churches often establishes a weak foundation for the church. Often conversion is the measure of success and new believers' lives are not transformed. Leaders may not be biblically qualified themselves because of a lack of character transformation to lead and pastor others. Sills notes, "Attempting to plant churches quickly to achieve these short-term goals may result in the planting of weak churches, with inadequately trained leaders, the shortcomings of which may discourage further church planting."[288]

Returning to the Center of Christ's Mission—
Beginning with the End in Mind

Hull maintains,

> It is painfully obvious that we have overlooked the single most important element for fulfilling the great commission. It seems we have been so busy trying to reach the world that there has been no time to focus on being like Jesus. So we haven't reached the world, and we aren't very much like Jesus. Since the great commission is driven by depth more than strategy, the mission of the church has been greatly weakened. Depth means passion; it means connection to God. Depth gives credibility that following Jesus matters as our immaterial nature is transformed into the characteristics of Christ—more compassion than

---

[288] Murray, 101.

detachment, more humility than hubris, less comparison and more unity.[289]

Jesus revealed his heart for mankind in the great commission. Jesus' desire remains the same today to save (justify) and shape (sanctify) believers into his likeness. Jesus in his sovereignty declared that the best way to transform the nations was through reproducing holistic disciples in disciple-making movements. "The great commission is not just about evangelism or church planting. Jesus said to make disciples of all the ethnic groups of the world and to do that by *teaching them to observe all that He commanded* us (Matthew 28:19-20)."[290] Hull states that Christ's divine will is that, "A commitment to be and make disciples must be the central act of every disciple and every church."[291] Sills highlights the priorities of the mission of Christ:

> A study of Jesus' life reveals that He spent several years with his disciples teaching them, discipling them and mentoring them, and then He sent them out. The need for speed and priming the pump for CPMs, where the ends often seem to justify the means, was not what Jesus did nor would do . . . . The biblical approach is to do God's will where He leads us to do it, according to his gifting. If teaching, teach the people to observe all that the Lord commanded us. If the speed at which missionaries are moving will not allow such thorough and deep involvement, the truly greater good should be to slow down and watch God do what only He can do.[292]

---

[289] Hull, *Choose the Life*, 82.
[290] Sills, 13.
[291] Hull, *The Complete Book of Discipleship*, 26.
[292] Sills, 150

This discussion could be summarized with the question, "What is the biblical evidence that we have been successful in our attempts to fulfill Christ's great commission?" Nelson suggests, "If we as a church succeed in every area, but fail to make disciples who can spiritually multiply, then ultimately we have failed. Yet, if we fail in every other area, but succeed in spiritual multiplication, then ultimately we have succeeded."[293] When we begin with the end goal in mind, the clear answer to this question is that obedient disciples of Christ have been made among all groups of people.

Sills provides this helpful analysis on contemporary church planting practices: "The task of international missions is not just to reach and leave, but rather to reach and disciple and teach the nations. The need for speed tempts us to evangelize and move on. New believers are often the first to see the error of such thinking."[294] The mission of Christ is not fulfilled simply by reaching people with the gospel. "He wants us to reach and teach—reaching them with the saving gospel message and teaching them to observe everything he has commanded."[295] Christ's mission will not be fulfilled quickly and without sacrifice. As Platt aptly states, "God's design for taking the gospel to the world is a slow, intentional, simple process that involves every one of his

---

[293] Tommy Nelson, quoted in "A Discipleship Revolution: The Key to Discipling All Peoples" by Rick Wood, ed. *Mission Frontiers* (January-February, 2011), 4.
[294] Sills, 219-20.
[295] Sills, 220.

people sacrificing every facet of their lives to multiply the life of Christ in others."[296]

A Call for Creating Disciple-Making Movements

Based on his post-resurrection authority, Jesus proclaimed his plan to make obedient disciples of all nations until the end of the age; he announced the creation of a divinely empowered movement that would reach all the nations of the earth. Christ was initiating something that he intended to be the priority of his followers. Hirsch states,

> To be effective, movements, and the central ideas associated with them, must take root in the lives of their followers. If they do not, the movement simply will not ignite.... In terms of the movement dynamics and mission of the Christian church, this notion of modeling the message is absolutely crucial to the transmission of the original message beyond our Founder to subsequent generations.[297]

For three years, Jesus set the pattern and demonstrated what it looks like to model a priority of disciple-making. He taught that this pattern was to obediently be followed to advance his universal movement and create a self-replicating movement. Teaching new believers to observe all that Jesus commanded (Matthew 28:19) requires time and consistent effort. Imitation of spiritual disciple-makers is crucial if disciple-making is to be entrusted to faithful men (2 Timothy 2:2).

---

[296] Platt, 104.
[297] Hirsch, *The Forgotten Ways*, 116.

The Apostle Paul understood that holistic disciples were foundational. In Acts 14:21-22, the first missionaries were teaching new believers to be obedient disciples and to follow Jesus wholeheartedly. This priority mirrored what Jesus taught as he gave the great commission. Wilkins notes that, "The Jesus movement of the first century continued as disciples made other disciples and they helped them to grow in faith until the time when they would enter into the glorified kingdom of God. Of such is what all true Jesus movements are made."[298]

The core element in the development of a disciple-making movement is the faithful reproduction of Christ-like disciples through a process of personal disciple-making. It is essential to understand that in order for church planting and growth goals to be reached, an intentional disciple-making process must be prioritized. Hirsch makes this point clear:

> If the heart of discipleship is to become like Jesus, then it seems to me that a missional reading of this text requires that we see that Jesus' strategy is to get a whole lot of little versions of him infiltrating every nook and cranny of society by reproducing himself in and through his people in everyplace throughout the world. But this issue goes much deeper than sociological models relating to the transmission of ideas into movements; it goes to one of the central purposes of Christ's mission among us . . . our eternal destiny to be conformed to this image of Christ (Rom. 8:29; 2 Cor. 3:18). But the relationship between Jesus and his people goes deeper still. Our mystical union with Christ and his indwelling with us lies at the very center of the Christian experience of God—this is seen in all of Paul's

---

[298] Wilkins, *Following*, 119.

teaching about being "in Christ" and he in us, as well as John's theology of "abiding in Christ." All the spiritual disciplines therefore aim us toward one thing—*Christlikeness*.[299]

Hirsch declares that it is the organizing principle of Christ's mission that provides the impetus for his global mission to become an ongoing movement:

> To preserve the movement ethos of God's people, it is fundamental that the church keeps mission at the center of its self-understanding. Without mission there is no movement, and the community dies a death of the spirit long before it dies a physical death. To forget mission is to forget ourselves, to forget mission is to lose our *raison d'etre* and leads to our eventual demise. Our sense of mission not only flows from an understanding of the mission of God and missional church, but forms the orienting inspiration of the church of Jesus Christ, keeping it constantly moving forward and outward.[300]

It is vital, therefore, to understand that the mission of Christ never separates the concepts of evangelism and discipleship as some advocate. A healthy, biblical ministry incorporates *both priorities* of Christ's mission. An overriding focus on evangelism and the need to get people "saved" but not trained to be holistic disciples means taking the path of least resistance and using whatever man-made pragmatic ministry strategy that seems to result in the most identifiable conversions to Christ.[301] Sills warns,

> When the pressure is on to produce the greatest number of churches, missionaries often choose techniques that result

---

[299] Hirsch, *The Forgotten Ways*, 113.
[300] Hirsch, *The Forgotten Ways*, 236-37.
[301] Sills, 138.

in the most churches in the least amount of time. However, because there is no quick shortcut to producing New Testament churches with biblically qualified leaders, the definition of what a church is becomes adjustable to the current reality.... Many missionaries burdened by the need for speed and freed by the greater good mentality have jettisoned the 1 Timothy 3:1-7 qualifications for pastors. In ever-increasing ways, the definition of a church, the qualifications of church leaders, and the mission agency's position on these matters are all subservient to the greater good.[302]

When any ministry goal, even a good goal, detours believers from prioritizing their command to make holistic disciples, then it is missing the heart of Christ's mission. Frost and Hirsch state that the challenge for obedient believers is to be "taken captive by the agenda of Jesus, rather than seeking to mold him to fit our agendas, no matter how noble they might be.... The challenge before us is to let Jesus be Jesus and to allow ourselves to be caught up in his extraordinary mission for the world."[303]

Sergeant provides a useful summary:

If we are living out the Great Commandment then we will be making reproducing disciples because part of the disciple-making process is "teaching them to obey everything [Christ] has commanded" and the commission itself is one of those commands. Hence, every believer should by definition be involved in making reproducing disciples. It is a short step from this toward starting reproducing spiritual communities (churches) because several of the other commands demand a spiritual

---

[302] Sills, 139.
[303] Frost and Hirsch, *ReJesus*, 10.

community to carry out. Reproducing disciples will result in reproducing churches as a matter of obedience.[304]

Essential Components to Growing a Disciple-Making Movement

A disciple-making movement that flows out of the making of holistic disciples is based upon the reproduction of mature believers whose ambition is to live for Christ. A transformed disciple lives, loves, looks, and longs to be like Jesus. As more and more disciples are transformed with Christ's character qualities and an others-centered commitment, a self-sustaining movement is formed.

Sills observes, "Many rapid-multiplication church planting efforts do not see intentional church leadership as necessary, and if they have leadership at all, biblical qualifications are rarely addressed.[305] However, mature, biblically transformed and faithful leaders form the foundation and impetus of a disciple-making movement. Hirsch maintains,

> If we stated this in terms of movement dynamics, it can be said that the reach of any movement is directly proportional to the breadth of its leadership base. And leadership in turn is directly related to the quality of discipleship. Only to the extent that we can develop self-initiating, reproducing, fully devoted disciples can we hope to get the task of Jesus' mission done. There is no other easy way of developing genuine transformational movements than through the critical task of disciple making. Or as Neil Cole wryly

---

[304] Curtis Sergeant, *Planting Rapidly Reproducing Churches*, <http//www.churchplantingmovements.com> (accessed July 26, 2010), 1.
[305] Sills, 59.

notes, "If you can't reproduce disciples you can't reproduce leaders. If you can't reproduce leaders, you can't reproduce churches. If you can't reproduce churches you can't reproduce movements."[306]

A disciple-making movement must maintain a balanced focus between a continuous outreach to make new disciples (evangelism) and a commitment to nurture obedient disciples (sanctification). The "teaching them to observe" Christ's commandments is indispensable in the process. As the mind is transformed by biblical truth, the believer's understanding and worldview are transformed to reflect the mind of Christ as a result (Romans 12:2). This transformation compels believers to live and minister for the sake of others through good works. Hirsch notes how the will for others-centered service is embedded in the making of holistic disciples. This is essential to create an ongoing movement:

> And this is exactly how Jesus does discipleship: he organizes it around mission. As soon as they are called he takes the disciples on an adventurous journey of mission, ministry and learning. Straightaway they are involved in proclaiming the kingdom of God, serving the poor, healing, and casting out demons. It is active and direct disciple making in the context of mission. And all great people movements are the same. Even the newest convert is engaged in the mission from the start; even he or she can become a spiritual hero. If we accept that Jesus forms the primary pattern of disciple making for the church, then we must say that discipleship is our core task. But if disciple making lies at the heart of our commission, then we must

---

[306] Hirsch, *The Forgotten Ways*, 119. Hirsch quotes Neil Cole from a lecture given by Cole in Melbourne, Australia, May 2006.

organize it around mission, because mission is the catalyzing principle of discipleship. In Jesus they are inexorably linked.[307]

Throughout the New Testament, the Apostle Paul demonstrated a balance between his desire to reach the lost and his commitment to train the saved so that he could leave behind a solid basis for a church—Christ-like lives. The Apostle Paul planted churches through disciple-making movements. Sills notes,

> Modeling Paul's practice of training young men and sending them into ministry situations multiplies our ministries and allows us to continue reaching into new areas without abandoning untaught new believers. It also utilizes trained local leadership and empowers them to preach, teach, pastor and disciple among themselves in culturally appropriate ways.[308]

For a movement to have continuity there must be committed individuals who are able to transfer the same level of commitment to others. Sills highlights Jesus' practice: "The first strategic reason for Jesus' focus on a few was to ensure the internalization of his life, and ministry in those who would be the foundation of the Jesus movement."[309] After internalization, multiplication was the second strategic reason why Jesus focused on a few.[310] Ogden observes that Jesus' strategy to build his church and reach the world would be fulfilled by training a few holistic disciples. Ogden describes why this principle is vital to understand:

---

[307] Hirsch, *The Forgotten Ways*, 120.
[308] Sills, 102.
[309] Ogden, 69.
[310] Ogden, 73.

However, Jesus knew the human limitation of his incarnate state. As a solitary human being his reach was limited. His strategy was designed to touch the whole world through the multiplication of disciples who were carefully trained. On the eve of his date with the cross, he saw how much fruit his deliberate strategy of multiplication would bear. He said to his disciples, "Very truly, I tell you, the one who believes in me will also to the works that I do and, in fact, will do greater works than these, because I am going to the Father" (John 14:12). How can it be that someone could do greater works than the son of God? The "greater works" were most likely a matter of quantity more than quality. By Jesus' multiplication of himself in the Twelve, they would geographically cover far greater territory than he ever did in his limited itinerant ministry. By the power of the indwelling Holy Spirit carrying them to the entire known world, the sheer volume of Jesus' ministry would expand exponentially. And so it has been.[311]

Platt makes the bold statement that, "We are fooling ourselves to think we can mass-produce disciples today. God's design for taking the gospel to the world is a slow, intentional, simple process that involves every one of his people sacrificing every facet of their lives to multiply the life of Christ in others."[312]

Conclusion

Two interdependent objectives constitute the *missio Christi*. The first—his divine promise to build his church—is based upon his person and sacrificial death to provide salvation for humanity (Matthew 16:18). His other missional goal, entrusted to his

---

[311] Ogden, 72
[312] Platt, 104.

followers, is to make obedient, Christlike disciples, taught to reproduce other disciples among all peoples (Matthew 28:18-20). This divine cause—the making of disciples of all peoples—is designed to achieve the divine effect: the building of his church.

The making of holistic disciples is the key to the establishment of healthy, reproducing churches. As Sills notes, "Rather than viewing theological education, pastoral preparation, leadership training, and in-depth discipleship as lesser forms of missionary activity, we must return to the biblical understanding of missions that incorporates them as primary and necessary ways of fulfilling the Great Commission."[313] When Christ's followers prioritize objectives other than, disciple-making as the means to growing healthy churches, the heart of his mission is weakened and the church is unhealthy. Ministries that seek to multiply churches based on the need for speed, the number of conversions, or a "going and reaching and leaving" strategy, leave the command of Christ to make obedient disciples unfulfilled. Sills describes how the quest for rapidly multiplying churches weakens the entire mission endeavor:

> Contemporary mission strategies emphasize reaching, preaching to, and leaving as many people groups as possible as fast as possible. In fact, the contemporary focus on speed influences all areas of missionary life and work. The qualifications and requirements for those who are to be sent as missionaries are also relaxed when speed is the highest value . . . . When missionaries or agency heads are reminded of the great commission duty to remain long

---
[313] Sills, 13.

enough to make disciples and teach them, they will often respond in frustration that they *have* taught them and ask, "How much is enough?"[314]

Although it may seem like describing holistic disciple-making as the heart of Christ's mission from a priority to plant churches is a trivial distinction, in practice the intended outcomes are vastly different. If national leaders are taught that fulfilling Christ's mission is tied to speed and number of conversions, they may never learn the importance of making holistic disciples who reproduce other faithful disciples. The disciple-making objective, established by Christ as the heart of his mission, forms the divinely ordained pathway through which he builds his church. Effective church planting *flows out of and is the necessary result of* holistic disciple making. By making disciples of the nations, Christ will build his church. Man-engineered strategies that devise artificial goals for completing Christ's mission through church planting and church growth are not centered on the heart of the great commission.

---

[314] Sills, 32-33.

CHAPTER 6
HISTORICAL EXAMPLES OF THE MAKING OF HOLISTIC DISCIPLES AND DISCIPLE-MAKING MOVEMENTS

Introduction

Chapters Three and Four of this study support the New Testament concept that the mission of Christ is most faithfully accomplished through the making of holistic disciples who create disciple-making movements. These movements share common features: obedient disciples are trained, biblically healthy churches are formed, and faithful disciples are equipped to reproduce holistic disciples. This self-replicating cycle forms the basis for additional disciple-making movements.

Since producing holistic disciples and disciple-making movements reflects the heart of Christ's mission, it is important to examine church history to discover if these missional principles were demonstrated. Four church history scholars[315] were asked to provide their input on people and/or groups throughout history

---

[315] These scholars included: Dr. John D. Hannah, Ph.D., Research Professor of Theological Studies, Distinguished Professor of Historical Theology at Dallas Theological Seminary; Dr. Scott M. Manetsch, Ph.D., Associate Professor of Church History, Chair of the Church History and the History of Christian Thought Department, Associate Professor of Church History, Trinity Evangelical Divinity School; Dr. Bruce Gordon, Ph.D., of Yale University, Professor of European and British History, and Dr. Garth M. Rosell, Ph.D., Professor of Church History, Gordon-Conwell Theological Seminary.

who advanced the mission of Christ through the making of holistic disciples. Based on the input received from these scholars, the following groups and people were included in this study: [1] the Irish piety in the sixth and seventh centuries; [2] the Cistercians of the twelfth century and Bernard of Clairvaux; [3] the German Pietists of the seventeenth and eighteenth centuries; and [4] the twentieth century German pastor, theologian, and author, Dietrich Bonhoeffer.

Irish Piety in the Sixth and Seventh Centuries

Introduction

The greatest advance of the mission of Christ in Northern and Central Europe during the "dark ages" of the sixth and seventh centuries came through the Irish church and the related monastic movement. Spiritual formation and missionary outreach were centered on the community monastery. The careful study of the Bible was central to Irish monasticism. Mayer notes that, "The chief subject of study in the monastic schools of early Christian Ireland was the Bible . . . all other studies, including that of the Fathers of the Church, were ancillary to the reading, comprehension, and exposition of the Scriptures."[316] Between A. D. 650 – 800, over forty works were written on the Scriptures as well as nine commentaries.[317] Both individuals and entire families were

---

[316] Maher, 35.
[317] Maher, 36.

trained with the Scriptures and it was a common practice to send new converts immediately back to their families to share the gospel with them.[318] Through the ministry of monks and spiritual leaders, new community monasteries were established with community churches that served as training centers, creating a system method for reproducing disciples. God raised up key leaders to make disciples and create a disciple-making movement in Northern and Central Europe through faithful missionary monks.

Patrick (387-461)

Although he was taken captive from Britain and enslaved in Ireland during his youth, Patrick returned to Ireland in 432 as a Bishop of the Roman Church where he ministered for nearly thirty years. Patrick traveled throughout the nation, preaching, founding churches, mentoring young spiritual leaders and developing a vibrant monastic movement. In 444, he established the cathedral at Armagh as the educational and ministry-outreach center of the Irish church from which he built a network of monastery-based churches with an outward missional focus. The monks in each monastic center were trained to be active by ministering in the community and winning people to Christ.[319] The monasteries, therefore, not only promoted Christian culture but also were

---

[318] Larry L. Lyons, *Redeeming Culture: An Examination of the Methodology and Effectiveness of the Irish Missionary Movement with their Application to Contemporary Urban Ministry* (Master's Thesis, Dallas Theological Seminary, 2001), 48.

[319] Robert G. Clouse, Richard V. Pierard and Edwin M. Yamauchi, *The Story of the Church* (London: Angus Hudson, Ltd, 2002), 73.

centers of training and missionary zeal.[320] Lyons describes Patrick's method of establishing new community monasteries that reached out to the community:

> He and his followers would request permission to settle in the area from the king or local opinion leaders. They would converse with the people, live and work in a community of faith, pray for people who were sick or demonized, and pray for success in fishing. They staged open-air presentations characterized by the use of Irish language, art, drama, stories, and songs, and would entertain people's questions and receive those who responded into their community. They then accompanied them to speak with family members. Once a sufficient group was gathered, they built a church. Reliable teachers would be left in charge of these Christian communities, having basic instructions for conduct within the community rule. Patrick did not limit himself to a particular region, but ordained clergy to baptize and exhort the new Irish Christians wherever necessary.[321]

Patrick did not follow the long time Roman practice of mass baptisms to "Christianize" the people. He and his coworkers sought to know the people and live with them to learn aspects of their culture, mindset, language and social structure so that they could preach the gospel and make disciples in ways that fit the lifestyles and cultures of the people.[322]

---

[320] J. Herbert Kane, *A Concise History of the Christian Mission* (Grand Rapids, MI: Baker Book House, 1982), 13.
[321] Lyons, 11.
[322] Lyons, 13.

For Patrick, the training of monks, nuns, and religious workers was his principal focus and ministry.[323] He modeled and taught that discipline and dedication were necessary to promote spiritual growth. His life, character and practice in ministry became the model that monks and clergy followed, taught, and faithfully reproduced. While bishops, priests and lay-clergy[324] were sent into new communities to develop the spiritual lives of new converts and establish new monasteries and churches, pious women were consecrated and placed in small groups to assist the clergy in the churches and monasteries.[325] As Pierson describes,

> He (Patrick) brought his most zealous converts into monastic communities where they were discipled and trained to go back out as evangelists. They adopted very rigorous spiritual disciplines, and were imbued with missionary passion. In addition, they put great emphasis on Bible study and learning. The system multiplied itself as Patrick's disciples established other monasteries that became new centers of mission. Houses for women were also established.[326]

Patrick taught his followers that their growth in Christ should produce a desire to serve others. Those whom Patrick and his disciples trained not only served to evangelize Ireland, but their ministry strategy spread throughout Europe. As Hunter noted,

---

[323] John Ryan, *Irish Monasticism: Origins and Early Developments* (Ithaca, NY: Cornell University Press, 1972), 91.

[324] A lay-clergy in that day is similar to the modern concept of a layperson or a lay minister in that they were not ordained ministers but worked alongside the priests and bishops. Ryan, 93.

[325] Ryan, 93.

[326] Paul E. Pierson, *The Dynamics of Christian Mission: History Through a Missiological Perspective* (Pasadena, CA: William Carey International University Press, 2009), 72.

Patrick and his people launched a movement. They baptized "many thousands" of people, probably tens of thousands .... An ancient document called the "Annuals of the Four Masters" reports that Patrick's mission planted about 700 churches, and that Patrick ordained perhaps 1000 priests. Within his lifetime, 30 to 40 (or more) of Ireland's 150 tribes became substantially Christian.[327]

Columba (521-597)[328]

Columba traveled with forty-two men to the isolated island of Iona off the west coast of Scotland and established a monastery there. He lived in a small hut within the monastery and sought to meet the needs of the poor residents of the island.[329] The monastery in Iona became one of the most effective missionary centers for spreading the gospel and making disciples in history. Membership was divided into three groups: the *Seniors* devoted themselves to copying and teaching the Scriptures; the *Working Brethren* provided manual labor; and the *Juniors* were new believers being discipled.[330] Edman describes the life of the monks and religious workers in Iona: "Manual labor and hard service were performed in field and kitchen, as well as study and worship in cell or chapel. All was done to bring the gospel to those among whom Christ had not been named."[331]

---

[327] Hunter, 23.
[328] "'Colum,' 'ColumCillle,' 'Colman,' and 'Columban' are all versions of the same name, the latter two being diminutives; in Latin the name means 'dove.'" Catherine Thom, *Early Irish Monasticism* (New York: T&T Clark, 2006). 125n3.
[329] Clouse, Pierard, and Yamauchi, 76.
[330] Kane, 38.
[331] Raymond V. Edman, *The Light in Dark Ages* (Wheaton, IL: Van Kampen Press, 1949), 149.

Through the influence of Columba a chain of monasteries were established throughout the island and spread to the northeast coast of England. From these missionary centers, monks traveled north to spread the gospel among the mountain tribes of Scotland and south throughout England.[332] As Thom observes, "His leadership, tough or compassionate, was inspired by the basic monastic principle enunciated throughout this work: prayer, work, penance in their varied forms, all in the name of a closer relationship with God and the other members of the monastic enclosure."[333]

Columba taught that obedience to God's Word was more important than penitential sacrifice and religious ritual. He promoted a radical lifestyle of self-denial as a spiritual exercise to lead one to inner spiritual transformation through dying to self. As his teaching and example grew, the monks under his supervision learned to live and serve by following his example.[334]

Aiden (d. 651)

Aiden, a disciple of Columba, emulated his discipline and spiritual instruction and began a mission to England thirty-eight years after his death.[335] Aiden's followers committed themselves to the in-depth reading of the Scriptures and the memorization of the

---

[332] Pierson, 74.
[333] Thom, 149-150.
[334] Thom, 139-140.
[335] *The Saintly Triad of the Lives of St. Patrick, St. Columbkille, and St. Bridget, Commonly Known as the Three Patron Saints of Ireland* (Dublin, Sold to the Booksellers, 1844), 137.

Psalms. He considered his "daily work" to be instructing others in the Scriptures.[336]

Aiden was known for pouring out his life in compassionate care and defense of the weak and the poor. He sought to deeply learn and apply all of the Bible to all areas of his life and he dedicated himself to teach others to follow his example.[337] His disciples created a disciple-making movement that spread far beyond Scotland. As is recorded in the historical record of *The Saintly Triad*:

> For at that time the whole anxiety of those teachers was to serve God, and not the world; their whole care was occupied in cultivation of the heart, and not the stomach.... Whenever any clergyman or monk would come... they would give diligent heed to their words of exhortation; and on the Lord's days they flocked together eagerly to the church or to the monasteries, not with a view to refreshing their bodies, but desirous to learn the Word of God. And if any of the priests happened to come into a village, the townspeople there would congregate together, and be sure to ask him to instruct them in the Word of Life.[338]

Columbanus (550-615)[339]

The motivation of Columbanus to make disciples originated in Ireland and had the distinctively Irish missionary

---

[336] *The Saintly Triad*, 137.
[337] *The Saintly Triad*, 144.
[338] *The Saintly Triad*, 162.
[339] Stephen Neill, *A History of Christian Missions* (New York: Penguin Books, 1964), 62. Columbanus was also known as "Columba" or as "Columban," named after Saint Columba of Iona.

concern to see a practical response to the gospel.[340] Columbanus and his followers established Irish missionary-style monasteries throughout France and in northern Italy as centers of evangelism and church planting. They reached barbarians arriving from the East and deepened the spiritual life of nominal Christians they encountered.[341] These monastic communities worshipped, studied, memorized Scriptures, and nourished each other through *contemplative prayer*. The monasteries were ministry stations to train and send missionaries to unreached areas where believers within the target communities worshipped, witnessed and learned the Scriptures together.[342]

Thom describes how Columbanus promoted spiritual formation with the monks. "They enjoyed obeying the abbot in the same spirit as one would obey Christ. Obedience was also promoted through the input of one's *anamchara* or soul-friend, without whom no personal decisions were taken."[343] The *anamchara* was crucial to the disciple-making practices of Irish missionaries and monks. Thom notes that,

> The Irish Church can claim to have introduced a unique form of penitential practice which . . . enabled people to form a relationship with God not based on fear of public exposure for human failings . . . . Each monk had a soul-friend, *anamchara*, to whom he went for counsel. This interaction, at times, included discussion of the monk's failings and the imposition of a penance. So the beginnings

---

[340] Thom, 162.
[341] Pierson, 76.
[342] Hunter, 29
[343] Thom, 176.

of private "confession" as opposed to "public confession" can be seen as making a substantial contribution to the inner life of the early Irish Church and indeed later to the Universal Church.[344]

As Tracey notes, a *disciple* would spend time with their *soul friend*, with whom they received support and counsel:

> A soul-friend is not just a relationship of friendship, it is much more one of mentor and disciple. The goal of the Christian life is conversion, and to ever deepens one's conversion to Christ. The role of the soul-friend is to help the Christian to remove what may be a block on that road. The penitential's growth began in this atmosphere and are an attempt to codify the teaching and insights of these spiritual guides.[345]

Ryan notes how the practice of having a "soul friend" grew to signify the role of a spiritual guide and doctor of souls. Through the "soul friend," the "sacrament of reconciliation emerges as an essential way toward spiritual development."[346] The *anamchara* assisted the younger disciple to grow in Christ, to love of his cross, and to reproduce the likeness of Christ in his life.

Columbanus taught that Christians are to live with wholehearted devotion as *slaves of Christ*, demonstrating Christ's love by living in strict discipline to the will of God. He taught that God's love alone saves people and that responding to his love

---

[344] Thom, 31

[345] Tracey Liam, "Celtic Spirituality: Just What Does it Mean?" *Thinking Faith*, Jesuit Media Initiatives, [March 14, 2008], p. 4, <http:www.thinkingfaith.org/searchresults.htm?/> (accessed 12/22/2010).

[346] Marguerite-Marie Dobois, "Saint Columbanus," in *Irish Monks in The Golden Age*, ed. John Ryan (Dublin, Ireland: Clonmore & Reynolds Ltd., 1963), 49-50.

produces a changed life characterized by asceticism, humility, and love.[347] Columbanus instituted rules and practices to promote obedience and "inner transformation."[348] The growing Irish monastic movement was driven by the conviction that believers are to dedicate themselves totally to live for God and imitate Christ who sacrificed himself for them.[349]

Conclusion

A remarkable feature of Irish Christianity in the sixth and seventh centuries was its fervent zeal of dedicated believers to fulfill the mission of Christ through the founding of ministry-oriented monasteries throughout Ireland, the British Isles, Belgium, France, northern Germany, and northern Italy.[350] As Hunter declares,

> This movement was fueled by "the burning zeal of the apostles of the country" and "their aim was wonderfully furthered by the ardent temperament of the newly won converts." In two or three generations, all of Ireland had become substantially Christian and Celtic monastic communities became the strategic "mission stations" from which apostolic bands reached the "barbarians" of Scotland, and much of England, and much of Western Europe.[351]

The emphasis of instruction in the monasteries concentrated on making disciples who were committed to serving

---

[347] Thom, 167.
[348] Thom, 169.
[349] Thom, 168.
[350] Clouse, Pierard and Yamauchi, 74-76.
[351] Hunter, 35

Christ in practical ways. As Pierson notes, "Because Celtic monasticism was oriented toward mission, it grew rapidly by planting new communities.... It was a highly evangelistic kind of monasticism, and the churches drew their leadership from the monasteries."[352] Maher notes that in the monasteries, there was

> ... a life of whole-hearted commitment to the following of Christ, a life built around the daily times of prayer, the Sunday Eucharist, the hours of working in the field, in the workshops, in the scriptorium, in the cells where so much study and teaching went on day by day. Its life was the life that attracted so many disciples so the monastic founders and the monastic cities which were their legacy.[353]

The monasteries of the Roman church were stagnant and inward focused. Irish monks pursued a vibrant disciple-making priority, focused on spiritual transformation. Their monastery-based, disciple-making movements targeted unreached areas by discipling believers with a commitment to ministry to the surrounding community.[354]

The Irish monks taught a life of asceticism and radical faith, lived-out in response to the gospel. They taught a whole-life dedication to the Lord and others as opposed to private religious solitude.[355] As Murray concludes,

> The Celtic missionary movement that emerged from Ireland and Scotland was characterized by a very different kind of monasticism, consisting of teams of church planting and evangelizing monks, who traveled all over England and

---

[352] Pierson, 72.
[353] Maher, 20.
[354] Hunter, 53.
[355] Thom, 163.

on into Western Europe and beyond. The mission work seems to have involved a self-replicating model, whereby teams of men and women established new churches and new monasteries, missionary communities and training centers from which further teams were sent out to continue the work. Team members became team leaders. All over England, the demise of the Roman churches gave way to the replacement planting achieved by their vibrant missionary movement. Although there were set-backs, many of their churches took root, survived, and flourished in these difficult times.[356]

Pierson summarizes the impact of Irish monasticism. "The Celtic movement had three important features. It exhibited deep devotion to Christ, a love of learning, and missionary passion. It can serve as a model of some of the best characteristics of any missionary movement."[357]

Cistercian Monasticism in the Twelfth Century: Introduction to the Cistercian Order

Cistercian monasticism began with a small group of Benedictine monks in 1098 at Citaeux, France, and grew to become the most significant monastic movement in the middle ages. The Cistercians sought to imitate the main features of the historic desert monastic movement establishing monasteries in secluded areas, promoting the zeal, purity and practices of the desert fathers and the patristic tradition. They established reformed monasteries throughout Europe with such speed and spiritual

---

[356] Murray, 93
[357] Pierson, 77.

impact that the twelfth century became known as "the Cistercian century."[358]

The Cistercians welcomed common, untrained working-class men into the monastery as a class of full members known as *converse.*[359] They believed that the love and fellowship of monastic life was necessary for spiritual growth. The monastic community was characterized by expressions of loving-kindness designed to help individuals become like the Lord.[360] Clouse, Pierard, and Yamauchi describe the impact of Bernard's emphasis on love:

> In spite of this strictness, the Cistercians were a phenomenal success, and by the end of the twelfth century there were hundreds of houses. Its most remarkable leader was Bernard of Clairvaux (1090 – 1153). Bernard described the Christian life as an experience of progress in love. Under him, the monks concerns were widened beyond contemplation to missionary work and pastoral care for their neighbors.[361]

The Cistercians developed a process to transform their understanding, desires and behavior by training their minds to be controlled by God's love. They believed that as people learned the true nature of God's love, they would develop humility, obedience and others-centered love. According to the reforms mentioned in *The Boundaries of Charity*, "This education in humility and

---

[358] Sellner, 229-230.
[359] Pennington, "The Cistercians," 206.
[360] Patricia Wittberg, *The Rise and Decline of Catholic Religious Orders* (Albany, New York: The State University of New York, 1994), 132.
[361] Clouse, Pierard and Yamauchi, 107-108

obedience was the central purpose of the Benedictine Rule; what the Cistercians emphasized was the idea that fraternal relationships could shape interior feelings as well as external behavior and transform obedience into love."[362]

Bernard of Clairvaux

At age twenty-one, Bernard of Clairvaux led thirty relatives to join him in ministry at the new monastery at Citeaux.[363] Esther de Waal also refers to Bernard in glowing terms as

> ... a complex, talented, combative looking man, a reformer in some things and a conservative in others. He is larger than life—though one thread holds it all together, and that is his zeal for the church which was simply an extension of the love of God which directed and informed his whole being.... Bernard was a prophet, a man who found in the Word of God the energy to open doors for his contemporaries and communicate to them something of his zest for living and his enthusiasm for the way of Christ.[364]

Bernard soon became the Abbot at Clairvaux and orchestrated phenomenal growth, incorporating hundreds of older monasteries into the Cistercian order. His great driving passion was the salvation of all mankind. He sought to do whatever was in his power to bring people to God. His love of souls demonstrated his desire to serve people. His love for God was displayed in his

---

[362] *The Boundaries of Charity: Cistercian Culture and Ecclesiastical Reform 1098-1180* (Stanford, CA: Stanford University Press, 1996), 55.
[363] M. Basil Pennington, *Bernard of Clairvaux: A Lover Teaching the Way of Love* (New York: New City Press, 1997), 7.
[364] Esther de Waal, *The Way of Simplicity: The Cistercian Tradition* (Maryknoll, New York: Orbis Books, 1998), 126-127.

longing for quiet, solitude, prayer and study. His love for God and man constituted the two great loves of his life.[365] Robson describes how Bernard was transformed to become a channel of love for others:

> The spark that gave Bernard's life meaning and direction was his encounter and increasing union with the Word. We would further contend that the fruit of this union—self-sacrificing love, *caritas*—transformed Bernard. As a consequence, he himself became a channel of *caritas*, bringing unity and integrity to the people, places and events he served in his complex ministry in the Church.[366]

Bernard believed in the absolute centrality of Christ for salvation and life. He taught that the whole of a person's life was to be lived for Christ's sake and patterned after Christ's example. The proof of authenticity was a spirit of charity displayed in the person's union and life with Christ.[367]

Bernard taught believers to imitate Christ and express their obedient love for God through compassionate acts of service for others. Bernard believed that Christ's incarnation and sacrificial death were examples of how his followers should live and love. He taught that to imitate Christ meant that Christ's followers imitate his compassion.[368] Bernard compared a person's progress toward Christ-likeness to the journey of a pilgrim on a pathway, making

---

[365] Sellner, 237.
[366] Stephen Robson, *"With the Spirit and Power of Elijah (Lk.1,17): The Prophetic-Reforming Spirituality of Bernard of Clairvaux as Evidenced Particularly in His Letters* (Rome: Editrice Pontificia Universita Gregoriana, 2004), 187.
[367] Pennington, *"The Cistercians,"* 210.
[368] de Waal, 119.

progress throughout his life towards perfection of love that should result in ever increasing loving service to others.[369]

Life for Bernard centered on the person of Christ. Bernard felt that the ultimate measure of a believer's connection with God occurred when their will was saturated with the love of God so that their character grew in Christ-likeness and reflected God's love to the world. At this point, the believer's soul is unified with the spirit of Christ so that they can will to live and desire what God has willed.[370] Sommerfeldt describes how Bernard understood the power of love to transform the believer's life:

> Love is the perfection of the will . . . . Love fulfills the lover; this fulfillment is the gift of God's, the indwelling of the Holy Spirit . . . . Love has so many facets and dimensions that Bernard is quite comfortable in using descriptions which differ—and even seem to contradict. But the teaching behind all of them is the same: love is the perfection of the will, free to choose the good . . . . Still more fundamentally, Bernard is sure that, in loving, one participates in the very being of God. For love is the principle of unity in the Trinity. Indeed, God is Love.[371]

Bernard taught that a mature believer who took on the responsibility to mentor and train others needed to demonstrate two aspects of love: On one hand, the spiritual guide needed a mother's type of love characterized by compassion. On the other hand, the spiritual guide needed to have a correcting and exhorting kind of father's love that would discipline a disobedient child.

---

[369] Sommerfeldt, 181.
[370] *The Boundaries of Charity,* 56.
[371] Sommerfeldt, 100-101.

Both aspects of love are necessary to train a disciple to be like Christ.[372] Bernard taught that growth in the spiritual life is about progress in the love of God. Believers are to pursue godly character intentionally, which they can experience through a process that develops deeper levels of communion with God.[373] Sommerfeldt comments on Bernard's priority of love: "Love for one's neighbor requires more than the desire for his or her well-being. Bernard teaches that one must also do all one can to bring about the neighbor's well-being. In loving one's neighbor, one increases one's capacity for love of God and thus for happiness.[374]

Bernard taught that believers could achieve fulfillment in their spiritual lives through pursuing a strenuous journey up a mountain showing progress toward maturity, and that all believers should intentionally and purposefully pursue spiritual transformation.[375] De Waal explains Bernard's view:

> Our earthly life is one of seeking, of seeking the good who is seeking us. That is the question that the novice entering the community is asked: "Are you truly seeking God?" Bernard tells us that God should be sought sincerely, frequently and perseveringly; that he would be sought by desires and deeds. The Lord is looking for his workman. So the search is a response. Bernard says we seek because we have been found, found out, called.[376]

---

[372] Sellner, 249.
[373] Sellner, 243.
[374] Sommerfeldt, 106.
[375] Sommerfeldt, 50-51..
[376] de Waal, 89.

Bernard challenged his disciples to contemplate the truth of their own relationship with God and with others, and to measure their progress in godliness against the teachings of the Gospel and church tradition. He believed the disciplined monastic life, under his supervision at Clairvaux, was the highest state of life and the best route to salvation. He believed that no follower of Christ was ever to be content with his or her spiritual state. He taught that all people were called by God to be holy and that no one should ever rest or be content with their own level of spiritual growth.[377]

Following the Benedictine Rule, the Abbot of each monastery was portrayed as the *spiritual father* or *wise physician* who promoted spiritual growth and obedience, intervened in abuses of the Rule, and showed concern and care for individuals as the spiritual *healer* in the community. As a spiritual director, Bernard interacted with each monk as he carried out his wider ministry.[378] Bernard taught that each Abbot spoke with the authority of God's word and was responsible to mentor each monk to promote growth in obedience through admonishing, rebuking, persuading, and reproving them.[379]

Bernard did not feel a formal process was needed to make disciples but that believers are formed into Christ's likeness by following the godly example of others and obeying the practices of the Benedictine Rule. Contrary to the older Benedictine model, the Cistercian communities had no organized system to pursue

---

[377] Robson, 378-79.
[378] Robson, 180-81.
[379] Robson, 170-71.

spiritual formation. Bernard trained young monks through teaching practical doctrinal faithfulness and through his daily preaching, personal exhortations, and writings. He believed that spiritual formation is a process that must be pursued for a lifetime.[380]

Conclusion

Schaff makes this bold statement about Bernard of Clairvaux: "There is no spotless saint in this world, and Bernard was furthest from claiming perfection, but he came as near the medieval ideal of ascetic holiness as any man of his century."[381] Bernard taught that spiritual formation was the pathway to the discovery of one's true self in God. He believed that "Even the greatest contemplative gifts, even the deepest personal intimacy with God, find their context within, and are to some sense, ordered to life in community, to the pure love of brothers of the Rule."[382] He believed, taught and exemplified the truth that a pursuit of spiritual maturity and holistic discipleship is evidenced in a life lived for the sake of others.

Bernard is a clear example of a believer who understood that the center of Christ's mission was to make holistic disciples who intentionally pursue spiritual transformation. He understood and exemplified the kind of godly leader Christ uses to make faithful disciples of others. Bernard understood that holistic

---

[380] Robson, 152-53.
[381] Philip Schaff, *History of the Christian Church, vol. V, The Middle Ages* (Grand Rapids, MI: Wm. B. Eerdmans Publishing Company, 1952), 343.
[382] de Waal, 115.

disciples who live obediently before Christ naturally seek to reproduce other faithful disciples through their teaching and life example. Bernard demonstrated that he was a strong advocate of disciple-making movements, as exemplified though his personal example and lasting impact.

Finally, Bernard understood that greater growth in spiritual maturity finds its ultimate expression and fulfillment in loving and living for others. Love expressed through humble service to others demonstrates Christ's character and will. Sommerfeldt maintained,

> Although Bernard insists on the primacy of one's love for God, that love must find expression in serving others . . . . Loving concern responds not to abstract formulations but to real, human need.
>
> In this, Bernard does not reject concern for one's own spiritual well-being, or the practices that promote it. Loving service builds on those practices and fulfills them . . . . Indeed, for Bernard, the expenditure of energy in the service of others does not diminish one's store of love but augments it. True love is sufficient for all . . . . Loving service for others is, in the end, a way in which God gives his love to them. The minister of that love is a means through which God acts in love. And a happy consequence is the growth of love in the minister.
>
> The realization that one's loving service is a mediation of God's love induces humility. Humility, knowledge of oneself, is necessary to the maintenance of a proper attitude toward those who one serves . . . .
>
> The response to all of these human miseries, Bernard teaches, must be loving service.[383]

---

[383] Sommerfeldt, 175-77.

German Pietists

During the seventeenth century in Germany, the state controlled Lutheran church was characterized by a stale intellectual orthodoxy. Pierson notes that for the parishioners of the Lutheran church, "The Christian life was understood as quite passive: one went to church, took the sacraments, and believed correct dogma . . . most sermons focused on obscure points of doctrine that were neither understood or relevant to the common people."[384] It was in this context that a religious movement developed, called by its critics "pietism." In essence, pietism promoted a biblically based faith that focused on personal conviction of sin and salvation, heart-felt repentance, true regeneration in Christ, and a new life in Christ lived under the control of the Holy Spirit. Pietism involved a pursuit of biblically defined faith and was a reaction against intellectualism, religious authorities and formalistic creeds. As Lindberg explains, "Pietism became a Bible movement that strove to activate the universal priesthood of all believers, shift the focus from the theory to the praxis of Christianity, limit confessional polemics, reform theological studies in the sense of the practice of piety, and finally redirect preaching to the edification and cultivation of the 'inner man.'"[385]

Pietism claimed that the state church had over emphasized "justification by faith apart from works."[386] Pietists taught that

---

[384] Pierson, 181-82.
[385] Carter Lindberg, *A Brief History of Christianity* (Malden, MA: Blackwell Publishing, 2006), 130.
[386] Stoeffler, 183-85.

salvation involved more than justification. It included a lifelong process of transformation into Christ's likeness. According to Stein, Spener was genuinely concerned, "that justification bear fruit in the sanctification and renewal of each believer. Spener's task therefore was not to dislodge the doctrine of justification from the central position of Christian piety, but to set it so deep in the individual's being that it would confirm and rule all his or her utterances from within."[387]

The orthodox state church viewed Pietism as a form of religious idealism. Pietists often described the nature of saving faith as the *whole, perfect* or *entire* life that God intends for all believers. They taught believers to commit themselves totally to live for God and to entrust their whole life to Christ.[388] Stoeffler notes that Pietists believed that to grow spiritually it was a believer's

> ... religious obligation, prompted by the love of God, to live on a higher moral plain than other people, but in addition he had to engage in a given set of devotional exercises calculated to keep him responsive to the divine will. To this end the use of edificatory materials, Bible reading, prayer, and the regular attendance of divine worship was a necessity .... To the typical Pietist these works were the inevitable and necessary results of the religious relationship into which man had been placed by the grace of God. They were man's thank offering for God's redemptive love.[389]

---

[387] K. James Stein, *Philipp Jacob Spener: Pietist Patriarch* (Chicago: Covenant Press, 1986), 186.
[388] Stoeffler, *The Rise of Evangelical Pietism* (Leiden, Netherlands: E. J. Brill, 1971), 16-17.
[389] Stoeffler, *The Rise of Evangelical Pietism*, 18.

Philipp Jakob Spener[390]

Philipp Jakob Spener (1635-1705) received a doctor of theology in 1664 as an assistant minister in Strasbourg.[391] As Beddington noted, his passion for theological education drove him to publically renounce the barren orthodoxy of the state church and call for four significant changes:

> 1) more intensive Bible study, individually and in *collegial pietatis* (*conventicles*); 2) The exercise of the universal priesthood of believers through increased lay activity; 3) The practice of Christianity in daily life and works of unselfish love; 4) Dealing with unbelievers and heretics with sincere prayers, good examples persuasive dialogue and the spirit of love instead of compulsion.[392]

As the pastor in Frankfort, Spener began the practice of inviting a group of believers to his home one evening each week to study a chosen biblical passage, discuss the previous Sunday's sermon, and pray for each other. These groups, consisting of men and women of different ages and social classes, were called *Collegia Pietatis* (College of Piety).[393] Spener not only encouraged personal Bible study but also claimed that a right feeling in the heart in devotion to God was more important than pure doctrine.[394]

---

[390] Alternate spelling for his first and middle names includes "Philip" and "Jacob." The most common spelling for his name found throughout the literature reviewed is "Philipp Jakob Spener."

[391] Clouse, Pierard and Yamauchi, 212.

[392] David W. Beddington, "Pietism" in *The New Dictionary of Theology*, edited by Sinclair B. Ferguson, David F. Wright and James I. Packer (Downers Grove, Illinois: InterVarsity, 1988), 515-16.

[393] Pierson, 182.

[394] Clyde L Manschreck, editor, *A History of Christianity, The Church from the Reformation to the Present* (Grand Rapids, MI: Baker Book House, 1964), 268.

In 1675, Spener wrote the introduction to the new edition of Johann Arndt's book, *True Christianity,* which was later published as a small book entitled *Pia Desideria* (Pious Desires). In *Pia Desideria,* Spener described the reform needed in the lifeless Orthodox Church, emphasized the biblical teaching about the priesthood of every believer and called for the formation of small groups of believers in every church to meet together for Bible reading, prayer, and mutual edification.[395] *Pia Desideria* was widely circulated and read during the seventeenth century, producing four editions and 80,000 copies.[396]

Spener's greatest passion in ministry was to teach orthodox doctrine and to apply biblical doctrine to the pursuit of personal godliness. As Brown notes, "Spener proposed to test each doctrine by whether faith in that doctrine led forth to piety through the grace of God in Christ."[397] He believed there was no value in studying about the spiritual life and sanctification without experiencing that truth in daily living.[398] As Way observed, "Spener sought a more complete Christianity than was prevalent at the time. He saw authentic Christian spirituality as encompassing not only the mind in its assent to right doctrine, but also the feelings and actions of the believer."[399]

---

[395] Pierson, 182-183.
[396] Kenneth B. Mulholland, "From Luther to Carey, Pietism and the Modern Missionary Movement." *Bibliotheca Sacra*, 156 (January-March, 1999), 91.
[397] Brown, 58.
[398] Way, 73-4.
[399] Way, 12-13.

Spener believed that conversion mandated the cultivation of a growing and vibrant faith. Stoeffler notes,

> Spener's most radical departure from orthodoxy had to do with their conception of sanctification . . . (he) believed uncompromisingly that Christ came not only to justify men but to sanctify them as well. Sanctification, he held, is not merely a test of true faith, it is a divine intention and hence a valid religious end. Nor it is something done by God alone. God initiates the action, to be sure. He provides the initial impulse and the strength the Christian needs from day to day to live in holiness. But the individual must respond to God's grace and bend his will toward the continuous amendment of life.[400]

Spener taught that the Lordship of Christ was to rule the life of the believer. Pietists believed the study of Christology should not only reveal biblical truth about Christ but also foster a personal evaluation of how much Christ controls every aspect of the believer's life.[401] He believed that obedience to Christ as King applied to every aspect of a believer's being and was ultimately expressed through love and service to others. In Pietist literature, obedience to Christ is often defined as the imitation of Christ's life in the believer's life.[402]

For Spener, righteous living motivated the believer's own will to cooperate with the will of God. He taught that God calls all believers to a life of self-denial and that effort and work are

---

[400] Stoeffler, *The Rise of Evangelical Pietism*, 241.
[401] Brown, 93.
[402] August Francke, *Nicodemus: Or a Treatise Against the Fear of Man . . .* (London: Joseph Downing, 1706), 98, quoted in *Understanding Pietism*, by Dale W. Brown, rev. ed. (Nappanee, IN: Evangel Publishing House, 1966), 62

necessary for the believer to obey God's commands faithfully. Spener taught that obedience required expending physical, intellectual, and spiritual power for the benefit of others. Stein notes how Spener believed that only God empowers believers to live an others-centered life: ". . . that their lives of obedience be marked by a denial of self to the advantage of their neighbors, there is no way in which they can allow the cry of the need about them to go unanswered. Obedience means involvement, as well as abstention."[403]

A. H. Francke in Halle

An equally important figure in the development of Pietism was August Hermann Francke (1663-1727). Through his teaching and example of love and good deeds, he spread the ideals and priorities of Pietism beyond Germany.[404] "Francke shaped the agenda and described the impact of Pietism in just twelve words, 'A life changed, a church revived, a nation reformed, a world evangelized.'"[405] Francke demonstrated that true spiritual growth has an inward as well as an outward dimension as believers live out their faith and piety in service to others.[406]

Francke believed that an individual's salvation should lead to progressive improvements. His primary interest was to see a

---

[403] Stein, 232.
[404] Clouse, Pierard and Yamauchi, 212.
[405] August Hermann Francke, quoted in "Gallery of Leading Figures," *Christian History* 5 (1986): 14.
[406] M.A. Noll "Pietism" in *Evangelical Dictionary of Theology* (Walter A. Elwell, ed. (Grand Rapids, MI: Baker Book House, 1984), 857.

believer grow in conformity to the will of God.[407] Stoeffler notes Francke's commitment to promote spiritual growth in his disciples:

> his tireless exhortation is that his hearers must grow in faith, grow in wisdom, grow in dedication, grow in good works, and by the same token, that they must dissociate themselves increasingly from the "world" and from the pleasures of the "flesh." Nor can this be the result of an occasional attempt to amend one's life, it must, rather, be a constant, a daily effort.[408]

For Francke, the guiding principle of the spiritual life was obedience to God. Francke saw no room for compromise in daily life as the obedient believer applied God's Word to all aspects of their life. For Francke, the ultimate goal for believers was to honor God by pursuing godliness.[409] As Stoeffer notes, he taught that the faith that sanctifies and causes spiritual growth requires a wholehearted dedication and investment of all of one's energy. He promoted the use of godly disciplines like "self-examination, daily repentance, and prayer, hearing the Word, and participating in the Sacrament" to produce maturity in Christ.[410] Francke believed that spiritual transformation was a lifelong, intentional process of pursuing Christ-likeness. As a believer grows in his or her love for God and fellow man, the more he or she will grow in obedience and submission to God and his Word.[411]

---

[407] Stoeffler, *German Pietism During the Eighteenth Century*, 8
[408] Stoeffler, *German Pietism During the Eighteenth Century*, 18.
[409] Stoeffler, *German Pietism During the Eighteenth Century*, 18-19.
[410] Stoeffler, *German Pietism During the Eighteenth Century*, 21.
[411] August Hermann Francke, *Sonn, Fest, und Apostel, Tags, Predigten. 3 Teile* (Halle 1704, I): 990 quoted in Gary R. Sattler, *Nobler Than the Angels, Lower Than a Worm: The Pietist View of the Individual in the Writings of Heinrich*

The Pietist believed that the spiritual life was to be lived from the inside out. A believer's new life in Christ begins on the inside of a person with the love of God and through spiritual growth and moves to the outside through actions to demonstrate love for others. Believers become a channel of Christ's love to their neighbors. Sattler notes Francke's view on God's love: "The love which originates in God and is poured out in Jesus Christ onto humanity is then channeled through the believer to his or her neighbor."[412] Loving neighbor means loving all people. Francke taught that the measure of a believer's life in the light of eternity was to be based, in part, on how others benefited spiritually and physically from the believer's life of love and good works. Francke demonstrated that loving one's neighbor must necessarily result in loving non-believers who live in the world.[413]

The *Pietist trinity* linked together the pursuit of God's glory, one's neighbor's good, and the believer's personal holiness, to characterize the obedient Christian's life.[414] The *Pietist trinity* became the motivation for active, loving engagement in the world. Pietists taught that inner spiritual transformation results in a vibrant, active and other's-centered life. Obedient believers are

---

Muller and August Hermann Francke (Lanhan, MD: University of Press of America, 1989), 89.

[412] Gary R. Sattler, *Nobler Than the Angels, Lower Than a Worm: The Pietist View of the Individual in the Writings of Heinrich Muller and August Hermann Francke* (Lanhan, MD: University of Press of America, 1989), 116-17.

[413] Stein, 230-231.

[414] Sattler, 129-30.

called to be a light in the dark world.[415] Brown emphasizes the priority Pietists placed on loving all people and having others-centered focused faith:

> A frequent stereotype of Pietistic Christianity portrays it as almost exclusively preoccupied with inward devotion and private moral scruples. On the contrary, the Pietist milieu resulted in a desire to transform the living conditions of the poor and oppressed, reform the prison system, abolish slavery, break down rigid class distinctions, establish a more democratic polity, initiate educational reforms, establish philanthropic institutions, increase missionary activity, obtain religious liberty, and propose programs for social justice . . . . Even among movements concerned only about personal spiritual growth and salvation, class barriers are transcended in lives reflecting the transforming power of the message. For example, at Halle the treatment of the poor and orphans as educable was in itself socially transforming.[416]

Gordon highlights Francke's unique commitment to others:

Touched with compassion over the ubiquitous human misery resulting from the Thirty Years War, Francke decided to teach the way of Christ outside the classroom, as well as from the university lectern. Orphans were everywhere, living in the streets and indulging in crime to survive. Francke established orphanages to care for your children, hospitals to care for the sick, and schools to educate pupils from ministry and the sciences. At his death in 1726, nearly three thousand people were involved at the Francke Foundation with these students becoming pastors, government officials, nurses, and professors.[417]

---

[415] Francke, Sonn, Fest und Apostle, III, 235, quoted in Sattler, 129.
[416] Brown, 86-87.
[417] Ronald J. Gordon, *Rise of Pietism in 17th Century Germany* <http:www.cob-net.org/pietism.htm> (accessed September 13, 2005).

Pietists believed that it is God's will that the gospel be shared with all people and particularly with the poor and oppressed. Francke was so committed to the great commission that he turned the seminary in Halle to a center for missionary training. Francke was instrumental in creating the first organized effort to reach the nations for Christ since the Protestant Reformation. Students were challenged with the great commission and 60 men through Francke's influence and another 220 through the leadership of his student—Nikolaus Ludwig Graf, count von Zinzendorf (1700-1760)—committed their lives to serve as missionaries throughout the world. The first Protestant missionaries, Bartholomaeus Ziegenbalg and Heinrich Pluetschau, were students at Halle, sent to India by King Frederick IV of Denmark. Francke also published the first mission journal, *Hallesche Corresponden* (Correspondence from Halle), which detailed missionary activities from letters received from the field and promoted interest in missions throughout Europe and the New World.[418]

Conclusion

Pietism represents a return to the authority and application of Scripture and the intentional pursuit of an active and vibrant personal spiritual life. The Pietist concern for obedience to the Bible and godliness lived-out in tangible ways shaped their

---

[418] Eric Jonas Swensson, "August Hermann Francke, Lutheranism's Forgotten Hero," Pietist Blogspot, entry posted September 15, 2010, <http://pietist.blogspot.com/2010/09/august-hermann-francke-lutheranism.html> (accessed 06/06/11).

application of Christology, sanctification, and ecclesiology. It transformed their worldview, preaching, education, discipleship, their approach to daily living and their relationships with others and the world. Their quest for practical holiness shaped their values and attitudes, their application of truth, their submission to Christ's Lordship and their understanding of his mission. The desire to faithfully study and obey the Word of God, submit to the presence and power of the Holy Spirit, and others-centered service distinguished Pietism and made it a model to follow by believers around the world for generations.[419]

Pietism emphasized that faith and spiritual growth should be demonstrated in a love for God and neighbor. Inward spiritual transformation necessarily expressed itself in obedience and submission to Christ's Lordship and mission. Pietism was an essential model from which William Carey, Von Zinzendorf, John Wesley, and many others prioritized the making of disciples and expressed a passion for the great commission.[420] Pietism centered evangelism, disciple-making and church planting on the church's agenda. It provided the model for multiplication that makes up disciple-making movements.

Dietrich Bonhoeffer

The teaching, writings and example of Dietrich Bonhoeffer have greatly influenced many evangelical churches and

---

[419] Stoeffler, *The Rise of Evangelical Pietism*, 23-24.
[420] Mulholland, "From Luther to Carey," 95.

denominations. Bonhoeffer demonstrated his wholehearted commitment to Christ through his insightful and compelling words, personal convictions, and his example of loving and sacrificial deeds. In the late 1930's, the state church in Germany had capitulated in its opposition to the all-out aggression of the Nazi regime against the innocent. Bonhoeffer could not stand idle and joined an effort to assassinate Hitler. The plot was discovered and Bonhoeffer was imprisoned and eventually killed.[421]

As Demarest notes, "Bonhoeffer held Christology at the center of his thinking." Demarest describes how Bonhoeffer viewed one's ability to know and comprehend God: "Unknowable in Himself, God is understood only through Jesus Christ."[422] For Bonhoeffer, it was the incarnation of Christ that placed Him as the unifying center of a Christian's reality and experience as Christ lives at the center of every aspect of a believer's being.

Bonhoeffer rejected the efforts of organized religion to impose rules to direct the behavior of believers. He believed that true and lasting spiritual formation that produces enduring moral and ethical change comes from inside the believer, brought about through the renewal of the mind. Bonhoeffer taught that spiritual transformation happens as a process in which the believer's mind is shaped to the mind of Christ. Bonhoeffer believed that this goes beyond merely imitating Christ. It involves having Christ's power so work within the obedient believer that he becomes what God

---

[421] Bruce A Demarest, "Devotion, Doctrine and Duty in Dietrich Bonhoeffer," *Bibliotheca Sacra*, 148:592 (October-December, 1991), 401.
[422] Demarest, 401.

intended for mankind—to be fully human which is to be Christ-like.[423]

Bonhoeffer referred to spiritual formation as formation into the "likeness of the Crucified."[424] The obedient believer who draws closer to Christ becomes aware of the indwelling sin that required Christ's death. Believers are not only to be conformed to Christ in his death as "the Crucified One," they also are to deal with their own sin in the process of being conformed to his victory over sin as the "Risen One." The believer in Christ is made a new person before God. As Bonhoeffer wrote, "In the midst of death, he is life. In the midst of sin, he is righteous. In the midst of the old, he is new. His secret remains hidden from the world. He lives because Christ lives, and, lives in Christ alone."[425] Bonhoeffer refers to the process of being formed into Christ-likeness as becoming fully man:

> The form of Jesus Christ takes form in man. Man does not take on an independent form of his own, but what gives him form and what maintains him in the new form is always solely the form of Jesus Christ Himself. It is therefore not a vain imitation or repetition of Christ's form but Christ's form itself which takes form in man . . . . Man becomes man because God became man. But man does not become God. It is not he, therefore, who was or is able to accomplish his own transformation, but it is God who changes his form into the form of man, so that man may become, not indeed God, but, in the eyes of God, man.[426]

---

[423] Dietrich Bonhoeffer, *Christ the Center* (New York: Harper & Row, Publishers, 1966), 14.
[424] Dietrich Bonhoeffer, *Ethics* (New York: The Macmillan Company, 1965), 81.
[425] Bonhoeffer, *Ethics,* 82.
[426] Bonhoeffer, *Ethics*, 82.

In *The Cost of Discipleship* (1937), Bonhoeffer commented on the teaching of the Sermon on the Mount (Matthew 5-7), identifying real life principles to be lived-out by every believer. Bonhoeffer felt that the common way of understanding justification by faith as the essence of salvation in the congregations of his day amounted to "cheap grace." He taught that people are saved by grace alone and that this grace is also to promote obedience to God's word and is therefore costly grace. Ultimately, he believed that grace "is costly because it cost God the life of his Son: 'ye were bought at a price,' and what has cost God much cannot be cheap for us . . . it is grace because God did not reckon his son too dear a price to pay for our life, but delivered him up for us."[427] In *The Cost of Discipleship*, Bonhoeffer wrote, "cheap grace" is "the grace which amounts to the justification of sin without the justification of the repentant sinner who departs from sin and from whom sin departs. Cheap grace is not the kind of forgiveness of sin, which frees us from the toils of sin. Cheap grace is the grace we bestow on ourselves."[428]

Bonhoeffer claimed that the Church throughout history has developed a "fatal conception of a double standard—a maximum and a minimum standard of Christian obedience."[429] He states that "Luther had said that grace alone can save; his followers took up his doctrine and repeated it word for word. But they left out its invariable corollary, the obligation of discipleship."[430] Regarding discipleship, Bonhoeffer wrote,

> Christianity without the living Christ is inevitably Christianity without discipleship, and Christianity without discipleship is always Christianity without Christ. It

---

[427] Bonhoeffer, *The Cost of Discipleship*, 48.
[428] Bonhoeffer, *The Cost of Discipleship*, 47.
[429] Bonhoeffer, *The Cost of Discipleship*, 49-50.
[430] Bonhoeffer, *The Cost of Discipleship*, 53.

remains an abstract idea, a myth which has a place for the Fatherhood of God, but omits Christ as the living Son. And a Christianity of that kind is nothing more or less than an end of discipleship. In such a religion there is trust in God, but no following of Christ.[431]

Bonhoeffer believed that the basic issue negatively affecting the spiritual life was, "The justification of the sinner in the world degenerated into the justification of sin and the world. Costly grace was turned into cheap grace without discipleship."[432] Bonhoeffer taught that the obedient disciple is to live by costly grace, grace that works, that grows, that sacrifices and is concerned with loving God and neighbor.[433]

Franklin notes Bonhoeffer taught that there were three obedient responses believers needed to pursue to be Christ's disciples. First, all disciples must dedicate themselves to study, contemplate, and pray through the Word to faithfully obey it.[434] Bonhoeffer wrote,

> It is evident that the only appropriate conduct of men before God is the doing of his will. The Sermon on the Mount is there for the purpose of being done (Matt. 7:24ff). Only in doing can there be submission to the will of God. In doing God's will, man renounces every right and every justification of his own; he delivers himself humbly into the hands of the merciful Judge. If the Holy Scripture insists with such great urgency on doing that is because it wishes to take away from man every possibility of self-justification

---

[431] Bonhoeffer, *The Cost of Discipleship*, 63-64.
[432] Bonhoeffer, *The Cost of Discipleship*, 53.
[433] Franklin, 150.
[434] Franklin, 150.

before God on the basis of his own knowledge of good and evil.[435]

Secondly, a disciple must understand that grace and obedience go together and must not cheapen grace by making it an abstract concept divorced from daily life. Bonhoeffer claimed that, "Jesus summons men to follow him not as a teacher or a pattern of the good life, but as the Christ, the Son of God . . . . We are not expected to contemplate the disciple, but only him who calls and his absolute authority . . . there is no road to faith or discipleship, no other road—only obedience to the call of Jesus." [436]

Thirdly, the obedient disciple is called to live a rigorous faith based on the example of the life, death and resurrection of Christ. A life of active faith demonstrates the reality of a believer's justification.[437] Franklin describes Bonhoeffer's opinion about the Christ-directed life: "We must be willing to live in radical obedience to the Living Christ, in constant communion with him, seeking him anew in every situation, and never relying upon our own systems, ideas, feelings, or experiences. We must seek him and his word alone."[438] Matthews describes Bonhoeffer's perspective on the disciple's relationship to Christ: "The solid foundation, Jesus Christ, is God incarnationally present in every

---

[435] Bonhoeffer, *Ethics*, 43.
[436] Bonhoeffer, *The Cost of Discipleship*, 62.
[437] Bonhoeffer, *Ethics*, 121.
[438] Franklin, 51-52.

nook and cranny of existence, within which his disciples are called to participate."[439]

Bonhoeffer believed that God's love alone has the divine power to transform a believer's entire existence and draw the believer into the world to live before God, and in God and through God.[440] Bonhoeffer taught that there is no true love that is separated from the love of God. Loving God and others, for Bonhoeffer, was simply living out the love which one receives through God's love.

Bonhoeffer stressed that the believer's service to others should address the needs of the *whole person,* and not be focused solely on a person's intellectual, or spiritual or physical needs. He taught that since Christ took humanity upon himself, he came to redeem and restore people according to God's original design as complete and whole disciples. Bonhoeffer understood that Christ saves people, not to rescue them from the world, but that they would now live to serve the world and to make other disciples. He therefore believed that spiritual growth and mission are to be lived out together.[441]

Bonhoeffer taught that believers are not called to live-out their Christian life in isolation but community—through the church of Christ. Thiselton, quoting Bonhoeffer, notes that Bonhoeffer

---

[439] Matthews, 20.
[440] Bonhoeffer, *Ethics*, 52.
[441] Geffrey B. Kelly and John C. Weborg, eds. *Reflections on Bonhoeffer: Essays in Honor of F. Burton Nelson* (Chicago: Covenant Publications, 1999), 261.

taught that, "Jesus Christ was 'there only for others'. 'Being there for others' is what really points to the reality of God."[442] However, Bonhoeffer strongly believed Christians are also called to serve people in the world who are *not yet* part of a church-community. Since Christ was in the world though his incarnation, Bonhoeffer claimed that the church needed to be in the world, ministering to the needs of those without Christ. Bonhoeffer stated,

> The Church's word derives its sole right and its sole authority from the commission of Christ, and consequently any word which she may utter without reference to this authority will be devoid of all significance . . . . The Church proclaims this commandment by testifying to Jesus Christ as the Lord and Savior of his people and of the whole world, and so by summoning all men to fellowship with Him.[443]

Bonhoeffer continues, "In view of the incarnation of God, to live as man before God can mean only to exist not for oneself but for God and for other men."[444]

Conclusion on Bonhoeffer's Influence

In the midst of tumultuous times in Nazi Germany, in the face of a compromised and paralyzed state church, and in opposition to a Christian faith that had become humanly comfortable yet biblically stagnant and passive, Dietrich Bonhoeffer issued forth a call for believers to pursue Christ's

---

[442] Anthony C. Thiselton, "An Age of Anxiety," in *Introduction to the History of Christianity: First Century to the Present Day—A Worldwide History,"* ed. Tim Dowley (Minneapolis, Fortress Press: 1995), 618.
[443] Bonhoeffer, *Ethics,* 296.
[444] Bonhoeffer, *Ethics,* 297.

mission passionately. Bonhoeffer taught the nature of holistic discipleship as a lifelong quest of living-out costly grace through obedience to Christ and sacrificial service for others. Bonhoeffer's emphasis on the character, example, love, and sacrifice of Christ provides a biblical understanding and compelling example for promoting holistic discipleship and the creation of disciple-making movements.

Conclusion

The four historical movements and persons studied demonstrate a remarkable similarity in their understanding of the person, work, and mission of Christ. Within their own historical, social, and religious contexts, each individual and group explored above made obedient disciples and initiated movements to train others to do the same. The historical record demonstrates how they were motivated principally by the love of God to intentionally and sacrificially advance the mission of Christ. Their example also confirms the importance of making holistic disciples through training, mentoring and leading believers to obey and follow all that Christ had commanded in the accomplishment of his mission.

Every individual and group explored above manifested a clear commitment to see Christ's church built, each in their own cultural and social contexts, making holistic disciples and nurturing disciple-making movements. These historical examples serve to validate the thesis of this study. The making of holistic disciples results in the creation of disciple-making movements and the building of Christ's church. This divinely ordained and biblical mission Christ has commanded his followers to fulfill among the nations must be pursued through Christ, obedience to his Word, and the power of the Holy Spirit.

CHAPTER 7
AN ANALYSIS OF CURRENT MISSIONAL THOUGHT INTERPRETED BY THE THESIS OF THIS STUDY

Introduction

The thesis of this study is that the heart of Christ's mission is the making of holistic disciples that results in disciple-making movements. Many scholars believe that God's mission is defined by his redemptive acts as seen in Scripture as he establishes his kingdom rule. This study demonstrates that the two-fold mission of Christ is the mission of God for all believers. It is therefore important to understand the perspective of those scholars who promote God's mission during this age as something other than that which Christ commanded.

The word, *missional*, denotes an activity related to or characterized by *mission*, or has the qualities, attributes or dynamics of mission. As Wright notes, *missional* as an adjective, "is to the word *mission* what covenantal is to *covenant*, or fictional to *fiction*."[445] When *missional* is used to delineate the mission of Christ, it should emphasize the center of Christ's mission—the making of holistic disciples and the creation of disciple-making movements. If the word *missional* does not define the mission of

---

[445] Wright, 24.

Christ, then it does not describe the mission of God. This chapter reviews the most prominent missional scholars and their views on the nature of the mission of Christ.

Central Tenets Used to Advance the Missional Church Concept

Introduction

In contemporary evangelical thought, a diversity of opinions exists over what constitutes the mission and work of God in the world. Added to this diversity is the justifiable compassion felt by many pastors and church leaders as they observe the needs and suffering of people in their communities. In recent years, scholars have promoted the fulfillment of Christ's mission through programs to foster church growth and health. Church leaders have focused their efforts on developing the seeker church, the simple church, the cell church, the emerging church, and the missional church. The missional church concept is having, perhaps, the greatest impact in redefining the nature and practice of many pastors and churches. Although the scholars who advocate for a missional church come from various theological persuasions, there are some common elements on which they base their missional philosophy. The standard for evaluating all missional activity is the mission of Christ.

The theological diversity among scholars can be traced to the interpretation of Scripture (hermeneutics), doctrinal traditions and convictions, and ecclesiastical background. One's position on these issues contributes directly to their understanding Christ's post-resurrection mandate and the ministry of the local church. The question of what is *missional* therefore cannot be adequately answered apart from a clear understanding of the mission of Christ. Only a literal hermeneutic and a biblically accurate perspective of salvation history in the Scriptures will correctly reflect what the word of God teaches about the centrality of Christ's mission.

The first part of this chapter begins with a synopsis of the *main* theological and interpretive beliefs that form the foundational perspective of scholars advocating missional ministry. This is followed by a survey of the growth of missional ministry and a presentation of its theological underpinnings. The second section will analyze the practical emphasis employed in developing missional churches. The third section presents a critique of the missional church movement. The basis of this critique is an understanding of the mission of Christ as presented in this study.

The Broad Theological Basis for Missional Church Ministry

Because of the wide range of perspectives on what constitutes the missional church, it is impossible to make definitive statements addressing all missional church perspectives. However, there are common theological and philosophical tenets that the majority of missional church proponents advocate.

The *Missio Dei* Emphasis in Missional Ministry
Historical Background on the Missio Dei Concept

A key result developed from the World Missionary Conference (Edinburgh, 1910) was the eventual creation of the "International Missionary Council" (IMC) in 1921. The IMC was the first Protestant international and ecumenical organization dedicated to global evangelism and missions.[446] After its founding, the IMC initiated various international conferences, generally held each decade, to promote ecumenical cooperation in missions. In Willingen, Germany (1952), the IMC significantly shifted its understanding on the nature of biblical missions. Hesselgrave observes that at this time the focus moved from a church-centered focus on mission to a global one. He notes that the place of the kingdom in the mission of Christ began to replace an emphasis on the church.[447] Scherer states that the church-centered concept was, "no longer adequate for dealing with the problems facing churches engaged in missions in, from, and to all six continents in the post-colonial era."[448]

Hesselgrave observes how the IMC leadership not only defined a new understanding of the nature of biblical mission; it subtly introduced a different theological perspective. God's mission and activity in salvation history began to be interpreted

---

[446] Hesselgrave, *Paradigms,* 318.
[447] Hesselgrave, *Paradigms,* 321.
[448] James A. Scherer, "Church, Kingdom, and Missio Dei," In *The Good News of the Kingdom. Mission Theology for the Third Millennium,* edited by Charles Van Engen, Dean S. Guilliland, and Paul Pierson (Maryknoll, New York: Orbis Books, 1993), 85.

from a Trinitarian framework on the mission of God in the world rather than from the more historic Christo-centric, New Testament perspective. The IMC was later incorporated into the World Council of Churches and the mission of God concept developed and was associated predominately with an ecumenical and theologically liberal interpretation.[449] From the 1960's through the 1980's, the concept of the *missio Dei* grew and was interpreted as the center of mission, promoted by mainline denominational leaders associated with the World Council of Churches. Over the past two decades, numerous moderate and evangelical leaders have studied and adopted much of what has been taught and developed from Scripture about the *missio Dei* concept.[450]

Contemporary Perspective on the Missio Dei Concept

The *missio Dei* concept makes the Trinity the starting point for missions. Bosch states,

> Mission was understood as being derived from the very nature of God. It is thus put in the context of the doctrine of the Trinity, not of ecclesiology or soteriology. The classical doctrine of the *missio Dei* as God the Father sending the Son, and God the Father and the son sending the Spirit expanded to include yet another "movement." Father, Son, and Holy Spirit sending the church into the world.[451]

---

[449] Hesselgrave, *Paradigms,* 321-22.
[450] Craig Van Gelder, *The Missional Church: Helping Congregations Develop Contextual Ministry* (Grand Rapids: William B. Eerdmans Publishing Company, 2007), 20.
[451] Bosch, 390.

The concept of the *missio Dei* views God in trinity as the creator of all things. God is also the creator of the church and it is through the Holy Spirit that the church is called, gathered and sent into the world to accomplish God's mission. Some scholars understand that in the *missio Dei,* his character and sovereign nature as well as the substitutionary sacrifice of his Son, Jesus, drive God's participation in mission.[452] Other scholars, such as Bosch, believed that the *missio Dei* is to be understood as defining a broad ministry focus for the church:

> We do need a more radical and comprehensive hermeneutic of mission. In attempting to do this we may perhaps move close to viewing everything as mission, but this is a risk we will have to take. Mission is a multifaceted ministry, in respect of witness, service, justice, healing, reconciliation, liberation, peace, evangelism, fellowship, church planting, contextualization, and much more . . . Whoever we are, we are tempted to incarcerate the *missio Dei* in the narrow confines of our own predilections, thereby of necessity reverting to one-sidedness and reductionism. We should beware of any attempt at delineating mission too sharply.[453]

Most missional scholars teach that the mission of the church is defined and governed by the *missio Dei* found throughout the scriptures. The church is Christ's agent to accomplish God's mission. A major tenet of many missional church scholars is that Christ's promise to build his church is a key element of the *missio Dei* . Christ sends the church as he was sent, to the world. Bosch maintains,

---

[452] Craig Van Gelder, *The Ministry of the Missional Church: A Community Led by the Spirit* (Grand Rapids, MI: Baker Books, 2007), 18.
[453] Bosch, 512.

Mission is *missio Dei*, which seeks to subsume into itself the *missiones ecclesiae*, the missionary programs of the church. It is not the church which "undertakes" mission; it is the *missio Dei* which constitutes the church. The mission of the church needs constantly to be renewed and re-conceived. Mission is not competition with other religions, not a conversion activity, not expanding the faith, not building up the kingdom of God; neither is it social, economic, or political activity. And yet, there is merit in all of these projects. So, the church's concern is conversion, church growth, the reign of God, economy, society and politics—but in a different manner![454]

As McNeal notes, "the missional church is the people of God partnering with God in his redemptive mission in the world."[455] McNeal believes that, "This characterization intentionally allows for a wide range of expression, as wide as God's interaction. Missional is not a place you arrive at but a direction in which you are moving. It is a way of being in the world."[456] God's overall interaction towards humanity forms the missional character of the church.

Many missional church scholars view the development of the *missio Dei* concept as contributing to a biblical understanding of mission. MacIlvaine states,

> In missional churches service is seen as a return to a historic value of the church, temporarily lost during the twentieth century. In the missional construct, service is especially local. "What are the needs in our immediate situation? How can we meet those needs as an expression

---

[454] Bosch, 519.
[455] Reggie McNeal, *Missional Renaissance: Changing the Scorecard for the Church* (San Francisco, Jossey-Bass, 2009), 24.
[456] McNeal, 38.

of God's common grace for long-term sustained culture change within our community?"[457]

The Kingdom and Reign of God in Missional Ministry

Many missional church advocates believe that Christ's sacrificial death for humanity announced the redemptive reign of God that is now available to all through faith in him.[458] Van Gelder continues,

> This redemptive reign of God in Christ is inherently connected to the *missio Dei*, which means that God is seeking to bring back into right relationship all of creation.... The Spirit-led, missional church is responsible to participate in this reconciling work by bearing witness to the redemptive reign of God in Christ as good news, and through inviting everyone everywhere to become reconciled to the living and true God.[459]

Missional advocates view the kingdom of God from a missional perspective. Christ and God's redemptive plan based on Christ's death are central in the larger biblical story of God's message of salvation. Van Gelder describes a missional perspective on Christ's redemptive reign:

> A missional understanding of God's work in the world from this perspective is framed as follows: God is seeking to bring his kingdom, the redemptive reign of God in Christ, to bear on every dimension of life within the entire world so that the larger creation purposes of God can be fulfilled—the *missio Dei*. This missional understanding has the world as its primary horizon and the church is placed at

---

[457] W. Rodman MacIlvaine III, "How Churches Become Missional," *Bibliotheca Sacra* 167 (April-June 2010), 232.
[458] Van Gelder, *The Ministry of the Missional Church,* 18.
[459] Van Gelder, *The Ministry of the Missional Church,* 18.

the center of the activity in relation the kingdom of God to the *missio Dei*.[460]

British missiologist Lesslie Newbigin most effectively delineated the relationship between the triune concept of the *missio Dei* and the reign or kingdom of God. Newbigin taught that a core activity of the triune God is to both call and send the church, through the Holy Spirit, into the world as his representative, to accomplish God's work throughout all of creation. Newbigin taught that under God's universal reign, the church exists as God's work in the world as a *sign* that points to the fact that the redemptive reign of God's kingdom is actually currently present in the world. Secondly, the church is a *foretaste* that manifests God's future redemptive and eschatological reign. Lastly, the church functions as an *instrument* to bring the ongoing redemptive reign of God over all that has been created, through the control of the Holy Spirit.[461]

The mission of God and the eventual redemption of all creation from the curse of sin are necessarily connected to Christ's reign as Sovereign and King. The church, therefore, is sent out as God's agent in the world, called to participate in his mission by "living into and announcing the redemptive reign of God in Christ (the kingdom of God)."[462]

---

[460] Van Gelder, *The Ministry of the Missional Church*, 85.
[461] Craig Van Gelder, ed., *The Missional Church and Denominations: Helping Congregations Develop a Missional Identity* (Grand Rapids: William B. Eerdmans Publishing Company, 2008), 3 quoting Lesslie Newbigin, The Open Secret (Grand Rapids: Eerdmans, 1978), 124.
[462] Van Gelder, *The Ministry of the Missional Church*, 85.

The Place of the Church in Missional Theology

The emphasis on the missional church has led to a renewed biblical and practical examination of God's contemporary mission. Many authors, theologians, and pastors are advocating for a missionally-based ministry that impacts people outside the walls of the local church. The theological concepts of the *missio Dei* and the reign or kingdom of God are applied to the essence of the church and its mission.

The following definitions define the main characteristics and priorities of a missional church that moves out to address needs in the community. Roxburgh and Romanuk state, "A missional church is a community of God's people who live into the imagination that they are, by their very nature, God's missionary people living as a demonstration of what God plans to do in and for all of creation in Jesus Christ."[463] The church is therefore sent into the world as God's agent and representative of Christ. Barrett adds, "A missional church is a church that is shaped by participating in God's mission, which is to set things right in a broken, sinful world, to redeem it, and to restore it to what God has always intended for the world."[464]

Most missional scholars focus the church's ministry on the immediate needs of the people outside the doors of the church.

---

[463] Alan J. Roxburgh and Fred Romanuk, *The Missional Leader: Equipping Your Church to Reach a Changing World* (San Francisco: Jossey-Bass, 2006), xv.

[464] Lois Y. Barrett, ed. *Treasure in Clay Jars: Patterns in Missional Faithfulness* (Grand Rapids: William B. Eerdmans Publishing Company, 2004), x.

Hunsberger notes that, "The heart of the missional character of the church anywhere it is located, is its recognition that in the gospel's encounter with its own culture, i.e. the culture the church shares with the immediate community around it, the church is that community which knows that it sits on both sides of the encounter."[465] Greene and Robinson clarify the church's role in its community:

> The call that comes to the missional church is to exegete the community in which it is located—to engage in what some call ethnography, such that the stories that make up a given community are well understood. The members of a given congregation need to be helped to see how their personal stories interact with the various community narratives. As this process develops it gradually becomes clear how the missional church can engage with its community to bring transformation to it.[466]

Understanding and addressing the needs of the context and culture surrounding the church is central in the thinking of most missional church scholars. The desire is for the whole church to be God's agent of transformation. Greene and Robinson continue:

> It is not about finding opportunities for evangelistic outreach, nor is it just a matter of healing the hurts of a given community. Both of these activities may form part of a transformational agenda and encounter, but the *key* issue becomes: How can the church, working with a gospel of grace, help to create transformed communities? With this

---

[465] George R. Hunsberger, "*Birthing Missional Faithfulness: Accents in a North American Movement,*" International Review of Mission, vol. XCII: 365, March 25, 2009, 149. http://onlinelibrary.wiley.com/doi/10.1111/j.1758-6631.2003.tb00390.x/full (Accessed June 13, 2011).

[466] Colin Greene and Martin Robinson, *Metavista: Bible, Church and Mission in an Age of Imagination* (Colorado Springs, CO: Authentic Media, 2008), 203.

go questions like what partnerships need to be developed, what problems need to be overcome, what resources will be required, and how can prayer and a creative reimagining of what a community could look like begin to create a new reality?[467]

Based on the perspective that the church is called and sent to accomplish God's mission in the world, a new understanding of ecclesiology has emerged. Most missional scholars approach the doctrine of ecclesiology as first and foremost an extension of the *missio Dei*. The church is placed under and responds to the *missio Dei* and the reign of Christ in the kingdom of God. A missional ecclesiology defines the nature and activity of the church. The church is Christ's agent, sent out to the world to accomplish God's mission.

Guder states that first, a missional ecclesiology is biblical because it is solidly grounded in the person and testimony of God and the formation of his missionary people as his witnesses and instrument in mission. Secondly, a missional ecclesiology is historical because it is designed to continue God's mission of redemption in a particular context. Thirdly, a missional ecclesiology is shaped by the contextual realities of a particular culture and should be based upon and developed from within a specific cultural context. Fourthly, a missional ecclesiology is considered eschatological. The church is created and inspired by God's Spirit and it is therefore creative and dynamic in its development and nature. The church is on the move with God as

---

[467] Greene and Robinson, 204.

he moves in creation history towards his promised consummation of all things. Fifthly, a missional ecclesiology can be practiced individually and applied to life. It can serve as a witness to "make disciples of all nations . . ." (Matt. 28:19-20).[468]

The concept of viewing the church as being *sent* into the world to promote the salvation and reign of Christ is central to most missional church philosophies. As Stevenson observes,

> To be missional is to participate in the ministry of Jesus to the world, and to be the "incarnational" presence of Jesus in the world . . . .
>
> Being missional is going out into the culture to engage the culture in order to connect those in the culture to Christ. In essence, it is Great Commission living (Go and Make) with a Great Commandment heart (Love your neighbor) . . . .
>
> Being sent and going out is central to the ministry of those who follow Christ. It is an extension of Jesus being sent by the Father into the world. God the Father sends God the Son and God the Son sends us empowered by God the Spirit. As Jesus *was* the incarnation of God in the world, the church *is* to be the incarnation of Jesus in the world.[469]

A Critique of the Missional Church Movement
Introduction

It is impossible to present a comprehensive critique of the missional church movement in one chapter. The growing diversity of missional scholars, their perspectives and distinctive theologies, make a thorough evaluation of missional philosophy unfeasible.

---

[468] Guder, 11-12.
[469] Phil Stevenson "Fit Churches Missionally Engaged," *Journal of the American Society for Church Growth*, Winter, 2009, 60.

However, based on the thesis of this study, it is possible to highlight key perspectives of many missional church scholars.

The Missional Church and the Mission of Christ

This study has demonstrated that the mission of Christ is defined by his mandate to make holistic disciples who reproduce disciple-making movements. The adjective "missional," as defined above, refers to the attributes, characteristics and activities of a "mission." The mission defines its missional expression. Therefore, based on the thesis of this study, all genuine missional activity contributes to and advances the mission of Christ.

The "Missio Christi" Accurately Expresses the Mission of Christ

The *missio Dei* concept has emphasized the essence and character of the triune God as displayed in salvation history throughout Scripture. The New Testament reveals that the post-resurrection mission of God is centered in the person and authoritative work of Christ until the end of the age. That mission is exclusively expressed in the *missio Christi* (Matthew 28:18-20). The ministries of the Father and the Holy Spirit are directed at supporting the *missio Christi* until Christ comes again for his church.

Many missional scholars use the concept of the *missio Dei* to refer to all that God desires to do in the world. Engel and Dyrness make this significant statement:

> First, missions grows out of all that God has done in creation and new creation. And since it has to do ultimately with God and God's purposes, the second corollary is that a complete understanding of missions (and therefore an appropriate mission strategy) must be sensitive to the breadth of God's activities from creation to consummation.[470]

When the mission of God is defined broadly from Scripture and the church is taught that their role is to be God's agent in fulfilling his mission, the centrality of Christ's mission is redefined and undermined. McQuilkin provides a helpful perspective:

> The typical evangelical expects a theology of the mission of the Church to be developed primarily from the data found in Acts to Revelation, not primarily from the Old Testament or the teaching of Christ prior to his resurrection. Though God's purpose of worldwide redemption is clearly enunciated in all sections of Scripture, and any legitimate theology of mission must be rooted in the Old Testament and expanded through the teachings of Jesus, the delineation of the specific task of the Church is found after the church has come into existence. Revelation is progressive, and the earlier is to be understood in light of the latter.[471]

The Reign of God and the Mission of Christ

Many missional church scholars agree that the church as God's agent, under his kingdom reign, is sent into the world to accomplish his purposes. Van Gelder states that,

---

[470] Engel and Dyrness, 37.
[471] J. Robertson McQuilkin, "An Evangelical Assessment of Mission Theology of the Kingdom" in *The Good News of the Kingdom*, eds. Charles Van Engel, Dean S. Gilliland, Paul Pierson (Maryknoll, New York: Orbis Books, 1993), 176.

> The kingdom of God, the redemptive reign of God in Christ, gives birth to the missional church through the work of the Spirit. Its nature, ministry, and organization are formed by the reality power, and intent of the kingdom of God. Understanding the redemptive purposes of God that are embedded within the kingdom of God provides an understanding of the church being missionary by nature. The church participates in God's mission in the world because it can do no other. It was created for this purpose. This purpose is encoded within the very makeup of the nature of the church.[472]

While missional church scholars state that the church is missional by nature, its role in relationship to Christ and his mission is rarely stressed as the main objective and central purpose of the church.

It is clear that God exercised an aspect of his reign and kingship through human leaders for Israel in the Old Testament. The New Testament describes Christ's kingship and reign over individual's lives through faith in Christ (Romans 2:28, 29; 4:12; 9:6-8). As McQuilkin notes, The Kingdom of God is "never coextensive with either Israel or the church, and the proportion of true Kingdom citizens varies from church to church and from time to time. A further agreement is that there is coming a time when God's reign will be visible and universal, and this will be accomplished by God alone."[473] Referring to the Greek term for *kingdom*, McQuilkin notes that "biblical scholarship for some time has recognized that the root idea and dominant force of *basileia*

---

[472] Van Gelder, *The Ministry of the Missional Church*, 93.
[473] McQuilkin, 173.

(kingdom) is better expressed as *kingship rather than kingdom.* God's reign, not God's realm, is the focus."[474]

Hesselgrave describes the mission of Christ in relationship to God's kingdom:

> Though God is always building his kingdom, he is in this age building his church as an expression of that kingdom. Nowhere in Scripture are we specifically called upon to obey "kingdom mission" in the way we are called upon to obey the great commission. "Kingdom mission" was and remains uniquely the mission of Christ, though we are to witness to it in very practical ways. "Great Commission mission" is uniquely ours and requires us to make disciples by preaching, baptizing, and teaching the peoples of the earth. Christ will *bring* his kingdom and so he teaches believers to pray that God's kingdom will come *on earth as it now is in heaven.* Christ is *building* his church so he commands believers to witness and work for its completion, now and in this age.[475]

Holistic Ministry and the Mission of Christ

The term "holistic ministry" is commonly used to describe ministry to every aspect of a person. Holistic ministry involves social, physical, emotional and spiritual needs. Salvation as described by Newbigin is a "making whole, a healing, the summing up all things in Christ."[476] Many missional scholars prioritize the meeting of physical and social needs seeing the mission of God as addressing the needs of body and soul. As a result, much of missional ministry is focused on meeting people's

---

[474] McQuilken 174.
[475] Hesselgrave, *Paradigms*, 347-48.
[476] Lesslie Newbigin, *The Household of God: Lectures on the Nature of the Church* (Grand Rapids, MI: Eerdmans Publishing Company, 1957), 140.

material and social needs. They believe this is the heart of Christ's mission. However, the mission of Christ, to make obedient disciples of all peoples, can be undermined when an emphasis on physical, or societal needs is elevated above or equal to the making of holistic disciples who live like Jesus.[477]

It is essential to understand that the mission of Christ to make obedient disciples encapsulates the activities and ministries normally referred to as *holistic* ministry. Believers, as obedient disciples, are called to love like Jesus loved, serve like Jesus served, sacrifice self-interest like Jesus did, and even suffer, in some way, like Jesus suffered. Obeying all things Jesus commanded results in humble, others-centered service. As this research has shown, holistic disciples manifest their maturity in Christ through doing good works that have been prepared before the foundation of the world for them to do (Ephesians 2:10). Holistic disciples do not live for themselves, but for the sake of others (2 Corinthians 5:14-15). Holistic disciples inherently and sacrificially do holistic ministry for the benefit of others and the glory of the Lord.

Contrary to the opinions of many missional scholars, there is no clear mandate or example in the New Testament where physical or social ministry is given equal status with the disciple-making mission of Christ for all peoples.[478] McQuilkin states,

---

[477] Franklin, 29-30.

[478] Some missional scholars could appeal to Acts 2:44-45 to argue for a mandate for social and physical ministry to the community. Yet, in context, the passage demonstrates that the activity to care for the needs of others was based upon the

What mainstream evangelicals resist strongly, however, is giving *co-equal status* to social action and evangelism as parts of the *missionary* mandate to the church. To change this will require more than an appeal to Kingdom Theology. It will need demonstration from the New Testament data on the meaning of the great commission. This resistance to a redefinition of the missionary mandate is based on biblical, theological, and historical reasons.[479]

McQuilkin continues:

If Christ intended to include in that evangelistic mission a responsibility to redeem society, to restructure the unjust structures of the Roman Empire, he certainly failed to communicate that to those who were there. In fact, he remonstrated with the Apostles because they were hung-up on that very vision of establishing the Kingdom at that time (Acts 1:6-8).[480]

Horton states,

In this time between Christ's two comings, the church's task is to "proclaim the gospel to the whole creation.' There is no mandate for the church to develop a political, social, economic or cultural plan. Although it teaches the whole Word of God, both the law and the gospel, the church's mission is not even to reform the morals of society. Whatever effects the gospel has in the lives of its hearers and in the wider society in which it is heard, *the Great Commission itself* is a very specific mandate to get the Good News to everyone who lies in darkness, to baptize them, and to teach them everything in God's word.[481]

---

spiritual growth that occurred from the disciple-making ministry of the Apostles (Acts 2:42-43).
[479] McQuilken 175.
[480] McQuilkin, 176.
[481] Horton, 88.

Making a clear distinction between "holistic ministry" and the heart of Christ's mission is not a trivial matter. Believers who live under Christ's Lordship obligate themselves to obey all that Jesus commanded (Mt. 28:19, 20). His commandments and example about showing love and mercy and promoting justice instruct his disciples how to live for others. Under the control of the Spirit, believers are to live as "salt and light" as they make obedient disciples.[482] McQuilkin emphasizes the need to prioritize the evangelistic task of Christ's mission:

> But if one insists that the transformation of society is an equal part of the *missionary* mandate, that person will meet with resistance. The resistance is based on biblical understandings, but it is intensified by an historic sense: the near-at-hand, visible, earthly has always crowded out the geographically distant, invisible, spiritual. Once the two are given equal emphasis, commitment to the evangelistic task is gradually eroded and what the missionary does looks less and less like that the early church and Paul the Apostle did in response to Christ's last great command.[483]

Ministering to people's physical and social needs is important but this type of holistic ministry should not compete with the central mandate of Christ's mission or the Father's desire to seek worshipers and save those who are perishing (John 3:16; 4:23).

---

[482] McQuilken 176.
[483] McQuilken 176-77.

The Disciple-Making Mandate—Obedience, Teaching, and Transformation into the Likeness of Christ,

There is a lack of emphasis in most missional church literature concerning Christ's mandate to make obedient disciples. A church that is truly missional exists to fulfill the mission of Christ. A missional believer lives to be and make obedient disciples of Christ. In some missional church books the words *disciple*, d*iscipleship*, *disciple-making*, and *spiritual formation*, are scarcely mentioned. For many missional scholars, the development and character of individual disciples is not highlighted as an objective nor as part of the ministry focus of a *missional church*.

An emphasis on spiritual transformation into Christ-likeness and an emphasis on the second aspect of a believer's salvation—the sanctification process into Christ-likeness—is also notably absent from most missional church literature. The emphasis is on the corporate ministry of the church, not on the transformation of individual believers. Hunsberger, a missional church advocate, makes this observation:

> The issue of discipleship is as much corporate as it is personal. A missional church asks, "How must *we* follow Jesus?" It knows itself to be a "corporate disciple," not merely a collectivity of individual disciples. Each one's personal commitments in following Christ are important to that but are understood to be part of a larger whole. Thus, the issue of communal discernment, grasping together the will of God for this particular Christian community and the path it follows, becomes an essential practice.[484]

---

[484] George R. Hunsberger, "Features of the Missional Church: Some Directions and Pathways," *The Reformed Review* (Autumn 1998), 8.

A missional perspective that honors the mission of Christ is centered on holistic disciple-making that leads to disciple-making movements. The omission of Christ's great commission mandate as the heart of his mission is a major weakness in the majority of missional literature. Any missional ministry that does not prioritize the heart of Christ's mission as presented in Matthew 28:18-20 cannot be called missional in a biblical sense.

A Critique of Missional Church Philosophy

This study has demonstrated that the mission of Christ for all of his followers is clear, measurable, and mandatory—the making of holistic disciples and the creation of disciple-making movements. Misunderstanding or minimizing the importance of Christ's mission negatively affects the fulfillment of God's will. The following critique presents the major weaknesses in missional church philosophy compared to the thesis of this study.

Noted above are two areas of theological perspective that form the foundation for most missional church scholars, namely, the interpretation of the *missio Dei* concept and the nature of the relationship of Christ's mission to the Kingdom of God. Adherence to the theological perspectives mentioned above, promoted by most missional scholars, is not advocated and supported in this study. Below are several additional theological and/or philosophical weaknesses, which are inherent in the prevailing missional church perspective, that are not supported by this study.

The Authority and Role of Scripture

A number of missional scholars fail to base their understanding and application of missional ministry on core theological positions and biblical passages that support the mission of Christ. In addition, many scholars do not base their perspective on a defined hermeneutic that demonstrates an understanding of the progressive nature of revelation. The great commission is not considered by many to be the determinative and final statement on God's mission and Christ's command to make disciples is rarely mentioned.

Many missional scholars also include relatively few biblical references and arguments to support their conclusions. Key passages from the New Testament, including the great commission accounts and related passages, are not used to define the nature of the mission of Christ. Scriptural support is limited to a selection of passages that do not concentrate on Christ and his post-resurrection missional priorities in this age.

The Strategic Basis of Missional Ministry

Many missional scholars base their missional strategy on the physical, material and social needs of people in their communities. A church is referred to as "missional" if it actively seeks to meet the needs those outside of its walls in the community. When an analysis of the material and social needs of the community is used as the key element to formulate missional strategy, the objectives and success of Christ's mission are weakened. According to some missional church scholars, an understanding of context and community is more important for missional ministry than a discovery of the biblical mandate and the authority of Christ.[485]

The Sanctification Process

Few missional scholars discuss the sanctification process as a significant aspect of God's mission in the lives of his followers. Because missional activity is focused primarily on physical and social needs and on evangelistic goals, the second aspect of salvation—growth into Christ's likeness through disciple-making—is not a priority. In most missional church literature, there is little discussion about spiritual transformation and spiritual maturity as goals of missional ministry. Since the objective of Christ's mission is that disciples of all peoples are both saved and sanctified, then the authoritative mandates of Christ must be prioritized individually and corporately. Spiritual transformation into Christ-likeness is not an emphasis in most missional literature.

Much of the literature that emphasizes the need to live under the reign of God emphasizes the importance of developing one's spiritual life. Apart from some references to the Sermon on the Mount, there is often little connection between living under God's reign and the believer's sanctification. The command given by Christ to make disciples by "teaching them to obey all that I have commanded you" (Matthews 28:19), is not found in most

---

[485] Franklin, 216-17.

missional church literature. This priority of "holistic ministry" significantly weakens the priority of evangelism and disciple-making in missional ministry. Caring for material and social needs is important but this focus flows out of the disciple being trained to live, love and look like Jesus.

The Role of the Local Church

Most missional literature is focused on helping local churches become active in their community by being missional. Attention is given to outward activities and programs that meet needs of people unrelated to the church. Being missional is characterized as an outward activity to meet material and emotional needs rather than on spiritual transformation into Christ-likeness. Many missional scholars seem to ignore certain Scriptures that do not fit their criteria for the missional character of the church. As Franklin describes, the missional ministry of the church is minimized by some scholars:

> While much is written in the *Gospel and Our Culture Series* about addressing North American culture and proclaiming and anticipating the kingdom of God, relative little is said about worship and spirituality, Christian fellowship, teaching and edification of the body, the place of the *charismata* (spiritual gifts), accountability and discipline, social justice, peace-making, and caring for the poor and needy. Even when such issues are mentioned, they are usually subordinated to the church's mission rather than considered as valid in themselves (i.e., in accordance with the heart of God).[486]

---

[486] Franklin, 224-25.

The Making of Disciples as the Central Priority of Christ

Perhaps the greatest weakness of many missional scholars is their lack of emphasis on the making of holistic disciples and their related disciple-making movements. From a careful reading of the New Testament it is difficult to understand how a person committed to missional ministry would not prioritize a disciple-making ministry. The fact that Christ's great commission is not central to the missional strategy of many scholars causes one to challenge the biblical integrity of their conclusions.

The Universal Nature of Christ's Mission

Christ gave his mission to his followers with the expectation that they, in obedience to his lordship, would spread the gospel and make obedient disciples. Christ's mission extends both locally and globally—focused on making disciples of all ethnic peoples. Biblically, a missional church strategy should reflect all of the priorities of Christ's mission. In most missional church literature, there is little focus on discipling the nations. Although the church is described as having been sent into the world as God's agent, there is little rationale for making disciples and creating disciple-making movements. Much of missional church literature focuses solely on God's desire to send the church into the world.

Christ is building his church by sending obedient disciples who reach, train, and reproduce others through the planting and growth of churches. Mature disciples live for the sake of others, motivated by the love of Christ (2 Corinthians 5:14-15). Christ has designed his church to emulate his loving character in community as well as to share his love with the world.[487]

Conclusion

Although scholars have written on the concept of missional ministry, few align their missional convictions with the clear teaching of the New Testament. A literal hermeneutic is essential to understanding the mission of Christ. It is apparent that many missional scholars minimize the clear mandates of Christ's mission. Actual ministry priorities of many missional churches give precedence to meeting social needs rather than the biblically mandated way those needs are to be addressed through the making of holistic disciples who live like Christ.

The mission of Christ in the world is centered on the making of holistic disciples who live to create more disciples—building Christ's church and fulfilling his will among all peoples. The Father, Son and Spirit are missional—characterized by their nature to redeem mankind, develop transformed saints who love, live and look like Jesus and prepare mature disciples to reproduce more disciples through others-centered service.

---

[487] Franklin, 217-18.

CHAPTER 8
SURVEY OF CONTEMPORARY AUTHORS CONCERNING THE MISSION OF CHRIST IN THE WORLD

Introduction

In order to provide additional validation for the thesis of this study, a three-question survey was given to twenty scholars who represented a wide spectrum of theological perspectives and ministry experience. Each scholar has written at least one book, chapters of books, and articles addressing subjects related to the thesis of this study. The perspective of these scholars has significantly influenced the dialogue and development of the missional church in Western evangelical thought. All of the participants in the survey are male and all but three were born in the U.S.

Approximately thirty scholars were contacted and asked to participate in this survey.[488] Each was contacted initially by phone with an explanation of the purpose and general theme of the survey. Twenty authors agreed to participate and responded to the survey questions. Most scholars participated by emailing their responses to the study's author, while three scholars preferred to be interviewed by phone by the author.

---

[488] See Appendix C.

The survey questions addressed three primary issues within the thesis of this study. Question #1 was written to discover how the respondent defined the mission of Christ. Question #2 sought to determine the priority that the respondent placed on the disciple-making mandate from their understanding of the mission of Christ. Question #3 probed the concept of missional movements to discover if the authors promoted a disciple-making focus as a reproducing movement. The questions were written broadly so as to not reveal the study's thesis or bias of the author.[489] The responses of each scholar are found in their entirety in Appendix C. The purpose of this chapter is to analyze the responses of the scholars to each question as compared to the thesis is this study.

Question #1: The Nature of the Mission of Christ

Introduction

According to this study, the mission of Christ or *missio Christi* is the great commission of Christ, recorded in its most complete form in Matthew 28:18-20. The mission of Christ is centered on the making of holistic disciples who reproduce faithful disciples and live for the sake of others through disciple-making

---

[489] 1) How would you describe what you understand to be the essence of the mission of Christ in the world?
2) What would you delineate as the missional objective(s) that believers/churches should pursue and prioritize to fulfill Christ's mission? 3) Some promote the importance of "missional movements" (i.e. Church Planting Movements) to advance Christ's mission. Do you think that individual believers and/or churches should prioritize missional movements, and if so, how is that done and what is the envisioned end product or result of this type of movement?

movements. Christ's mission is God's central activity in the world during this age

The first survey question was, "How would you describe what you understand to be the essence of the mission of Christ in the world?" This question is focused on the product and the process of Christ's mission. This question was written to demonstrate the scholar's understanding of the unique nature and obligation of Christ's great commission command. The question, dealing with the essence of the mission of Christ received the greatest variety of responses from the scholars surveyed.

Summary of Responses

Nearly one-third of the survey participants identified the essence of Christ's mission with the kingdom of God or the kingdom reign of Christ in the present age. Ott sees the essence of Christ's mission as "the restoration of all things under the rule of God (the kingdom of God), which only comes to pass as men and women are reconciled to God through the redemptive and reconciling work of Christ." Hirsch aligns the mission of Christ with the mission of the church and states, "the agenda of the kingdom is the agenda of the mission of the church." Stetzer agrees with this view and describes the essence of Christ's mission to glorify God by, "establishing the kingdom of God on the earth through the life, death, and resurrection and through the sending of the spirit-empowered Church." Frost defines the Christian mission by quoting the words of Bosch: "alerting of people to the reign of

God through Christ." He continues by stating that "the mission of God and therefore the church is anchored in God's kingly reign and rule . . . . Mission therefore is our participating in God's work of bringing everything to fulfillment that he began at creation."

Hirsch underscores Christ's relationship with the kingdom of God by noting, "In the issue of the kingdom of God, Jesus demonstrates the agenda." However, Hirsch's perspective is unique because he emphasizes the importance of Jesus' relationship to the kingdom of God. Hirsch believes that a kingdom emphasis should be reflected through a wholehearted commitment to the great commission that has at its core discipleship.

As noted above, several authors believe the mission of Christ is an important part and fulfillment of the kingdom of God and his reign on the earth. Christ is understood as extending the kingdom of God through his reign and authority based on his redemptive death. The church is understood as God's agent in establishing and advancing his kingdom purposes on the earth through Christ.

Several of the authors relate the kingdom of God with the mission of God (or the *missio Dei*). Strauss mentioned that the mission of Christ is "another way of talking about the 'mission of God' as revealed throughout Scripture." Strauss emphasizes that the nature of God's mission in the world "is his project of redeeming humankind and creation from humankind's fall into sin and all its deadly effects, and restoring humankind and the creation to its original intent of bringing glory to him."

Several of the authors defined the mission of God as including the total revelation of Scripture. Roxburgh, for example, observed that mission cannot be defined "in one or two sentences . . . because the bigger narrative, the story of what God is up to, it's a whole story, the story of what the Bible is about." Matthews answered this question by identifying the messianic statement of Christ in Luke 4:43 as the definition of Christ's mission in this age. Matthews, referring to Christ stated, "He said, 'This is why I am doing what I am doing.' The gospel of the kingdom was the great mission of Jesus, the extension of that redeeming humanity and the redemption of all things—the proclamation of the present availability of the kingdom—that takes on the agenda of God for the world."

Another perspective on the issue of the essence of mission of Christ is that of being a witness. Guder responded to this question by stating, "The essence of Christ's mission is . . . to witness corporately and personally to the good news of God's healing love for all creation made concrete in the life, death, resurrection and reign of Jesus Christ." Roxburgh shares similar thoughts because he sees "the mission of God in Christ is that the whole creation is invited into doxological relationship with its creator and Jesus comes and forms a people that are a sign and witness and demonstration of the movement of God."

Adsit believes that there are other biblical passages that define the mission of Christ. Adsit noted from Luke 19:10 that "the Son of Man has come to seek and to save that which was lost." He also quotes 1 John 3:8b, that "the Son of God appeared for this purpose, to destroy the works of the devil . . . to rescue the kidnapped and expose and render harmless the kidnapper." He believes the mission of Christ includes salvation for mankind and the defeat of Satan and his evil work on the earth. Strauss identified the mission of Christ as "God's mission is his project of redeeming humankind and creation from humankind's fall into sin and all its deadly effects, and restoring humankind and the creation to its original intent of bringing glory to him."

Only nine of the twenty authors surveyed identified the great commission and the making of disciples as the essence or heart of the mission of Christ. McDonald noted that the mission of Christ is "to be disciples who make disciples—lifelong learners or intentional imitators of everything associated with the Son of God, including words, actions, motives, and transforming vision for the healing of this broken world." Sills shares a perspective supportive of this study's thesis. He stated, "Christ commissioned his church to be obedient to making disciples among all the peoples of the world, teaching them to obey all He has commanded us. We see in Matthew 28:19-20 and Acts 1:8 the parameters of this mission." Smith answered in a way that demonstrates an understanding of the two aspects of a believer's salvation when he wrote, "The aim of missions has often been conversion, which is great but has often failed to preach a gospel that naturally leads to discipleship."

Hirsch also presents the importance of discipleship in the mission of Christ:

> Taking the great commission very seriously and very literally. Matthew 28—"Go into all the world and make disciples of all the nations".... Rather than reading it as an evangelistic text which is the way we have read it, is to read it as a disciple-making text. Discipleship is a major part of the deal, it is like the elephant in the room, and we never get to do it properly and yet it is so key to what we are to be about.

Ott as well shares the perspective that the mission of Christ "entails gospel proclamation, discipleship of believers, and gathering them into churches (kingdom communities) that manifest the reign of God in word and deed."

Hesselgrave stated that answering this question is "easy, at least for me. You see I'm stuck in the past and, I think, in Scripture. The fulfillment of the great commission is my mission; and Missionary Paul is still my model. For [sic] a matter of fact, I am still happy with, 'The gospel for every person and a church for every people group.'"

Of all of the respondents, Ogden provided the most complete answer that supports the thesis of this study:

> The essence of the mission of Christ is the same as what Jesus gave to us in the great commission, which I consider the mission statement for the church which parallels Paul's personal mission statement in Colossians 1:28-29. Make disciples of Jesus is what we are to be about. Jesus tells us that this is done by going to the nations (evangelism),

baptizing in the name of the triune God (our identity and life is found in being engrafted to the life of the relational God who is the basis for a new community, the church), and being taught to obey all that Jesus commanded (aligning our lives with Jesus' intention).

Conclusion

There was a variety of definitions on the essence of the mission of Christ. Several scholars believed the mission of God was connected to the kingdom of God and made effective through the redemptive work of Christ. Several also noted how the church represented and witnessed to Christ's reign. Only Hirsch clearly connected the central priority of making disciples in the mission of Christ as the way the kingdom of God is demonstrated today.

Hirsch underscored the foundational role of one's theological perspective in answering this question. He stated, "Define the kingdom of God to me and I will give you a definition of mission." The validity of this statement is demonstrated in the nature of the responses received for this first question. The diversity of answers highlights how one's theological understanding of the *missio Dei* and particularly the kingdom and the mission of God throughout the Scriptures affects one's understanding of Christ's post-resurrection mission to make disciples of all peoples. If the mission of Christ in Matthew 28:18-20 is not understood as distinct and primary in the mission of God in this age, and the Lordship and authority of Christ do not govern the lives of believers, then the great commission will not obeyed as the exclusive mission of Christ and essence of God's program in the world. Of the twenty scholars who answered this question, just over half stated, in some fashion, that the essence of Christ's mission is found in his great commission and they believed it was the responsibility of every believer is to obey Christ by making disciples of all peoples.

Question #2 Missional Objectives to Fulfill Christ's Mission

Introduction

The second question focused on which objectives should be pursued to fulfill Christ's mission. This question was written to build upon the information shared in response to the first question concerning the essence of Christ's mission. This question asked the participants to provide more specific information concerning what activities and priorities are needed to fulfill Christ's mission. The responses to this question were more extensive than those of the first question and were more pragmatic as each scholar delineated their understanding of the missional priorities of Christ's mission.

According to this study, the missional objective that all believers and churches should prioritize is the making of holistic disciples who reproduce other disciples through divinely ordained movements. The second question was, "What would you delineate as the missional objective(s) that believers/churches should pursue and prioritize to fulfill Christ's mission?"

Summary of Responses

As with the first question, several of the scholars also identified a relationship between God's kingdom and churches as they seek to prioritize Christ's mission. Strauss, for example, stated, "The missional objectives are to proclaim and live the Gospel, the good news of the kingdom of God, seeking to disciple individuals into Christ-like citizens of the coming kingdom, to establish mature New Testament churches as 'beachheads of the kingdom' and to impact society by infusing into it the values of the coming kingdom." Stetzer emphasized that the "missional objective(s) of the church are to be the sign and instrument of the kingdom of God." He observed that through their transformed lives believers share the redemptive message of the gospel and live out their faith for the good of their world through the church.

Hirsch also unites the reign of God and the ministry of the church to identify the missional purposes of Christ:

> A missional church should be measuring its effectiveness by its impact on those outside of the church. It is not just internal measurements that institutional church uses (buns, bucks, and buildings).... Are we impacting truancy at school; or violence in our area? That kind of thing would be very interesting to measure the impact of our effectiveness. The church is not the kingdom of God, it is an expression of the kingdom of God.... Properly obeying that is what we are meant to be about. We as a church must be living in the kingdom as much as we can.

Others like Guder, Hirsch, Frost, Roxburgh, and Van Gelder shared answers that define the objective of Christ's mission for his followers to "serve as a faithful, understandable, and credible witnesses to God's love in Christ, that is, to be signs, instruments and foretastes of God's good reign under the Lordship of Jesus Christ" (Guder).

Frost connected the missional priority of Christ's mission with the reign of God and the ministry of the local church:

> If mission is the alerting of others to the reign of God through Christ then I think the church does this by embracing two broad missional objectives: the announcement of that reign, which includes such actions as evangelism, witness, and worship, and the demonstration of that reign, which includes acts of kindness and compassion, the alleviating of suffering, the work of correcting unjust political and economic structures and the protection of the environment . . . . When it comes to demonstrating God's reign, a simple equation is to ask what would the world look like if God's reign through Christ was completely recognized and understood and then for the church to create foretastes of this world in the midst of unbelief, fear, violence and hatred.

United to the kingdom of God, Frost described the essence of the mission of Christ:

> Our mission is to draw people's attention to the unfurling kingdom of God and demand that people come under his kingship and acknowledge it as the way, the truth and the life . . . . I think that the mission of the church is to both alert others to the reign of God through Jesus, emphasizing the reconciliation, justice and beauty of the Gospel in our announcement (evangelism/witness/worship) and creating examples of reconciliation, justice and beauty in our demonstration (kindness, justice, peace, art, music etc).

Others like Guder stated that the priority of Christ's mission was to demonstrate a credible and faithful witness of

God's love. Roxburgh noted two priorities. First, as people shape their lives around the practices of the Christian life, they are a demonstration, sign, and foretaste of the kingdom of God. Secondly, Roxburgh asserts that believers need to continue to ask, "What is God up to in needy communities and how can we begin to join Him in these efforts?"

Van Gelder declared that the Spirit leads the believer to discern what God desires him or her to do to accomplish his mission. He states, "the mission of God . . . invites the church into participation," following the Spirit by using good stewardship "of resources to participate more fully in God's mission in the context of where the Spirit of God is already at work." He believes that believers can participate in the mission of God "by bearing witness of the reign of God" through a demonstration of "a holistic gospel of good news . . ." and by "unmasking the principalities and powers that have already been defeated by God through Christ."

Several scholars highlighted a church planting priority and the disciple-making ministry of the church to accomplish the missional objective of Christ's mission. McDonald noted that "the first item on the priority list should be the establishment of new congregations around the world . . . we cannot live into the mission of being disciples who make disciples unless this is strategized and applied via community."

Several other scholars stated that disciple-making is the key missional objective to fulfill Christ's mission. Most of these authors articulated the relationship between disciple-making and the development of local churches. Kincaid linked the missional objective to the church and stated, "Churches should put an emphasis on mentoring-disciple-making. More mature Christians help younger Christians grow in their faith." He stated, "If churches would internationalize this effort of discipling by pairing up people . . . they would each find someone else to disciple, the church would grow more solidly and quickly." McCallum outlined three missional priorities to fulfill Christ's mission: "1) Evangelism, 2) Disciple-making, and 3) Development of a full-orbed community where gifts and ministries can flourish."

Several authors strongly advocated for disciple-making as the central priority to fulfill the mission of Christ. Ogden declared,

> The mission objectives should parallel the definition of a disciple that Jesus gave us. A disciple goes, roots his or her identity in "Christ, and seeks to obey all that Jesus commanded. Every mission statement should reflect these priorities. Train people to share their faith; have people rooted in the life of the triune God in the midst of a discipleship community—so everyone should have a small group of fellow followers who are trying to orient who they are to the One they follow; and finally live in a lifetime of dying to self while Christ is coming alive in them."

Willard provided a succinct response to the question of priorities: "Make disciples to Jesus and develop them to the point where they do everything He said."

Sills stated that, "Believers must not only recognize the inerrancy of God's Word, but also the authority of it, deriving their ministry objectives from the commands, principles, and parameters found within it." Sills calls for maintaining "a focus on the gospel, the transformational power of God in the life of individuals, and the recognition that we are not obedient unless we are faithful to not only reach, but to teach all that Christ has commanded us." He stated, "Ultimately, our missiological objectives should reflect the progression of a believer's life. We should seek to engage and reach lost people in culturally appropriate ways with the gospel, disciple and teach them as Christ has commanded us and then training them to continue the work with others."

Ott stated that "the primary missional objectives are Gospel proclamation, discipleship, church planting, and holistic transformation; logically in that order." He stated that believers receive the power of the Holy Spirit to live under the lordship of Christ. None of the previous respondents had emphasized the authority or lordship of Christ. He also declared, "Holistic transformation will include personal holiness, acts of compassion, salt and light witness and work in the larger society." This was the answer that most closely reflects the thesis of this study. Regarding the making of disciples, McDonald notes that:

> We cannot live into the mission of being disciples who make disciples unless this is strategized and applied via community. The tragedy of the North American church is that we have substituted knowledge for wisdom, occasional fellowship for authentic community, and making decisions for making disciples . . . . true community . . . will require a level of obedience and risk-taking — that is, thinking and working outside the current Western box of Christian experience . . . .

McDonald expresses several valid concerns that pastors have when they look at the current state of many evangelical churches. He believes that "we can be a part of whatever God is doing right now to grow a new wave of congregations and community here and around the world."

Matthews notes, "We have wrongly made our objective in mission to make converts and we have not turned the corner in any way in making disciples." He states, "If we do not make disciples who are taking on the mission of the agenda of their Rabbi their teacher Jesus, we will then see mission happen, but we are not going to get there if we just make converts who are forgiven of their sins to go to heaven."

Hesselgrave challenged the common use of the term "missional" and its use in defining ministry objectives. "I think that 'missional' has become the plaything of evangelicals just as Scherer said that '*missio Dei*' became the plaything of ecumenists. Like most neologisms, it means whatever one puts into it. And that bothers me . . . . Decide what your mission is and then settle on a theology that will support and further it. If that is missiology it is also heresy."

Conclusion

As was observed from the responses in the previous question, the theological perspective of the respondents largely determines their understanding and interpretation of Christ's mission. There were several authors, like Matthews who defined the missional priority of Christ as disciple-making:

> We talk about discipleship as being for the advanced Christian but we have made converts and then expect people to move into discipleship. And that usually doesn't happen. If we make disciples who are taking on the mission of the agenda of their teacher Jesus we will then see mission happen, but we are not going to get there if we just make converts who are forgiven of their sins and go to heaven.

For most of these authors, the missional purpose of making disciples was closely related to the ministry of a local church. The church is described by several scholars as the training ground for the making of disciples who constitute and strengthen the church.

Several of the authors connected the missional priorities of Christ with the reign of God through Christ and the compassionate ministry of the church. Several other authors believed the missional goal for the church involved meeting the physical and social needs of the community outside of the church. This compassionate ministry provides a foretaste of the kingdom of God and the church of God's love.

Question #3 The Place of Missional Movements in Christ's Mission.

Introduction

The last question sought to discover what each scholar understood regarding a process or mechanism necessary to fulfill the mission of Christ. The question was also written to determine if the scholars who identified disciple-making as a priority, recognized the need for disciple-making movements in order to advance the mission of Christ. Embedded within this question is a reference to *Church Planting Movements*. This was included to give the respondent a conceptual frame of reference for what type of movement could be envisioned.

The third question was, "Some promote the importance of "missional movements" (i.e. Church Planting Movements) to advance Christ's mission. Do you think that individual believers and/or churches should prioritize missional movements, and if so, how is that done and what is the envisioned end product or result of this type of movement?"

Survey of Responses

Because the term *missional* in contemporary scholarship is used broadly with diverse applications, several scholars were hesitant to answer this question concerning *missional movements*. For some, words like *movement*s conjure up the thought of man-made strategies, devoid of God's leading and power. Stetzer expressed this sentiment. "I think we can plan and strategically work towards movements through networks and denominations, but we should remain rightly aware that true spiritual movements are not planned and organized by us. They are a gracious work of God for the building of his church." Others indicated that a movement is a special work of God that cannot be planned or anticipated in advance. Hesselgrave, for example, stated,

There's that word again (missional). I really can't deal with it until I know the nature of a "missional movement." Logically, the meaning of "missional" has to be consonant with "mission" so logically what we have here is something akin to "churchly church." That being the case, one either ends up as a holist or a prioritist. But as McGavran said, there are multitudes of good Christian things to do that are not mission.

Hesselgrave dealt with this question in his answer to the first question when he stated that the essence of the mission of Christ was "the fulfillment of the great commission" along the lines of Apostle Paul's ministry.

> Roxburgh, pushed against the use of the word "movement": I dislike the word "movement" intensely. The people who use it to me demonstrate that they don't understand how social or cultural change takes place. A movement is something to write about after the fact. You can say, oh look what happened . . . . I am concerned about a lot of these people who keep using that language as if they are creating something. They are pointing to something and saying . . . . I just think that is highly barbaric and what it tells you is that they already have a pattern in their mind of those things will look like. So I struggle with all of that language. I find what it does is create a nice neat box to put things. I find that what people are looking for are what are the three, four or five points and that's what a missional movement looks like. God is up to all kinds of stuff in all kinds of ways across different kinds of church systems. How do you listen to what's going on out there?

Strauss objected to the word "priority" to describe a missional movement:

> Whenever we use the word "priority," we imply that something is ultimately optional. None of the Gospel/Kingdom commands of Jesus is optional. Further,

different strategies and means for fulfilling the mission of God have been advanced over the centuries; many are both biblical and effective ways to fulfill God's mission. Different labels have been used at different times, and people define those labels differently. So I'm also hesitant to either endorse or condemn any strategy or method.

Van Gelder stated that a movement is important if it is focused on "the mission of the Triune God within all of life." He stated that, "This keeps God as the 'acting subject' with our seeking to live into and out of God's agency in pursuing such movements. The question is framed in such a way that human agency or church agency is the primary acting subject, which misses, from my perspective, the true meaning of what it means to be '*missional*.'"

Regarding the end product of a missional movement, Guder stated that "the only priority to be established is faithfulness in carrying out our vocation as witnesses . . . the purpose of Christian mission is that we should walk worthy of the calling with which we have been called."

Ott equates his idea of "kingdom communities" to missional movements. He declared, "I have a strong conviction that the establishment of 'kingdom communities' is absolutely central to the task of missions and is indeed the best and most biblical way to fulfill the great commission and advance God's kingdom." Ott is an advocate of Church Planting Movements. "Under the sovereign work of God, we hope, pray and work to the end that not only isolated communities of believers are established, but that multiplying indigenous movements are launched that are a witness for Christ and foretaste of the kingdom." For Ott, these multiplying movements have to do primarily with the rapid planting of new churches. "We see such movement happening in Ephesus and the Lycos Valley and other places in the New Testament." Ott believes there is a biblical mandate for church planting and that "the result of church planting movements is reproducing, gospel-centered churches that spontaneously grow and multiply, largely under local leadership."

Kincaid also believes that church planting is central to missional movements. "I believe churches should plant new churches." Lewis bases the idea of missional movements out of the ministry of local churches. "Every church should strive to be missional . . . in sharing the gospel, in meeting needs of the community and the world, and in planting churches. Whether they can do the latter may depend on their ability at the moment but every church should strive to do all three."

Frost also sees church planting as the key to promoting missional movements:

> Bosch once said that mission is intrinsically ecclesial (and therefore that ecclesiology must be intrinsically missional), so what we're seeing now is the era of the great church planting movements (the big 21st Century missional movement?). Rather than the church sending out missioning [author's wording] communities (what Roland Allen called the great divorce), we're now seeing the church sending out missional church planting teams. As soon as this catches on and we have church planting

churches being planted across the world we will have a serious missional movement.

Hirsch sees the nature of the church as missional:

> I think the church in the New Testament is clearly a movement and the sweetest and best expressions of church seem to be more movemental . . . . My understanding is that the term *ecclesia* (church) is a very movemental term. It can express itself in a local house, *ecclesia* is across the city and *ecclesia* is the universal people of God . . . . The future of the Western church is bound up in whether we can discover ourselves as a movement again."

Stetzer believes that God-honoring movements occur when God blesses a leader to mobilize individuals and churches. He states, "The church needs clear and courageous godly examples to point us to what God wants to do and is doing in our world. When God raises us such examples, the church should pay attention." Stetzer cautions, "The danger is always to see the movement as an end in itself rather than a mobilizing force for the cause of the kingdom for God's glory (which is the ultimate end)." He believes that "Movements, networks, and denominations are tools that God uses to encourage the church in its mission and to strengthen churches to accomplish more for the kingdom than they are able to alone."

Strauss focused his answer on disciple-making that leads to church planting. "Any means or strategy that is discipling individuals into Christ-like citizens of the coming kingdom, establishing mature New Testament churches that 'show off' the coming kingdom and is impacting society with the values of the kingdom is a good thing that should be commended and practiced."

Several authors mentioned discipleship as the heart of a missional movement of God. McDonald claimed that disciples must pursue missional movements. "I believe that missional movements should be the central priority of disciples. Church history has demonstrated that the Spirit is able and willing to use a number of means of advancing such movements."

Adsit understood that the end product of a missional movement is to see the kingdom of God birthed into the lives of unbelievers. He stated, "If we're doing a good job of discipling this new population of Christians, we'll see them getting fixed, healed, strengthened and eventually thrust into influential leadership positions."

Willard underscored the place of transformed individuals in a missional movement. "There would always be a place for special efforts with a special focus, dictated by the circumstances for the 'success' of Jesus' work the radical transformation—what one would naturally expect from reading the New Testament—of multitudes of individuals is what is required."

Matthews' answer supported the thesis of this study. "If we can really make disciples and help empower people to be disciples 24/7—that's the ultimate movement! Where people are really seeing their Monday to Monday lives (not their Sunday to Sunday lives) but their Monday to Monday lives as being salt and light, in their work places, their leisure time, etc." Ogden provided the closest answer in support of the thesis:

> Jesus told us to make disciples. The only thing I see that Jesus told us to multiply was followers of him. There are no short cuts to growing up in Christ. Certainly part of that is having a missional mindset. So to the extent that a "missional movement" creates an ethos of multiplication, all the better . . . a missional movement under the sovereignty of God, then the church should be a part of it to advance Christ's mission.

Conclusion

Those authors who accepted the concept of missional movements favorably believed that they could be used by God to advance the mission of Christ. Several authors understood church planting and the biblical ministry of the church as keys to the health and growth of missional movements. Ogden, Matthews and Adsit advocated for the making of disciples and, at least in part, the idea of disciple-making movements to advance the mission of Christ. Those authors, who base their perspective on the kingdom of God and the *missio Dei*, did not, for the most part, prioritize the making of disciples nor see disciple-making as a movement to fulfill the mission of Christ

Conclusion

The scholars surveyed displayed a diversity of perspectives and convictions. There were also several themes and convictions that were mutually shared by most of these authors. It is clear that the biblical perspective and theological presuppositions of a person, as well as their background and ministerial experience, influence their understanding and convictions on the nature of God's mission. Those who advocated for placing the great commission as the mission of Christ for this age were the strongest proponents for prioritizing the making of disciples. Several authors shared opinions that supported the thesis of this study. Those who identified the mission of Christ with the overall reign of God in the world and the *missio Dei*, did not, for the most part, promote either the great commission or disciple-making as a central priority to fulfill Christ's mission.

CHAPTER 9
SUMMARY AND CONCLUSION

Introduction

The motivation for this study was to clarify and apply the biblical teaching on the mission of Christ and what he ordained his followers to do to fulfill his mission. This study has demonstrated that growth in Christ-likeness does not result from a passive process of spiritual osmosis in the church but an active and purposeful alignment of one's life with Christ's mission.

The thesis of this study is based on the conviction that the New Testament clearly delineates Christ's mission. This mission concentrates on the making of holistic disciples and the creation of disciple-making movements. Scripture defines Christ's great commission mandate to make disciples as his unique mission during this age through which he builds his church.

In order to understand both the process and product of disciple-making, the goal of Christ-likeness and spiritual transformation was explored. The two-faceted nature of salvation and the lordship of Christ were highlighted to assist the reader to understand the obligation of believers to pursue lifelong spiritual maturity. The nature of spiritual maturity was described as a commitment to an others-centered life, pursuing and prioritizing good deeds for the benefit of others.

The study demonstrated how the biblical priorities of making of holistic disciples and disciple-making movements are validated through the four unique examples from church history. These examples demonstrate the importance of making holistic disciples and training faithful disciples to pursue disciple-making movements and to live for the benefit of others through good deeds.

It was demonstrated that the term "missional" describes the essence of Christ's mission. Thus, the writing of prominent scholars on topics related to the mission of Christ were evaluated from the perspective of the study's thesis. A three-question survey of scholars was also presented that demonstrated the variety of positions and perspectives related to the making of holistic disciples and the creation of disciple-making movements.

The Validation of the Study

This study is important to demonstrate that the heart of the mission of Christ during this age is the making of holistic disciples and the creation of disciple-making movements. It is vital to understand that Christ has commanded his followers to obediently grow into his likeness and reproduce other disciples of all peoples. The product—becoming a disciple, and the process—making other disciples, constitute the life Christ has designed for all believers.

The study also demonstrated the essential need for church leaders to understand that the promotion of spiritual growth and health of its members accomplishes Christ's purpose to pursue his disciple-making mission. As disciples grow into Jesus' likeness and reproduce other disciples, churches are established and Christ's mission is advanced. However, when the planting and development are prioritized over disciple-making, the overall mission and disciple-making purpose of Christ is weakened. Church Planting Movements were analyzed as missional movements that did not prioritize disciple-making and thus missed Christ's great commission strategy.

The historical survey of four exceptional examples of groups and individuals who pursued the mission of Christ provided strong support for the thesis of the study. These examples demonstrated that the making of holistic disciples and the creation of disciple making movements has been practiced and prioritized, in some form or another, throughout church history.

This study sought to prove that it is essential for Christians to understand that holistic disciple-making and the propagation of disciple-making movements are Christ's divine strategy to fulfill his mission. The normative pursuit for every believer should be to pursue spiritual transformation into Christ's likeness and to reproduce his godly character in other's lives.

This study also addressed how the local church is related to Christ's mission. The study emphasized that Christ, as the sovereign Lord, has been given authority over all things during this age. Christ alone defines the nature and character of his mission. He commands obedience to that mission from all of his disciples. One of the intended outcomes of the study was to encourage those who are seeking to be "missional," to evaluate their overall ministry from a biblical and Christo-centric understanding of the *missio Dei* in the world. It was demonstrated that the missional efforts of the church must be centered firmly on the mission of Christ. Only then can we ensure that the priority to make holistic disciples and disciple-making movements is central to their missional endeavors in the world. Hull provides validation for this study: "The reason the mission languishes is the acceptance of a nondiscipleship Christianity that creates shallow believers with hollow lives who don't affect those around them. This has led to the marginalization of the gospel and his retarded its spread because of its lack of authentic and power."[490]

Implications for Believers and Churches Today

Central to the mission of Christ is that all believers find their God-designed purpose and destiny. This study has demonstrated that the making of holistic disciples is the center of the mission of Christ and must therefore be the central priority and activity of the local church. When disciple-making is not the central priority of the church, individual disciples may never understand their purpose to become like Christ and to live obediently for him. Centering the mission of Christ on the *missio Dei* and the Kingdom of God does not focus believers on the singular mission of Christ and their disciple-making obligation. Other priorities and activities will occupy the attention and

---

[490] Hull, *Choose the Life,* 215.

resources of the church and the disciple-making mandate, on which the church is to be built, will suffer.

The implications of this study are significant because they directly impact the successful fulfillment of the mission of Christ. There are also important implications related to the nature of the believer's spiritual life. Having a biblical understanding of the process of sanctification is vital for a believer to be transformed into Christ's likeness. The recognition of a *"sanctification gap"* (disciple-making gap) in the teaching and practice of the church has negatively affected a biblical understanding of the nature of the spiritual life. Believers need to be taught how to intentionally work out their salvation (Philippians 2:12-13) and to pursue spiritual transformation into Christ's likeness. The minimum standard for spiritual life must be replaced with the biblical truth that disciples of Christ are to obey all that He commanded and teach others to do the same. All believers are to be holy, pursue a life of godliness, and imitate Christ as they serve and glorify Him.

Another implication of this study involves the need for a renewed biblical understanding of the nature and responsibility of a disciple. All believers must be taught that they are a disciple. God predestined believers to be conformed into the likeness of his Son. Jesus expects holistic disciples to be complete, mature, obedient and to become like him and accomplish his will. The great commission demands that all believers understand that they are called to obey him and make disciples of others regardless of their place or position in life. Personal discipleship and the making of disciples should be the most normal and common endeavor seen at the local church. The model of the Apostle Paul seeking to make disciples should be the common practice of all local churches and believers. The Apostle Paul had a singular focus: "Him we proclaim, warning everyone and teaching everyone with all wisdom, that we may present everyone mature in Christ. For this I toil, struggling with all his energy that he powerfully works within me" (Colossians 1:28-29).

A vital part of the mission of Christ is the "building" of his church. As holistic disciples are made, the obedient reproduce other disciples, which builds (establishes) Christ's church. As Christ's church is established, more holistic disciples are naturally produced. Through relationships with other believers and through ministry in the church, holistic disciples are made. According to Ephesians 4:11-12, God has given the church gifted men whose role it is to train and equip the believers. When this is being done, believers are enabled to do the work of the ministry while being used by God to edify the body. Disciples are made and new churches are birthed in this atmosphere.

Another implication is to understand that maturity in Christ is expressed through an others-centered life. Through obedience and a life controlled by the Holy Spirit, holistic disciples arrive at the place where the love of Christ continually compels them to live for him and others for his glory. In the church, we must recognize the others-centered life as the life Christ modeled and desires for all of his disciples. Christ has designed his disciples, his works of art, to live a life of good works. Those good works are focused on the making of disciples and creating disciple-making movements.

One final implication for mission agencies or local churches is to center their ministry strategy on diligently pursuing the creation of disciple-making movements. The study has demonstrated how disciple-making movements have been designed by Christ to reach and make disciples of all peoples. The Lord's promise to build his church is designed to be accomplished when disciples are made and serve their Lord to make other disciples through the church among all peoples. As has been demonstrated, when goals related to the planting and development of churches become first priority, the focus on disciple-making and the effectiveness of this crucial ministry is negatively affected.

Conclusion

The intended outcome of this study was not to provide the final treatise on the topic of the mission of Christ, holistic discipleship, disciple-making movements or the missional church. This study is presented as a call to the church to return to its biblical roots. It is a call for believers and churches to return to Christ's missional center. It is a call to consider thoughtfully that only through the making of holistic disciples will his mission be fulfilled. It is a call to the local church and mission agency to evaluate their ministry priorities to ensure that the discipleship mandate is always the center of the ministry—to make disciples of all people and build his church.

APPENDIX A
NEW TESTAMENT PASSAGES
ON GOOD WORKS[491]

Matthew 3:10	Even now the axe is laid to the root of the trees. Every tree therefore that does not bear **good** fruit is cut down and thrown into the fire.
Matthew 5:13, 16	You are the salt of the earth; but if the salt has become tasteless, how can it be made salty again? It is no longer **good** for anything, except to be thrown out and trampled under foot by men. Let your light shine before men in such a way that they may see your **good** works, and glorify your Father who is in heaven
Matthew 12:12	Of how much more value is a man than a sheep! So it is lawful to do **good** on the Sabbath.
Matthew 12:35	The **good** man brings out of his **good** treasure what is **good**; and the evil man brings out of his evil treasure what is evil.

---

[491] These verses are The Holy Bible, English Standard Version Copyright © 2001 by Crossway Bibles, a division of Good News Publishers. They were copied from <http://www.biblegateway.com/keyword/index.php?search=good&version.html> (accessed August 22, 2011).

Mark 3:4	And he said to them, "Is it lawful on the Sabbath to do **good** or to do harm, to save life or to kill?" But they were silent.
Mark 9:50	Salt is **good**; but if the salt becomes unsalty, with what will you make it salty again? Have salt in yourselves, and be at peace with one another.
Luke 3:9	Even now the axe is laid to the root of the trees. Every tree therefore that does not bear **good** fruit is cut down and thrown into the fire.
Luke 6:27	But I say to you who hear, love your enemies, do **good** to those who hate you...
Luke 6:35	But love your enemies, and do **good**, and lend, expecting nothing in return; and your reward will be great, and you will be sons of the Most High; for He Himself is kind to ungrateful and evil men.
Luke 6:45	The **good** man out of the **good** treasure of his heart brings forth what is **good**; and the evil man out of the evil treasure brings forth what is evil; for his mouth speaks from that which fills his heart.
Luke 14:34	Therefore, salt is **good**; but if even salt has become tasteless, with what will it be

		seasoned?
John 5:29		. . . and will come forth; those who did the **good** deeds to a resurrection of life, those who committed the evil deeds to a resurrection of judgment.
Acts 10:38		You know of Jesus of Nazareth, how God anointed Him with the Holy Spirit and with power, and how He went about doing **good** and healing all who were oppressed by the devil, for God was with Him.
Romans 2:7		to those who by perseverance in doing **good** seek for glory and honor and immortality, eternal life.
Romans 2:10		but glory and honor and peace for everyone who does **good**, the Jew first and also the Greek.
Romans 8:28		And we know that God causes all things to work together for **good** to those who love God, to those who are called according to his purpose.
Romans 10:15		How will they preach unless they are sent? Just as it is written, " HOW BEAUTIFUL ARE THE FEET OF THOSE WHO BRING **GOOD** NEWS OF **GOOD** THINGS!"
Romans 12:21		Do not be overcome by evil, but overcome

	evil with **good.**
Romans 13:3	For rulers are not a cause of fear for **good** behavior, but for evil. Do you want to have no fear of authority? Do what is **good** and you will have praise from the same.
Romans 15:2	Each of us is to please his neighbor for his **good**, to his edification.
Romans 15:4	I myself am satisfied about you, my brothers, that you yourselves are full of **good**ness, filled with all knowledge and able to instruct one another.
1 Corinthians 10:24	Let no one seek his own **good**, but that of his neighbor.
1 Corinthians 12:7	To each is given the manifestation of the Spirit for the common **good**.
2 Corinthians 5:10	For we must all appear before the judgment seat of Christ, so that each one may be recompensed for his deeds in the body, according to what he has done, whether **good** or bad.
2 Corinthians 9:8	And God is able to make all grace abound to you, so that always having all sufficiency in everything, you may have an abundance for every **good** deed.
Galatians 5:13	For you were called to freedom, brothers.

	Only do not use your freedom as an opportunity for the flesh, but through love **serve** one another.
Galatians 5:22	But the fruit of the Spirit is love, joy, peace, patience, kindness, **good**ness, faithfulness, . . .
Galatians 6:9-10	Let us not lose heart in doing **good**, for in due time we will reap if we do not grow weary. So then, while we have opportunity, let us do **good** to all people, and especially to those who are of the household of the faith.
Ephesians 2:10	For we are his workmanship, created in Christ Jesus for **good** works, which God prepared beforehand so that we would walk in them.
Ephesians 4:28-29	He who steals must steal no longer; but rather he must labor, performing with his own hands what is **good**, so that he will have something to share with one who has need. Let no unwholesome word proceed from your mouth, but only such a word as is **good** for edification according to the need of the moment, so that it will give grace to those who hear.
Ephesians 5:9	(for the fruit of the Light consists in all

	goodness and righteousness and truth),
Ephesians 6:7-8	With **good** will render service, as to the Lord, and not to men, knowing that whatever **good** thing each one does, this he will receive back from the Lord, whether slave or free.
Philippians 2:2-4	Do nothing from rivalry or conceit, but in humility count **others** more significant than yourselves. Complete my joy by being of the same mind, having the same love, being in full accord and of one mind. Do nothing from rivalry or conceit, but in humility count others more significant than yourselves. Let each of you look not only to his own interests, but also to the interests of others.
Philippians 2:13	. . . for it is God who is at work in you, both to will and to work for his **good** pleasure.
Colossians 1:10	. . . so that you will walk in a manner worthy of the Lord, to please Him in all respects, bearing fruit in every **good** work and increasing in the knowledge of God.
1 Thessalonians 5:15	See that no one repays another with evil for evil, but always seek after that which is **good** for one another and for all people
2 Thessalonians 1:11	To this end also we pray for you always, that our God will count you worthy of your

	calling, and fulfill every desire for **good**ness and the work of faith with power
2 Thessalonians 2:17	. . . comfort and strengthen your hearts in every **good** work and word.
2 Thessalonians 3:13	But as for you, brethren, do not grow weary of doing **good**.
1 Timothy 1:18-19	This command I entrust to you, Timothy, my son, in accordance with the prophecies previously made concerning you, that by them you fight the **good** fight, keeping faith and a **good** conscience, which some have rejected and suffered shipwreck in regard to their faith.
1 Timothy 2:10	. . . but rather by means of **good** works, as is proper for women making a claim to godliness.
1 Timothy 5:10	. . . having a reputation for **good** works; and if she has brought up children, if she has shown hospitality to strangers, if she has washed the saints' feet, if she has assisted those in distress, and if she has devoted herself to every **good** work.
1 Timothy 5:25	So also **good** works are conspicuous, and even those that are not cannot remain hidden.
1 Timothy 6:2	Those who have believing masters must not

	be disrespectful on the ground that they are brothers; rather they must serve all the better since those who benefit by their **good** service are believers and beloved.
1 Timothy 6:18-19	Instruct them to do **good**, to be rich in **good** works, to be generous and ready to share storing up for themselves the treasure of a **good** foundation for the future, so that they may take hold of that which is life indeed.
2 Timothy 2:21	Therefore, if anyone cleanses himself from these things, he will be a vessel for honor, sanctified, useful to the Master, prepared for every **good** work.
2 Timothy 3:17	so that the man of God may be adequate, equipped for every **good** work.
Titus 1:8	. . . but hospitable, a lover of **good**, self-controlled, upright, holy, and disciplined.
Titus 1:16	They profess to know God, but they deny him by their works. They are detestable, disobedient, unfit for any **good** work.
Titus 2:3	Older women likewise are to be reverent in their behavior, not malicious gossips nor enslaved to much wine, teaching what is **good** . . . .
Titus 2:7	. . . in all things show yourself to be an

	example of **good** deeds, with purity in doctrine, dignified.
Titus 2:11-14	For the grace of God has appeared, bringing salvation to all men, instructing us to deny ungodliness and worldly desires and to live sensibly, righteously and godly in the present age, looking for the blessed hope and the appearing of the glory of our great God and Savior, Christ Jesus, who gave Himself for us to redeem us from every lawless deed, and to purify for Himself a people for his own possession, zealous for **good** deeds.
Titus 3:1	Remind them to be subject to rulers, to authorities, to be obedient, to be ready for every **good** deed . . . .
Titus 3:8	This is a trustworthy statement; and concerning these things I want you to speak confidently, so that those who have believed God will be careful to engage in **good** deeds. These things are **good** and profitable for men.
Titus 3:14	Our people must also learn to engage in **good** deeds to meet pressing needs, so that they will not be unfruitful.
Philemon 1:6, 14	They profess to know God, but they deny

	him by their works. They are detestable, disobedient, unfit for any **good** work.
	... but I preferred to do nothing without your consent in order that your **good**ness might not be by compulsion but of your own accord.
Hebrews 10:24	... and let us consider how to stimulate one another to love and **good** deeds.
Hebrews 13:16	And do not neglect doing **good** and sharing, for with such sacrifices God is pleased.
Hebrews 13:21	... equip you in every **good** thing to do his will, working in us that which is pleasing in his sight, through Jesus Christ, to whom be the glory forever and ever. Amen.
James 2:13	What **good** is it, my brothers, if someone says he has faith but does not have works? Can that faith save him?
James 3:13	Who among you is wise and understanding? Let him show by his **good** behavior his deeds in the gentleness of wisdom.
James 3:17	But the wisdom from above is first pure, then peaceable, gentle, reasonable, full of mercy and **good** fruits, unwavering, without hypocrisy.
1 Peter 2:12	Keep your behavior excellent among the

	Gentiles, so that in the thing in which they slander you as evildoers, they may because of your **good** deeds, as they observe them, glorify God in the day of visitation.
1 Peter 2:15	For this is the will of God, that by doing **good** you should put to silence the ignorance of foolish people.
1 Peter 3:13	Keep your behavior excellent among the Gentiles, so that in the thing in which they slander you as evildoers, they may because of your **good** deeds, as they observe them, glorify God in the day of visitation.
1 Peter 3:16, 17	and keep a **good** conscience so that in the thing in which you are slandered, those who revile your **good** behavior in Christ will be put to shame. For it is better to suffer for doing **good**, if that should be God's will, than for doing evil.
1 Peter 4:10	As each one has received a special gift, employ it in serving one another as **good** stewards of the manifold grace of God.
1 Peter 4:19	Therefore let those who suffer according to God's will entrust their souls to a faithful Creator while doing **good**.
1 John 3:17	But if anyone has the world's **good**s and sees

| | his brother in need, yet closes his heart against him, how does God's love abide in him? |

APPENDIX B
RESEARCH SURVEY QUESTIONS

The survey questions below were responded to by twenty scholars who have written on the topics of the missional church, discipleship, spiritual formation, and the mission of the church. Their responses are recorded in Appendix C. These questions were written to elicit a broad range of perspectives regarding the mission of Christ: (question #1), the priority of making holistic disciples (question #2), and the reality and need to pursue making disciple-making movements to fulfill the mission of Christ (question #3).

1. How would you describe what you understand to be the essence of the mission of Christ in the world?
2. What would you delineate as the missional objective(s) that believers/churches should pursue and prioritize to fulfill Christ's mission?
3. Some promote the importance of "missional movements" (i.e. Church Planting Movements) to advance Christ's mission. Do you think that individual believers and/or churches should prioritize missional movements, and if so, how is that done and what is the envisioned end product or result of this type of movement?

APPENDIX C
RESPONSES TO RESEARCH SURVEY QUESTIONS

Glenn McDonald		
The essence of the mission of Christ in the world today?	The missional objective(s) to prioritize to fulfill Christ's mission?	Should believers prioritize missional movements? How? What result?
Twenty centuries have left the mission of Christ unchanged. We are called to be disciples who make disciples—lifelong learners or intentional imitators of everything associated with the Son of God, including words, actions, motives, and transforming vision for the healing of this broken world. Is this mission one of personal conversion to the way of Christ or the transformation of the social order? That is a false dichotomy. The redemption of human hearts should help inspire multiple	I believe the first item on the priority list should be the establishment of new congregations around the world. These may be as humble and under the radar as a few family members and friends gathering daily or weekly at a kitchen table, out of sight of local authorities. We cannot be ourselves by ourselves. We cannot live into the mission of being disciples who make disciples unless this is strategized and applied via community. The tragedy of the North American church is that we have substituted knowledge for wisdom, occasional fellowship for	My response will be all too brief and perfunctory, since the "how" and "what" questions deserve extraordinary insight and reflection. But yes, I believe that missional movements should be the central priority of disciples . Church history has demonstrated that the Spirit is able and willing to use a number of means of advancing such movements: from carefully planned multi-year efforts established by denominations or parachurch groups, to new forms of the church that spring up amongst indigenous

movements of redemption in every culture and amongst every ethnicity. At the same time, little if any good can happen in the social order unless individuals choose (in the memorable words of Eugene Peterson) "to pursue the Jesus life displaying the Jesus truth by means of the Jesus way."

authentic community, and making decisions for making disciples. The great challenge, of course, is that Americans will tend to pursue this goal by launching various seminars and classes with titles like, "How to create true community." We will all take notes and feel we have accomplished something. But the flame of true community is passed only in the context of existing true community, and that will require a level of obedience and risk-taking—that is, thinking and working outside the current Western box of Christian experience—that will almost surely take another generation to bring about. But, we can be part of whatever God is doing right now to grow a new wave of congregations and community here and around the world.

cultures—seemingly out of nowhere, to individuals graced with sufficient chutzpah and differentiation to "go their own way" and follow God where 99% of us fear to tread. The exciting thing about being a disciple in the 21st century is to "watch and pray" as God does things that no eye has seen, no ear has heard, nor have any such tactics even been imagined by the most creative amongst us.

Craig Ott		
The essence of the mission of Christ in the world today?	**The missional objective(s) to prioritize to fulfill Christ's mission?**	**Should believers prioritize missional movements? How? What result?**
The essence of mission is the restoration of all things under the rule of God (the kingdom of God), which only comes to pass as men and women are reconciled to God through the redemptive and reconciling work of Christ. Thus, mission practically and necessarily entails gospel proclamation, discipleship of believers, and gathering them into churches (kingdom communities) that manifest the reign of God in word and deed. This will impact all aspects of life, personal, familial, societal.	As indicated in the definition above, the primary missional objectives are Gospel proclamation, discipleship, church planting, and holistic transformation; logically in that order, though not always temporally in that order. The gospel is, so to speak, the source from which all else flows as people are reconciled with God and one another and receive the power of the Holy Spirit to live under the lordship of Christ. Holistic transformation will include personal holiness, acts of compassion, and salt and light witness and work in the larger society.	As I have spelled out in "Encountering Theology of Mission" (pp.156-70). I have a strong conviction that the establishment of "kingdom communities" is absolutely central to the task of missions and is indeed the best and most biblical way to fulfill the great commission and advance God's kingdom. Under the sovereign work of God, we hope, pray, and work to the ends that not only isolated communities of believers are established, but that multiplying, indigenous movements are launched that are a witness for Christ and foretaste of the kingdom. We see such movements happening in Ephesus and the Lycos valley and other places in the NT. I

		have a book to be released in January with coauthor Gene Wilson "Global Church Planting" that spells out the biblical mandate for church planting and biblical examples of church planting movements. The result would be (and often is) reproducing, gospel-centered churches, that spontaneously grow and multiply, largely under local leadership. The missionary often changes roles from pioneer to facilitator and empoweror (see also Tom Steffen's new book, "The Facilitator Era" 2010).
Darrell Guder		
The essence of the mission of Christ in the world today?	**The missional objective(s) to prioritize to fulfill Christ's mission?**	**Should believers prioritize missional movements? How? What result?**
The essence of Christ's mission is the same as it has been since Pentecost: to witness corporately and personally to the	The objective of Christian mission is to serve as faithful, understandable, and credible witnesses to God's love in Christ, that is, to be signs,	The only priority to be established is faithfulness in carrying out our vocation as witnesses. In Paul's words, the purpose of Christian

good news of God's healing love for all creation made concrete in the life, death, resurrection, and reign of Jesus Christ.	instruments and foretastes of God's good reign under the Lordship of Jesus Christ.	mission is that we should walk worthy of the calling with which we have been called.
Ron Kincaid		
The essence of the mission of Christ in the world today?	**The missional objective(s) to prioritize to fulfill Christ's mission?**	**Should believers prioritize missional movements? How? What result?**
Christ's mission in the world is for us to take the gospel to all nations. Jesus wants us to share the news of his love and forgiveness with all people who do not know him. The church's mission is to develop Christians who are strong in their faith so they have the ability to go and share their faith with others.	I believe churches should put an emphasis on mentoring/disciple-making. More mature Christians help younger Christians grow in their faith. If churches would internationalize this effort of discipling by pairing up people and having them meet together for a year or more with the expectation that at the end of that time they would each find someone else to disciple, the church would grow more solidly and quickly. All churches should place an emphasis on teaching the	I believe churches should plant new churches. New churches tend to be the fastest growing churches in the world because everyone in the church feels a responsibility to help the church grow.

	Scriptures and teaching people how to feed themselves daily from the Scriptures. Churches should emphasize prayer and teaching people how to pray. Churches should emphasize the great commission and teach people how to build relationships with non-believers and share their faith with them. Churches should emphasize worship and make the worship service the centerpiece of the church and how to worship during the week.	
Chris Adsit		
The essence of the mission of Christ in the world today?	**The missional objective(s) to prioritize to fulfill Christ's mission?**	**Should believers prioritize missional movements? How? What result?**
The essence of Christ's mission on earth has not changed in two thousand years. It is a two-fold seek-and-destroy mission: (1) Luke 19:10—for the Son of Man has come to	Down through the ages Christ has always chosen to pursue his mission in partnership with his church. In keeping with Christ's two-fold mission, and taking into account the current societal	If by "missional movements" you mean the strategy of infiltrating the various secular networks in the world and becoming outward-looking *communitas*, I think the church

seek and to save that which was lost. And (2) 1 John 3:8b—The Son of God appeared for this purpose, to **destroy** the works of the devil. His mission is to rescue the kidnapped and expose and render harmless the kidnapper. But, while his mission has not changed, his tactics have had to, based on the changing themes of society and the changing strategies of the devil.

emphasis, mindset and proclivities, the church needs to focus on the following pursuits:

a. **Become like Christ.** This isn't a process that can be finished, but it is one that *must* be begun. It involves helping the church to be distinctive salt and light in bold contrast with the unsavory and dark world. This will necessitate an intentional shift *away* from worldliness and *toward* godliness as defined in God's Word. We must foment this attitude within our churches. As Henry Blackaby wrote: "The world is getting darker because the light is growing weaker." I'm not speaking of a move toward religiosity, Phariseeism or adopting a "holier-than-thou" attitude, but a move toward true humility, selfless love, and sacrificial acts of kindness and finding ways to be "an

should make them a priority, but it will not be easy to induce most churches to budge from their "holy huddle" mentality. The transition can be accomplished if four elements are employed: (1) do it gradually, (2) accompanied with much prayer and a dependence of the Holy Spirit to accomplish it, (3) with the senior pastor referring to the need for this trend frequently and with increasing passion from the pulpit, and (4) with the leadership and the church's movers-and-shakers leading by example. The transition needs to happen on both the individual and corporate level. If it is only happening at the individual, grass-roots level, it's hard to establish momentum. If it's coming "from the top down" only, people can ignore it and stay away from its influence simply by

aroma of life to life." We have to buck the trend to make our churches more and more like the world. We must become not only "different from" but in a literal, God-energized way, "better than." This is where true, consequential disciple-making comes in.

b. **Infiltrate the world.** This distinctiveness won't happen in a positive way if the church adopts a fortress mentality, hiking their holy robes up about them and avoiding the spoilage of the world—but by infiltrating all networks, living with, interacting with, serving, providing an anchor. "Come out from among them and be separate," God enjoins us (2 Cor. 6:17), but He does not say, "…be isolated." We can be *with* them but not *of* them. As we are *among* them but distinct, then and only then will we truly be not showing up at church-sponsored events/ministries. A pincer movement strategy is needed. The envisioned end product would be that the kingdom of God is coming much closer to those who need it the most, they will be drawn to it, they will start pursuing and hanging out with the Christians, trying to find out more about "what they have", they will be drawn to Christ, then drawn to the churches, and will begin bringing others to the kingdom. We might see a strong influx of sinners in our churches—but that's what we're looking for! A hospital with no sick people in it should close down! But, if we're doing a good job of discipling this new population of Christians, we'll see them getting fixed, healed, strengthened and eventually thrust into influential leadership positions.

able to act as Christ's incarnational eyes, ears, mouth, feet and hands, intent on seeking and saving the lost. Most of the world is immune to the church's typical approaches of "sharing the gospel" (tracts, churches, crusades, radio & TV preachers, door-to-door, street corner, etc.). The current society wants honesty, relationship, openness, give-and-take, talk to me & listen to me—all of which happen best in an informal life-on-life approach. The church needs to become outward-looking communities (or *communitas,* as Alan Hirsch puts it), focusing on the needs of the lost around them—which, by the way, will deepen and strengthen the bonds *within* the communities.

c. **Train to speak and fight.** The church needs to train its members how to share Christ in this life-on-life context—how to make Christ the issue, and how to make Christ's two pursuits (search & destroy) the foundation of his message to the world. It must also train its members how to put on their spiritual armor before embarking on a ministry of infiltration. They are truly going into battle, and they will be lost to the cause if they are not prepared. Someone wants to devour them.

d. **Actively oppose the forces of darkness.** Though the church must infiltrate as much of society's networks as possible, it must find ways to resist compromise. No matter where we are or what we are doing, we are truly front-line troops in the battle against the forces of darkness, and we must actively oppose the works of the devil whenever we have the opportunity to do so. We are extensions of the will of Christ in this matter. It's *very* important, however, to distinguish between the kidnapped and the kidnappers. We don't shoot the victims—we show them love, care, compassion and a way out. But we target the forces behind them, the ones animating them and holding them down. We don't wrestle with flesh and blood, but against principalities, etc. (Eph. 6:12). We must stand firm against various influences that find their origin in Satan and seek to railroad people into death and hell: slavery, prostitution, racism, drug and alcohol abuse, adultery, radical Islam and terrorism, despotism, homosexuality, eradication of God & Christ from our society, the coarsening of our society in their communication and entertainment, the creeping lowering of standards regarding

	honesty, sex, theft, cheating, etc. This resistance should take place on both individual and corporate levels.	
Robert Lewis		
The essence of the mission of Christ in the world today?	**The missional objective(s) to prioritize to fulfill Christ's mission?**	**Should believers prioritize missional movements? How? What result?**
I believe the mission is to share the gospel and win people to Christ, build them in their faith, and then release them back into the world to do the work of ministry according to their passion and gifting . . . whatever that may be. We need to be in the "catch and release" business not the "catch and keep" business which so many churches do.	The holy grail of church ministry that I have followed all my life is Ephesians 4:11-12. This is the churches' game plan given by apostolic leadership and it has never been fully fleshed out.	Every church should strive to be missional . . . in sharing the gospel, in meeting needs of the community and the world, and in planting churches. Whether they can do the latter may depend on their ability at the moment, but every church should strive to do all three.
Greg Ogden		
The essence of the mission of Christ in the world today?	**The missional objective(s) to prioritize to fulfill Christ's mission?**	**Should believers prioritize missional movements? How? What result?**
The essence of the	Our church's mission	Jesus told us to make

mission of Christ is the same as what Jesus gave to us in the great commission, which I consider the mission statement for the church, which parallels Paul's personal mission statement in Colossians 1:28-29. **Make disciples of Jesus** is what we are to be about. Jesus tells us that this is done by **going** to all nations (evangelism), **baptizing** in the name of the triune God (our identity and life is found in being engrafted to the life of the relational God who is the basis for a new community, the church), and **being taught** to obey all that Jesus commanded (aligning our lives with Jesus' intention).

statement is: *Gathering in communities of disciples who worship, grow, and serve. Going into all the world as witnesses of the life-changing love of Jesus Christ.* The mission objectives should parallel the definition of a disciple that Jesus gave us. A disciple **goes, roots his or her identity in Christ, and seeks to obey all that Jesus commanded.** Every mission statement should reflect these priorities. Train people to share their faith; have people rooted in the life of the triune God in the midst of a discipleship community—so everyone should have a small group of fellow followers who are trying to orient who they are to the One they follow; and finally live in a lifetime of dying to self while Christ is coming alive in them.

disciples. The only thing I see that Jesus told us to multiply was followers of him. There are no short cuts to growing up in Christ. Certainly part of that is having a missional mindset. So to the extent that "missional movement" creates an ethos of multiplication, all the better. But I am suspicious of anything that says we can short cut the process of what it takes to grow people carefully and personally over time. If missional movements were Jesus' intention, he must not have done a very good job. Jesus focused in on 12 to whom he gave his life. The Holy Spirit certainly took hold of them and caused their message to convict the hearts of people in great numbers. So, if that is a missional movement under the sovereignty of God, then the church should be a part of it to advance Christ's mission.

Alan Hirsch

The essence of the mission of Christ in the world today?	The missional objective(s) to prioritize to fulfill Christ's mission?	Should believers prioritize missional movements? How? What result?
A friend of mine used to say, "Define the kingdom of God to me and I will give you a definition of mission." He was saying whatever the agenda of the kingdom is that is the agenda of the mission of the church. It encompasses issues of evangelism, service of the poor and needy, representing God in the public sphere as good witness without being control freaks. Living consistently in the kingdom, what does it mean to love God in every sphere and domain of society? What does Jesus do and do likewise. It takes to the issue of the kingdom of God, Jesus demonstrates the agenda. Another way to look	It goes back to the issue of the Kingdom of God—I'm not sure how that is measured. Jesus is the judge in the end—of the effectiveness of things. What a missional church should be doing is to measure its effectiveness by its impact on those outside of the church. It's not just internal measurements that the institutional church uses, (buns, bucks and buildings). There in nothing wrong with that itself but they are not measurements of a missionality. Are we impacting truancy at school? Or violence in our area? That kind of thing would be very interesting to measure our effectiveness. The church is not the kingdom of God. It is an expression of the kingdom of God. It is	I would say—I am for the movement idea of a church—we need to rethink ourselves as a movement. I think the church in the New Testament is clearly a movement and the sweetest and best expressions of church seem to be more movemental. We have basically a very institutional idea of the church, and I don't mean that in a pejorative sense. It is what it is. We tend to see the church as expressing itself in its rituals, its theologies, its creeds, structures, liturgy buildings, programming—that's what we think church is, which I think are external expressions but they are easily substituted by what the New Testament means by *ecclesia*. My understanding is that the term *ecclesia*

301

at that is if you go the great commission when discipleship is really at the core of it. Evangelism reframed in the context of discipleship is more of a kingdom kind of approach. Taking the great commission very seriously and very literally. Matthew 28, "Go into all the world and make disciples of all the nations . . ." Rather than reading it as an evangelistic text, which is the way we have read, it is to be read it as a disciple-making text. Discipleship is a major part of the deal. It is like the elephant in the room, and we never get to do it properly and yet is it so key to what we are to be about.	a profound heresy to identify entirely the church with the kingdom. The kingdom of God is God's work in every sphere everywhere. His rule over the entire universe. His government, his will, is being exercised. Properly obeying. That is what we are meant to be about. We as a church must be living in the kingdom as much as we can.	is a very movemental term. It can express itself in a local house, ecclesia is across the city and ecclesia is the universal people of God. So I think it is very movemental, its multi-dimensional, very fluid. As least part of the answer is discovering ourselves as a movement and living into it. In *Forgotten Ways* I outlined six ways the phenomenology of movements. When those six elements come together, you have the inevitability of movement. When those elements are freely expressed and interrelated as a system then you have the movement happening. Exponential growth is what would be the result. The future of the Western church is bound up in whether we can discover ourselves as a movement again.

Michael Frost

The essence of the mission of Christ in the world today?	The missional objective(s) to prioritize to fulfill Christ's mission?	Should believers prioritize missional movements? How? What result?
I follow David Bosch in defining Christian mission as the "alerting of people to the reign of God through Christ", meaning that the mission of God and therefore the church is anchored in God's kingly reign and rule, inaugurated in the very act of creation, demonstrated by the covenant with Israel and established in the life, teaching, death and resurrection of Jesus. Mission therefore is our participating in God's work of bringing everything to fulfillment that he began in creation.	If mission is the alerting of others to the reign of God through Christ then I think the church does this by embracing two broad missional objectives: the *announcement* of that reign, which includes such actions as evangelism, witness, and worship, and the *demonstration* of that reign, which includes acts of kindness and compassion, the alleviating of suffering, the work of correcting unjust political and economic structures and the protection of the environment. In this way the debate regarding the so-called competing priorities of evangelism and social justice is irrelevant, since they are simply two facets or expressions of a	The approach to mission I've outlined is so organic and non-institutional that it is hard to imagine it being contained by the traditional church's structures. As a result it leaks out and finds itself catalyzing missional movements. I'd say the Student Volunteer Movement of the 19th Century is one such example. Likewise, the Para-church Movement of the mid-to-late 20th Century, a similar movement is occurring but this time mission is being anchored more helpfully in ecclesiology. Bosch once said that mission is intrinsically ecclesial (and therefore that ecclesiology must be intrinsically missional), so what we're seeing now is

higher calling, that being the alerting of people to God's reign. I also think it includes worship as part of the mission of the church since worship is the spoken (and sung) announcement of God's reign. It also includes an ecological dimension because that is a demonstration of God's reign over creation.

When it comes to *demonstrating* God's reign, a simple equation is to ask what would the world look like if God's reign through Christ was completely recognized and understood and then for the church to create foretastes of this world in the midst of unbelief, fear, violence and hatred. In this way, feeding the poor isn't just an act of kindness, not even just a political act: it is an act of worship, since it is a demonstration of the world-that-is-to-come in the return of Christ.

the era of the great church planting movements (the big 21st Century missional movement?). Rather than the church sending out missioning communities (what Roland Allen called the great divorce), we're now seeing the church sending out missional church planting teams. As soon as this catches on and we have church planting churches being planted across the world we will have a serious missional movement.

As Jesus said then, it is done for him. Likewise, *announcing* the reign of God through Christ can't be reduced to recruiting people to our brand of religion. Rather, evangelism has to be seen as an articulation of God's reign—as a worshipful response to his kingship—rather than as a "winning of scalps" for the church. In this respect I'm also very influenced by N T Wright's inaugurated eschatology, believing that in the resurrection of Jesus, God is putting "everything to rights" (Wright's expression) and our mission is to draw people's attention to the unfurling kingdom of God and demand that people come under his kingship and acknowledge it as the way, the truth and the life. Wright identifies three broad areas where God's reign is most clearly recognized (putting

	things right)—reconciled relationships (with God and others), reestablished justice, and rediscovered beauty. In this way, I think that the mission of the church is to both alert others to the reign of God through Jesus, emphasizing the reconciliation, justice and beauty of the Gospel in our announcement (evangelism/witness/ worship) and creating examples of reconciliation, justice and beauty in our demonstration (kindness, justice, peace, art, music etc.).	
Alan Roxburgh		
The essence of the mission of Christ in the world today?	**The missional objective(s) to prioritize to fulfill Christ's mission?**	**Should believers prioritize missional movements? How? What result?**
The question itself is problematic. It assumes that you can define that in one or two sentences, but I don't know that you can because the bigger narrative the	I think that there are two interacting journeys that go on. One of the people—my language would be that the way a people can be a demonstration, sign	I may not understand what you mean by movement but it seems to me that church planting is only one very small specific effort that is happening in

story of what God is up to, it's a whole story, the story of what the Bible is about. If I am forced into that kind of mode—the mission of God in Christ is that the whole creation is invited into doxological relationship with its creator and Jesus comes and forms a people that are a sign and witness and demonstration of the movement of God.

and foretaste of the kingdom is that they more and more and more are shaped around the practices of the Christian life. Second part of the middle are the continuing asking of the question what is God up to in needy communities and how can we begin to join with God in those places? And it is that reciprocity between those two things which is ultimately shaping and reshaping, forming and reforming us as a people. They would be the criteria I am looking for in trying to answer your question.

impacting all kinds of local churches and parishes—the form in which missional life can be expressed is very diverse and flexible. Church planting is only one small form of that. There are all kinds of things going on across many forms of local congregations and even in existing church systems. One, I dislike the word "movement" intensely; The people who use it (to me) demonstrate that they don't understand how social or cultural change takes place. A movement is something to write about after the fact. You can say, oh look what happened . . . I am concerned about a lot of these people who keep using that language as if they are creating something. They are pointing to something and saying . . . I just think that is highly barbaric and what it tells you is that they already have

		a pattern in their mind of those things will look like. So I struggle with all of that language. I find what it does is create a nice neat box to put things. I find that what people are looking for are what are the three four or five points and that's what a missional movement looks like. God is up to all kinds of stuff in all kinds of ways across different kinds of church systems. How do you listen to what's going on out there?
	Steve Strauss	
The essence of the mission of Christ in the world today?	**The missional objective(s) to prioritize to fulfill Christ's mission?**	**Should believers prioritize missional movements? How? What result?**
I would describe the "mission of Christ" as another way of talking about the "mission of God" as revealed throughout Scripture. God's mission is his project of redeeming humankind and creation from	Our missional objectives are to proclaim and live the Gospel, the good news of kingdom of God, seeking to disciple individuals into Christ-like citizens of the coming kingdom, to establish mature New Testament	I'm hesitant to use the word "priority" for any of the missional tasks that we should be doing. Christ has given us a number of commands related to the Gospel, and he expects us to do them all. Whenever we use the word "priority,"

humankind's fall into sin and all its deadly effects, and restoring humankind and the creation to its original intent of bringing glory to him.	churches as "beachheads of the kingdom" and to impact society by infusing into it the values of the coming kingdom.	we imply that something is ultimately optional. None of the Gospel/Kingdom commands of Jesus is optional. Further, different strategies and means for fulfilling the mission of God have been advanced over the centuries; many are both biblical and effective ways to fulfill God's mission. Different labels have been used at different times, and people define those labels differently. So I'm also hesitant to either endorse or condemn any strategy or method. I understand a "church planting movement" as defined by, say, Garrison. But what does that mean to someone else? I understand "missional movement" as defined by, say, Frost, but what does that mean to someone else? I'm for any means or strategy that will fulfill the objectives I have listed under #2 in

		a biblical manner. Any means or strategy that is discipling individuals into Christ-like citizens of the coming kingdom, establishing mature New Testament churches that "show off" the coming kingdom and is impacting society with the values of the kingdom is a good thing that should be commended and practiced.
	Dennis McCallum	
The essence of the mission of Christ in the world today?	**The missional objective(s) to prioritize to fulfill Christ's mission?**	**Should believers prioritize missional movements? How? What result?**
I go to 2 Cor. 5 where Paul talks about how God was in Christ reconciling the world to himself, and that he has committed to us the ministry of reconciliation. It makes total sense that the body of Christ would be commissioned to do the same thing Jesus came to do. I	1. Evangelism 2. Disciple making 3. Development of a full-orbed community where gifts and ministries can flourish.	I think movements arise when God moves in unpredictable ways. The best thing we can do is be ready in case movemental force develops. If we have the quality leaders developed and the right ethos, we are in position to move on any opening God provides. Individual duplication should lead to group

understand reconciliation as involving more than evangelism. In addition to evangelism, ongoing reconciliation is fostered through disciple making and building up the body of Christ. All this is needed for full reconciliation to God.		multiplication eventually. Experts I have talked to (including Garrison and his strategy coordinator trainer) admit there is no true church planting movement in America. I think that is probably true (we sure haven't found one) and a very fascinating thing. Every proclaimed movement we have checked out has turned out to be fictitious. We haven't really succeeded either.

Jim Smith

The essence of the mission of Christ in the world today?	The missional objective(s) to prioritize to fulfill Christ's mission?	Should believers prioritize missional movements? How? What result?
The same as it always has been: go and make disciples, teach them to do what Jesus said, and immerse them in Trinitarian life. The aim of missions has often been conversion, which is great, but has often	The objectives should be what I mentioned in the previous answer: make Christ-followers. Not merely people who believe in Jesus, or things about Jesus, but those who believe and respond to that belief through their willingness to	Whatever the lead pastor is promoting tends to become the priority of the church, so it begins with leadership, and those who have a clear vision of the value of missions. If it is not a priority of the pastor, it is not likely to

failed to preach a gospel that naturally leads to discipleship.	practice what Jesus taught, through his power.	become the priority of the people.
Aubrey Malphurs		
The essence of the mission of Christ in the world today?	**The missional objective(s) to prioritize to fulfill Christ's mission?**	**Should believers prioritize missional movements? How? What result?**
Mt. 28:19-"Go and make disciples". Making disciples consists both of evangelism and edification.	First, as Mt. 28:19 says to "Go!" Our church people must get out into and involved with their communities/Jerusalem's (Acts 1:8). Gone are the days when we could sit back and invite them to our churches. Far too many aren't interested!	Depends on what you mean by "missional movements." Does this involve forays by the church out into their communities? If this is the case, yes, this should be a priority. It's accomplished by casting this vision and developing a strategy to implement the same. The envisioned end product is the picture of believers "rubbing shoulders with" unbelievers as we serve them in our communities. This could be serving in a soup kitchen, adopting a family, or even a school.

Craig Van Gelder		
The essence of the mission of Christ in the world today?	**The missional objective(s) to prioritize to fulfill Christ's mission?**	**Should believers prioritize missional movements? How? What result?**
God and God as a redeeming God. The creation and the cross are complementary aspects of God's mission—care for all of creation and bringing redemption to bear on every dimension of life. Understanding both the "sending" aspect of the Triune God— God the Father sent Son, Father and Son sent the Spirit, and the Spirit of Christ sends the church into the world for the sake of the world, and the "social reality" of God as a relational community of equality and mutuality that we are invited to participate in as the church of Jesus Christ.	The mission of God described above invites the church into participation, which includes congregations: (a) Discerning the leading of the Spirit— asking and answering the questions, "What is God up to in our context?" and "What does God want to do." (b) Stewarding their resources to participate more fully in God's mission in their context where the Spirit of God is already at work. (c) Bearing witness to the reign of God that is already present in redemptive power through the Spirit while also not yet in terms of final judgment; and enacting the realities of the redemptive reign of God in Christ within their context— a holistic gospel of	I would be interested in promoting the importance of movements that are shaped by a missional imagination--the mission of the Triune God within all of life. This keeps God as the "acting subject" with our seeking to live into and out of God's agency in pursuing such movements. The question is framed in such a way that human agency or church agency is the primary acting subject, which misses, from my perspective, the true meaning of what it means to be "missional."

	good news. (d) Contributing to unmasking the principalities and powers that have already been defeated by God through Christ.	
	David Sills	
The essence of the mission of Christ in the world today?	**The missional objective(s) to prioritize to fulfill Christ's mission?**	**Should believers prioritize missional movements? How? What result?**
Ultimately, the essence of the mission of Christ in the world is no different than it has been since He walked the earth. Christ has commissioned his church to be obedient to making disciples among all the peoples of the world, teaching them to obey all He has commanded us. We see in Matthew 29:19-20 and Acts 1:8 the parameters of this mission. We are to make disciples, which we are to do by going into all the world, and as we do	Believers must not only recognize the inerrancy of God's Word, but the authority of it, deriving their ministry objectives from the commands, principles, and parameters found within it. As such, our first objective within the context of missiology must be to be a people of the Word. The nature of missiology and global ministry is that we are often compelled by trends and the challenges that emerge from intercultural ministry and contextualization. However, we must	Paul, could you clarify what you mean by "missional movements" here? I have seen the term used in many different ways and want to be certain of your meaning. I am not sure if you are referring to the trend of stepping away from programmatic church movements to more individual/community focused church movements or to one of the alternative terms used for what is in Southern Baptist circles typically referred to as Church Planting Movements. I think probably the

we are to baptize and to teach them all He has taught us.	maintain a focus on the gospel, the transformational power of God in the life of individuals, and the recognition that we are not obedient unless we are faithful to not only reach, but to teach all that Christ has commanded us. Ultimately, our missiological objectives should reflect the progression of a believer's life. We should seek to engage and reach lost people in culturally appropriate ways with the gospel, disciple and teach them all Christ has commanded us, and then train them to continue the work with others.	best way to capture my thoughts on the aspects that are needed or central to a movement such as you describe is found in quotes within the book. Given the complexities of the issue and without knowing the exact context in which it will be used, I'm hesitant to branch out to give such a specific response to a complex issue. Since I've written on the subject, I think I'll just stand with what has been published since that has been thought through and reasoned with care. I need to run, but hope that is agreeable to you and doesn't cause any difficulties.
Dallas Willard		
The essence of the mission of Christ in the world today?	**The missional objective(s) to prioritize to fulfill Christ's mission?**	**Should believers prioritize missional movements? How? What result?**
His mission is to deliver "his people"—those who have confidence in	Make disciples to Jesus and develop them to the point where they do	Most, not all, of the efforts are misguided because they are attempting to do what

Him as Lord—from sin: the power of sin over their lives.	everything He said.	could only be done by responses to question 1) and question, 2) above. The natural effect of questions 1) and 2) would be "missions" of various appropriate kinds. There would always be a place for special efforts with a special focus, dictated by the circumstances for the "success" of Jesus' work the radical transformation—what one would naturally expect from reading the New Testament—of multitudes of individuals is what is required.
	Keith Matthews	
The essence of the mission of Christ in the world today?	**The missional objective(s) to prioritize to fulfill Christ's mission?**	**Should believers prioritize missional movements? How? What result?**
I tend to look at Luke 4:43 where Jesus said, "I have come to preach the good news of the kingdom because this is why I was sent." It is actually the place the first time He said, "This is why I am	We have wrongly made our objective in mission to make converts and we have not turned the corner in any way in making disciples. We talk about discipleship as being for the advanced Christian but we have	I am working with networks. I am working with younger missional leaders that part of networks. I'm a part of a network called ecclesia a church planting network. For tipping points to happen, we

doing what I am doing." The gospel of the kingdom was the great mission of Jesus, the extension of that of redeeming humanity and the redemption of all things—the proclamation of the present availability of the kingdom—that takes on the agenda of God for the world.	made converts and the expect people to move into discipleship. And that usually doesn't happen. If we make disciples who are taking on the mission of the agenda of their Rabbi their teacher Jesus, we will then see mission happen, but we are not going to get there if we just make converts who are forgiven of their sins to go to heaven.	cannot rely on our old denominations to make it happen. If we can really make disciples and help empower people to be disciples 24/7—that's the ultimate movement—where people are really seeing their Monday to Monday lives (not Sunday to Sunday lives) as being salt and light, in their work places, their leisure time, etc.

	David J. Hesselgrave	
The essence of the mission of Christ in the world today?	**The missional objective(s) to prioritize to fulfill Christ's mission?**	**Should believers prioritize missional movements? How? What result?**
This one is easy, at least for me. You see I'm still stuck in the past and, I think, in Scripture. The fulfillment of the great commission is my mission; and Missionary Paul is still my model. For a matter of fact I am still happy with "The gospel for every person and a church for every people	This question is a bit more complex for me. I think that "missional" has become the plaything of evangelicals just as Scherer said that *missio Dei* became the plaything of ecumenists. Like most neologisms, it means whatever one puts into it. And that bothers me because for some of its initiators and	There's that word again. I really can't deal with it until I know the nature of a "missional movement." Logically, the meaning of "missional" has to be consonant with "mission" so logically what we have here is something akin to "churchly church." That being the case,

group."	especially for Emergents, it means that mission is the mother of theology. Decide what your mission is and then settle on a theology that will support and further it. If that is missiology it is also heresy. I don't believe it. And I think that my answer to question 1 should be determinative in answering question 2.	one either ends up as a holist or a prioritist. But as McGavran said, there are multitudes of good Christian things to do that are not mission. Or as the Pope has recently written, today's world has need of many, many things but the one thing it needs most is . . . **God!** At that point I'm a good Catholic because I am that kind of prioritist.
	Ed Stetzer	
The essence of the mission of Christ in the world today?	**The missional objective(s) to prioritize to fulfill Christ's mission?**	**Should believers prioritize missional movements? How? What result?**
Christ's mission is to glorify God by establishing the kingdom of God on the earth through his life, death, and resurrection and through the sending of the spirit-empowered Church. He accomplishes this mission primarily by redeeming people from their sins and	The missional objective(s) of the church are (in Lesslie Newbigin's words) to be a sign and instrument of the kingdom of God. The believers/church do this by showing the redemptive power of God through transformed lives that are lived in the community of faith for	God-honoring Christian movements occur because God in his kindness and wisdom chooses to bless a leader or leaders to mobilize people and churches. The church needs clear and courageous godly examples to point us to what God wants to do and is doing in our world. When God

equipping them to live a life of love for the advancement of the kingdom.	the good of their world. They also do this by sharing the redemptive message of the gospel which is necessary for the eternal salvation of people.	raises up such examples, the church should pay attention. I believe God is doing this now in our generation with a number of different leaders and movements. The danger is always to see the movement as an end in itself rather than a mobilizing force for the cause of the kingdom for God's glory (which is the ultimate end). Movements, networks, and denominations are tools that God uses to encourage the church in its mission and to strengthen churches to accomplish more for the kingdom than they are able to alone. I think we can plan and strategically work towards movements through networks and denominations, but we should remain rightly aware that true spiritual movements are not planned and organized by us. They are a gracious work of God for the building of his church.

APPENDIX D
TOKYO 2010 DECLARATION[492]
VISION STATEMENT

Making Disciples of Every People in Our Generation

"Therefore go and make disciples of all nations, baptizing them in the name of the Father and of the Son and of the Holy Spirit, and teaching them to obey everything I have commanded you."
—Matthew 28:19-20 (NIV)

The vision statement of the Tokyo 2010 Global Missions Consultation is "Making disciples of all peoples in our generation." While this statement maintains the "closure" focus of Edinburgh 1910 and 1980—represented by the phrase "all peoples"—it also captures an equally important dimension of the great commission-the purpose of our going, which is to *teach all peoples to obey everything Jesus commanded.*

Discipling peoples is a process, not a one-time event or accomplishment. It is something that has to revisited in and by every new generation. The often repeated truism that the Christian faith is just one generation away from extinction is a reality not

---

[492] The Tokyo 2010 Global Missions Consultation celebrated the 100th anniversary of the first international mission consultation held in Edinburgh, Scotland in 1910, to analyze the progress and advance the great commission One of the outcomes of the Tokyo 2010 Global Missions Consultation was the "Tokyo 2010 Declaration." This represents a significant statement on the priority of disciple-making as the heart and foundation of Christ's mission in the world. This statement supports the thesis of this study. <http://www.tokyo2010.org/conference/htm> (accessed August 5, 2010).

only for the Church where it is, but for those seeking to build it where it is not.

Thus, it is imperative that we continually ask ourselves: What kind of Christianity are we seeking to establish around the world? Is it a copy of our own-one in which we can't even keep our own young people who have been raised in Christian homes? Or is it built on more solid foundations? The kind laid down by the Master himself, who took twelve young men, and said, "Come, follow me." Or the kind laid down by the Apostle Paul, who said to the church in Philipi, "Whatever you have learned or received or heard from me, or seen in me-put into practice" (Phil. 4:9). And again to the Church in Corinth, "I urge you to imitate me" (1 Cor. 4:16). How many of our leaders would be willing to say that! But that is the goal, and until we get there we are not fulfilling the great commission.

Making disciples is a three-step process: first by going to those who have had no exposure to the gospel; second, by calling them into a relationship with Jesus that culminates in baptism; and third by teaching them to observe his commands. There is an overwhelming need and challenge to the missionary endeavors to reach those who have not heard—the unreached *ethne* of our times. In doing that we expect to see the church planted and in turn reaching out to others. But the challenge does not stop there. Making disciples includes a process that follows to keep that new follower learning and growing in his new faith, what some call "spiritual formation." The important thing is that there is an ongoing growth experience. A new believer's worldview must be changed; his lifestyle adjusted to increasingly conform to the image of Christ; and his ethical conduct increasingly marked by integrity. When transformation is apparent in these areas, that believer in turn is in a position to teach others also and thus duplicate the process.

The Tokyo 2010 Global Missions Consultation will look at how we can work together to finish the task. How do we keep the conversation going and develop cooperative plans to move forward? How can we make sure that every people is properly engaged by disciple-making teams over the next decade? How can we help strengthen missions movements around the world which are just developing?

We thus embrace a vision of Making Disciples, with a time schedule of the generation of each one of us. We don't put a specific date on the vision, but realize that as we work together in love and increasing effectiveness and obedience to the Master's plan, the vision is both reachable and Biblical.

(See "Where Do We Go From Here: The Challenges of Tokyo 2010" for a longer discussion of the Vision of Tokyo 2010, <http://www.tokyo2010.org/conference/#3>, 08/05/10 Tokyo 2010 Declaration: Making Disciples of Every People in Our Generation.)

Preamble

We affirm that mission is the central theme of Scripture, through which God reveals Himself to be a God who communicates and works through us by action and word in a world estranged from Him. Furthermore, we recognize that fulfilling and bringing completion to Jesus' great commission (Mt. 28:18-20; Mk. 16:15; Lk. 24:44-49; Jn. 20:21; Acts 1:8) has been the on-going responsibility of the Church for 2000 years.

In this era of missions, we of the Tokyo 2010 Global Mission Consultation value and commemorate the 1910 Edinburgh World Missionary Conference, a hallmark event which stands out as an inspiration and impetus to the modern global mission movement. We celebrate a legacy of 100 years of mission that has transpired since that first world missionary conference.

However, the world has dramatically changed since that conference was convened a century ago. Missions is no longer the predominant domain of Western Christianity. Rather, the preponderance of mission activity is being engaged by Majority World Christians outside of the West. Christ's ambassadors are coming from everywhere around the world and going to anywhere and everywhere in the world. We rejoice that Christ's mission force is global in composition, bearing a diversity of thought, practice and resources that enriches and energizes Christ's global Cause as never before.

Yet, the corresponding reality is that the present day mission task is so large and complex that no one church, agency, national missions movement, or regional mission block can take it on alone or independently. Also, the understanding of the essence of what is entailed in the remaining task has altered considerably in recent years.

Declaration

We, representatives of evangelical global mission structures, being intent on fulfilling the ultimate objective of the great commission, have gathered in Tokyo May 11-14, 2010 at this Global Mission Consultation to make the following declaration. We set forth this declaration in obedience to Christ's final command, as a means of calling Christ-followers everywhere to whole-heartedly embrace and earnestly engage in "making disciples of every people in our generation."

Mankind's Need

We affirm that all people are lost apart from faith in Christ. The clear statements of Scripture reveal that every individual, without exception, is a sinner by nature, choice and practice (Rom. 3:9-18, 23). As such, all are under God's wrath and condemnation (Jn. 3:18) because their sin is an affront to the perfect and holy nature of God (Rom. 1:18; 2:2-5). The tragic result of sin is man's alienation from God, leading to everlasting death (Rom. 6:23), and creation's bondage to corruption, subjecting it to futility (Rom. 8:18-21).

God's Remedy

We further affirm that out of love, God sent his only Son, Jesus Christ (Jn. 3:16), to reconcile the world to Himself, so that mankind's sin will not be counted against them (2 Cor. 5:19). God's justice for the penalty of sin was satisfied by the atoning death of Christ as a sacrifice on man's behalf. Through Jesus' vicarious death and victorious resurrection, mankind is brought into a restored relationship with God. God offers forgiveness and salvation to all who, through faith, repent of their sin and believe solely in the redemptive work of Christ on the cross on their behalf (Rom. 1:5,16,17; 3:21-26; Eph. 1:7; 2:8-10). Therefore the message of the great commission is that "repentance and forgiveness of sins will be preached in his name to all peoples" (Lk. 24:47). Salvation is found in none other (Acts 4:12), nor in any other way (Jn. 14:6).

Our Responsibility

Because of the reality of mankind's dire need and God's gracious remedy, Jesus left with his followers the missional priority of making disciples of every people (Mt. 28:18-20). By this mandate we acknowledge both the breadth of the unfinished task—all peoples—and the depth of the task—making disciples, as its focus.

We recognize the breadth of our task as geographical, by going "into all the world" (Mk 16:15); as ethnical, by engaging "all peoples" (Mt. 28:19; Lk. 24:49); and as individual by proclaiming the gospel to "every creature" (Mk. 16:15).

Furthermore, we recognize that the depth of the task contains three essentials that comprise aspects in discipling peoples (Mt. 28:19-20):

Penetration ("go"): making a priority of going to those who have had little or no exposure to the gospel. Messengers go and encounter non-believers by way of personal encounters, broadcasts, podcasts, printed material, recordings, electronic communications, or any other innovative means used as a channel of penetrating witness. Thus, the importance of the ministry of evangelizing.

Consolidation ("baptizing"): gathering new believers into a relationship with Jesus and other believers, which is evidenced by the identifying rite of baptism. To conserve the fruit of evangelism and then be able to systematically disciple believers takes a local body of believers living in corporate harmony. Thus, the importance of the ministry of establishing churches.

Transformation ("teaching to obey"): teaching Christ-followers to observe his commands with the outcome of transformed lives. The new believer's worldview must be adjusted to a biblical worldview; his lifestyle changed to increasingly conform to the image of Christ; and his ethical conduct progressively marked by biblical morals. Ideally, this results in individuals applying the gospel of the kingdom to every sphere and pursuit of life—from government to economics, from education to health, and from science to creation care. As a consequence whole communities, cultures and countries benefit from the transforming power of the gospel. Thus, the importance of the ministry of teaching.

Finishing the Task

Although none dare predict when the task of making disciples will be brought to completion, we leave Tokyo cognizant of two realities:

1) We are closer now to finishing the task than at any time in modern history.

2) God has entrusted this generation with more opportunities and resources to complete the task than any previous one. We have more mission-minded churches, more sending structures and bases, more missionaries, more material resources, more funding, more and better technology, more information and data, a deeper understanding of the task, and a clearer focus of our responsibility than previous generations. God will require much of our generation.

However, we caution that all these advantages must be matched with a corresponding will to serve and sacrifice, coupled with genuine reliance upon the Holy Spirit. We acknowledge that we are engaged in spiritual warfare in which the presence and empowering of the Holy Spirit is essential (Acts 1:8). We give evidence of our reliance on God and his Spirit through frequent and fervent prayer on behalf of the world, the work and the workers (Jn. 17:20-21; Col. 4:3-4; 1 Th. 5:17).

Our Pledge

Therefore, as representatives of this generation's global mission community, we pledge to obey the great commission. We covenant together to use all that God has entrusted to us in this obedience. We will seek to know where people are unreached, overlooked, ignored, or forgotten. We will pray for the Holy Spirit to give strength and guidance as we join with others in changing that neglect, to love and make disciples in the way of the Cross.

We confess that we have not always valued each other or each other's work. We repent of those wrongs and will endeavor to bring an end to competition where it exists, and reconcile where there is hurt, misunderstanding and mistrust. Furthermore, we will endeavor to recognize that each part of the Body has its very own purpose, whether risking their very lives to show God's passion for the salvation of others, or supporting those who lead us forward, or caring for those who quietly support, or fervently pray that his will be done throughout the whole earth. We will respect all mission-engaging individuals and groups as special vessels for God's glory, each endowed with abilities that extend his Kingdom in multiple ways.

Finally, we recognize that finishing the task will demand effective cooperative efforts of the entire global body of believers. To facilitate cooperation and on-going coordination between mission structures worldwide, we agree to the necessity of a global network of mission structures.

With this in mind, we leave Tokyo pledging cooperation with one another, and all others of like faith, with the singular goal of "making disciples of every people in our generation."

BIBLIOGRAPHY

Adsit, Christopher B. *Personal Disciple-Making: A Step-by-Step Guide for Leading a Christian from New Birth to Maturity.* San Bernardino, CA: Here's Life Publishers, Inc., 1989.

Allen, Scott. "William Carey: A Missionary Who Transformed a Nation." *Mission Frontiers* 33: 5 (September-October 2011): 15-18.

Andrews, Alan. ed. *The Kingdom Life: A Practical Theology of Discipleship and Spiritual Formation.* Colorado Springs, Colorado: NavPress, 2010.

Arndt, William F. and F. Wilbur Gingrich. *Greek-English Lexicon of the New Testament.* Chicago: University of Chicago Press, 1957.

Atkinson, Donald A. and Charles L. Roesel. *Meeting Needs Sharing Christ: Ministry Evangelism in Today's New Testament Church.* Nashville, TN: LifeWay Press, 1995.

Barna, George. *Growing True Disciples.* Colorado Springs, CO: WaterBrook Press, 2001.

Barnett, Mike and Michael Pocock, eds. *The Centrality of Christ in Contemporary Missions.* Pasadena, CA: William Carey Library, 2005.

Barrett, Lois Y., ed. *Treasure in Clay Jars: Patterns in Missional Faithfulness.* Grand Rapids, MI: William B. Eerdmans Publishing Company, 2004.

Beddington, David W. "Pietism." *The New Dictionary of Theology*, ed. by Sinclair B. Ferguson, David F. Wright and James I. Packer. Downers Grove, IL: InterVarsity, 1988, 515-16.

"Good." BibleGateway.com <http://www.biblegateway.com/key word/index.php?search=good&version.html> (accessed August 22, 2011).

Bietenhard, H. "Lord." In *The New Testament Dictionary of New Testament Theology*. Grand Rapids, MI: The Zondervan Corporation, 1976.

Blaising, Craig A. and Darrell L. Bock. *Dispensationalism, Israel and the Church: A Search for Definition*. Grand Rapids, MI: Zondervan Publishing House, 1992.

_____. *Progressive Dispensationalism: An Up-to Date Handbook of Contemporary Dispensational Thought*. Wheaton, IL: A BridgePoint Book, 1993, 112-13.

Blomberg, Craig L. *Matthew*. The New American Commentary, 22. Nashville, TN: Broadman Press, 1992.

Bonhoeffer, Dietrich. *Christ the Center*. New York: Harper & Row Publishers, 1966.

_____. *The Cost of Discipleship*, New York: Macmillan Publishing Company, 1963.

_____. *Ethics*. New York: The Macmillan Company, 1965.

_____. *Life Together*. New York: Harper & Brothers, Publishers, 1954.

_____. *No Rusty Swords: Letters, Lectures and Notes 1928—1936*. Edwin H. Robertson, ed., translated by John Bowden and Eberhard Bethge. London: Collins, 1965.

Bosch, David J. *Transforming Mission: Paradigm Shifts in Theology of Mission*. Maryknoll, NY: Orbis Books, 2002.

_____. "Witness to the World." In *Perspectives on the World Christian Movement: A Reader*. 4th ed. Pasadena, CA: William Carey Library, 2009.

The Boundaries of Charity: Cistercian Culture and Ecclesiastical Reform 1098-1180. Stanford, CA: Stanford University Press, 1996.

Breen, Mike and Walt Kellestad. *The Passionate Church: The Art of Life-Changing Discipleship*. Colorado Springs, CO: Cook Communications Ministries, 2005.

Brown, Dale W. *Understanding Pietism*. Nappanee, IN: Evangel Publishing House, 1996.

Bruce, F. F. *The Epistle to the Hebrews*. The New International Commentary on the New Testament. Grand Rapids, MI: Wm. B. Eerdmans Publishing Co., 1964.

Cairns, Earle E. *Christianity Through the Centuries: A History of the Christian Church*. Grand Rapids, MI: Zondervan Publishing House, 1981.

Clouse, Robert G., Richard V. Pierard, and Edwin M. Yamauchi. *The Story of the Church*. London: Angus Hudson, Ltd., 2002.

Cole, Neil. *Organic Church: Growing Faith Where Life Happens.* San Francisco: Jossey-Bass, 2005.

Coleman, Robert. *The Master Plan of Evangelism.* Grand Rapids: Revell, 2006.

_____. "The Master's Plan." In *Perspectives on the World Christian Movement: A Reader,* 4th ed. San Bernardino, CA: William Carey Library, 2009.

Curran, Michael. "Early Irish Monasticism." In *Irish Spirituality,* edited by Michael Maher. Dublin, Ireland: Veritas Publication, 1981.

de Reuver, Arie. *Sweet Communion.* Grand Rapids, MI: Baker Academic, 2007.

de Waal, Esther. *The Way of Simplicity: The Cistercian Tradition.* Maryknoll, NY: Orbis Books, 1998.

Demarist, Bruce A. "Devotion, Doctrine and Duty in Dietrich Bonhoeffer." *Bibliotheca Sacra,* 148: 592 (October-December, 1991): 399-408.

Derickson, Gary. "The New Testament Church as a Mystery." *Bibliotheca Sacra* 166:664 (October-December 2009): 436-45.

DeYoung, Kevin and Greg Gilbert. *What is the Mission of the Church? Making Sense of Social Justice, Shalom, and the Great Commission.* Wheaton, IL: Crossway, 2011.

"Osmosis." Dictionary.com, <http://dictionary.reference.com/browse/osmosis.html> (accessed January 25, 2010.)

Dobois, Marguerite-Marie. "Saint Columbanus." In *Irish Monks in The Golden Age,* edited by John Ryan, Dublin, Ireland: Clonmore & Reynolds Ltd., 1963, 44-50.

Earle, Ralph. "1 Timothy." In *The Expositor's Bible Commentary,* vol. 11, edited by Frank E. Gaebelein. Grand Rapids, MI: Zondervan Publishing House, 1978, 341-390.

_____. "2 Timothy." In *The Expositor's Bible Commentary,* vol. 11, edited by Frank E. Gaebelein, Grand Rapids, MI: Zondervan Publishing House, 1978, 392-418.

Edman, Raymond V. *The Light in Dark Ages.* Wheaton, IL; Van Kampen Press, 1949.

Edwards, Jonathan. *Religious Affections: How Man's Will Affects His Character Before God.* Portland, OR: Multnomah Press, 1984.

Engel, James F. and William A. Dyrness. *Changing the Mind of Missions: Where Have We Gone Wrong?* Downers Grove, IL: InterVarsity Press, 2000.

Erb, Peter C., ed. *Pietists: Selected Writings.* New York: Paulist Press, 1983.

Ferdinando, Keith. "Mission: A Problem of Definition." *Themelios,* 33.1 (2008): 46-63.

Francke, August Hermann, quoted in "Gallery of Leading Figures," *Christian History 5* (1986), 14.

_____. *Nicodemus: Or a Treatise Against the Fear of Man.* London: Joseph Downing, 1706.

_____. *Sonn, Fest, und Apostel, Tags, Predigten. 3 Teile,* (Halle, 1704, I): 990 quoted in Gary R. Sattler, *Nobler Than the Angels, Lower Than a Worm: The Pietist View of the Individual in the Writings of Heinrich Muller and August Hermann Francke.* Lanhan, MD: University of Press of America, 1989, 89.

Franklin, Patrick S. *Bonhoeffer for the Missional Church: An Exposition and Critique of the Missional Church Movement's Ecclesiology in Light of the Ecclesiology of Dietrich Bonhoeffer.* Master's Thesis, Regent College, 2004.

Frost, Michael and Alan Hirsch. *ReJesus: A Wild Messiah for a Missional Church.* Peabody, MA: Hendrickson Publishers, Inc., 2009.

_____. *The Shaping of Things to Come.* Peabody, MA: Hendrickson Publishers, 2003.

Gangel, Kenneth and James Wilhoit, eds. *The Christian Educator's Handbook on Spiritual Formation.* Grand Rapids, MI: Baker Academic, 1998.

Garrison, Alton. *The 360° Disciple: Discipleship Going Full Circle.* Springfield, Missouri: Gospel Publishing House, 2009.

Garrison, David. *Church Planting Movements.* Richmond, VA: Office of Overseas Operations International Mission Board of the Southern Baptist Convention, 1999.

_____. *Church Planting Movements.* Midlothian, VA: WiGTake Resources, 2004.

George, Timothy and Allister McGrath, eds. *For All the Saints: Evangelical Theology and Christian Spirituality*. Westminster: John Knox Press, 2003.

The Gospel and Our Culture Network. "About The Network. . . ." The Gospel and Our Culture Network. <http://www.gocn.org/network/about.html> (accessed July 28, 2010).

Gordon, Ronald J. *Rise of Pietism in 17th Century Germany.* <http:www.cob-net.org/pietism.htm> (accessed September 13, 2005).

Greene, Colin and Martin Robinson. *Metavista: Bible, Church and Mission in an Age of Imagination*. Colorado Springs, CO: Authentic Media, 2008.

Guder, Darrell L., editor. *Missional Church: A Theological Vision for the Sending of the Church in North America*. Grand Rapids, MI: Eerdmans Publishing Company, 1998.

Gundry, Robert H. *Matthew: A Commentary on His Literary and Theological Art.* Grand Rapids, MI: Eerdmans, 1982.

Hendricksen, William. "Exposition the Gospel According to Matthew." In *A New Testament Commentary.* Grand Rapids, MI: Baker, 1973.

Hesselgrave, David J. "Challenging the Church to World Mission." *International Journal of Frontier Missions* 13:1 (January-March 1996): 27-32.

_____. "Confusion Concerning the Great Commission." *Evangelical Missions Quarterly* 15:4 (October 1979): 197-205.

_____. "Great Commission Contextualization." *International Journal of Frontier Missions* 12: 3 (Jul-Sep. 1995): 139-144.

_____. *Paradigms in Conflict: 10 Key Questions in Christian Missions.* Grand Rapids, MI: Kregel Publications, 2005.

_____. "Redefining Holism." *Evangelical Missions Quarterly* 35: 3 (July 1999): 278-284.

_____. "Will we Correct the Edinburgh Error?" *Southwest Journal of Theology.* 49:2 (Spring 2007): 121-149.

Hiebert, Edmond D. "An Expository Study of Matthew 28:16-20," *Bibliotheca Sacra* 149: 595 (July-September, 1992): 338-54.

Hirsch, Alan. *The Forgotten Ways: Reactivating the Missional Church.* Grand Rapids, MI: Brazos Press, 2006.

Horton, Michael. *The Gospel Commission: Recovering God's Strategy for Making Disciples.* Grand Rapids, MI Baker Books, 2011.

Hughes, R. Kent. *Ephesians: The Mystery of the Body of Christ.* Wheaton, IL: Crossway Books, 1990.

Hughes, R. Kent and Bryan Chapell. *1 & 2 Timothy and Titus.* Wheaton, IL: Crossway Books, 2000.

Hull, Bill. *Choose the Life: Exploring a Faith that Embraces Discipleship.* Grand Rapids, MI: Baker, 2004.

_____. *The Complete Book of Discipleship: On Being and Making Followers of Christ.* Colorado Springs, CO: NavPress, 2006.

_____. *The Disciple Making Church*. Grand Rapids, MI: Revell, 1988.

_____. "Spiritual Formation from the Inside Out." In *The Kingdom Life*, edited by Alan Andrews. Colorado Springs, CO: NavPress, 2010, (107-38).

Hunsberger, George R. "Birthing Missional Faithfulness: Accents in a North American Movement." *International Review of Mission*, vol. XCII: 365 (March 25, 2009), 149. <http://onlinelibrary.wiley.com/doi/10.1111/j.1758-6631.2003.tb00390.x/full> (accessed June 13, 2011).

_____. "Features of the Missional Church: Some Directions and Pathways." In *Developing the Missional Church*. Holland, MI: The Gospel and Our Culture Network, 1999, (5—13).

Hunsberger, George R. and Craig Van Gelder, eds. *Church Between Gospel & Culture: The Emerging Mission in North America*. Grand Rapids, MI: William B. Eerdmans Publishing Company, 1996.

Hunter III, George G. *The Celtic Way of Evangelism: How Christianity Can Reach the West . . . Again*. Nashville: Abingdon Press, 2000.

Johnson, Alan. "Analyzing the Frontier Mission Movement and Unreached People Group Thinking. Part V: A Model for Understanding the Missionary Task." *International Journal of Frontier Missions*, 18:3 (Fall 2001): 133-140.

Jones, Scott J. *The Evangelistic Love of God and Neighbor: A Theology of Witness and Discipleship*. Nashville, TN: Abingdon Press, 2003.

Kane, J. Herbert. *A Concise History of the Christian Mission*. Grand Rapids: Baker Book House, 1982.

Kelly, Geffrey B. and John C. Weborg, eds. *Reflections on Bonhoeffer: Essays in Honor of F. Burton Nelson*. Chicago: Covenant Publications, 1999.

Kimball, Dan. *The Emerging Church: Vintage Christianity for New Generations*. Grand Rapids, MI: Zondervan, 2003.

Kincaid, Ron. *A Celebration of Disciplemaking*. Wheaton, IL: Victor Books, 1990.

Köstenberger, Andreas J. *The Mission of Jesus and the Disciples According to the Fourth Gospel*. Grand Rapids, MI: Eerdmans, 1988.

Köstenberger, Andreas J. and Peter T. O'Brien, *Salvation to the Ends of the Earth: A Biblical Theology of Mission*. Downers Grove, IL: InterVarsity, 2001.

Kuhne, Gary W. "Follow-up—An Overview." In *Discipleship: The Best Writing from the Most Experienced Disciple-Makers*. Grand Rapids, MI: Zondervan, 1981.

Ladd, George Eldon. *Theology of the New Testament*. Grand Rapids, MI: William B Eerdmans Publishing House, 1993.

Lenski, R.C.H. *The Interpretation of St. Matthew's Gospel*. Minneapolis, MN: Augsburg, 1943.

Lewis, Robert. *The Church of Irresistible Influence*. Grand Rapids, MI: Zondervan, 2001.

Liam, Tracey. "Celtic Spirituality: Just What Does it Mean?" *Thinking Faith*. Jesuit Media Initiatives, March 14, 2008 <http:www.thinkingfaith.org/searchresults.html> (accessed December 22, 2010).

Liftin, Duane A. "1 Timothy." In *The Bible Knowledge Commentary: New Testament,* eds. John F. Walvoord and Roy B. Zook. Wheaton, IL: Victor Books, 1983.

Lin, Tony. *The Teleios as a Goal of Pauline Spiritual Formation*. Master's Thesis, Dallas Theological Seminary, 2005.

Lindberg, Carter. *A Brief History of Christianity.* Malden, MA: Blackwell Publishing, 2006.

Lovelace, Richard. *Dynamics of the Spiritual Life: An Evangelical Theology of Renewal*. Downers Grove, IL: Inter-Varsity Academic, 1979.

Lyons, Larry L. *Redeeming Culture: An Examination of the Methodology and Effectiveness of the Irish Missionary Movement with Their Application to Contemporary Urban Ministry*. Master's Thesis, Dallas Theological Seminary, 2001.

MacDonald, Glenn W. *The Disciple Making Church: From Dry Bones to Spiritual Vitality*. Grand Haven, MI: Faith Walk Publishing, 2004.

MacIlvaine III, Rodman W. "How Churches Become Missional." *Bibliotheca Sacra* 167 (April-June 2010): 216-33.

Maher, Michael, editor. *Irish Spirituality.* Dublin: Veritas Publications, 1981.

Manschreck, Clyde L. ed. *A History of Christianity, The Church from the Reformation to the Present.* Grand Rapids, MI: Baker Book House, 1964.

Martin, Dennis. "The Spirituality of St. Bernard of Clairvaux." *Christianity Today* (October 1, 1989). <http//www.ctlibrary.com/ch/1989/issu24/2413.html> (accessed June 08, 2010).

Matthews, John W. *Anxious Souls Will Ask: The Christ-Centered Spirituality of Dietrich Bonhoeffer.* Grand Rapids, MI: William B. Eerdmans Publishing Company, 2005.

Matthews, Keith J. "The Transformational Process." In *The Kingdom Life*, ed. Alan Andrews. Colorado Springs: NavPress, 2010.

McCallum, Dennis and Jessica Lowery. *Organic Disciplemaking: Mentoring Others into Spiritual Maturity and Leadership.* Houston, TX: Touch Publications, 2006.

McClung, Floyd. "Disciple Making & Church Planting: God's Way to Transform Nations." *Mission Frontiers* 33: 5 (September—October 2011): 19-23.

McElderry, Justin Kaine. *Theology of Mission in Matthew.* Master's Thesis, Talbot School of Theology, 2003.

McManus, Erwin. "Broken People Can Become Whole Disciples." *Leadership* 21:2, (Spring 2000): 48-54.

_____. *An Unstoppable Force: Daring to Become the Church God Had in Mind.* Loveland, CO: Group Publishing, 2001.

McNeal, Reggie. *Missional Renaissance: Changing the Scorecard for the Church.* San Francisco, Jossey-Bass, 2009.

McQuilkin, J. Robertson. "An Evangelical Assessment of Mission Theology of the Kingdom." In *The Good News of the Kingdom*, edited by Charles Van Engel, Dean S. Gilliland, and Paul Pierson. Maryknoll. NY: Orbis Books, 1993.

Meyer, Keith. "Whole-Life Transformation." In *The Kingdom Life*, edited by Alan Andrews. Colorado Springs: NavPress, 2010, (139-164).

Mitchell, Robinson W. *Mission: A Mark of the Church? Toward a Missional Ecclesiology.* Master's Thesis, Reformed Theological Seminary, 2008.

Moreau, A. Scott, Gary R. Corwin and Gary B. McGee. *Introducing World Missions: A Biblical, Historical, and Practical Survey.* Grand Rapids, MI: Baker Academic, 2004.

Moulton, Harold K. ed., *The Analytical Greek Lexicon Revised.* Grand Rapids: Zondervan, 1981.

Mulholland, Kenneth B. "From Luther to Carey, Pietism and the Modern Missionary Movement." *Bibliotheca Sacra* 156: 621 (January-March 1999): 85-95.

_____. "Moravians, Puritans and the Modern Missionary Movement." *Bibliotheca Sacra*, 156: 622 (April-June 1999): 221-32.

Murray, Stuart. *Church Planting: Laying Foundations.* Scottdale, PA: Herald Press, 2001.

Neill, Stephen. *A History of Christian Missions.* New York: Penguin Books, 1964.

Newbigin, Lesslie. *The Household of God: Lectures on the Nature of the Church* (Grand Rapids, MI: Eerdmans Publishing Company, 1957.

_____. *The Open Secret.* Grand Rapids: Eerdmans, 1978.

Noll, M.A. "Pietism." In *Evangelical Dictionary of Theology.* Grand Rapids, MI: Baker Book House, 1984.

Ogden, Greg. *Transforming Discipleship: Making Disciples a Few at a Time.* Downers Grove, IL: InterVarsity Press, 2003.

Ortberg, John. *The Life You've Always Wanted.* Grand Rapids, MI: Zondervan, 1997.

Ortlund, Raymond C. "Priorities for the Local Church." *Bibliotheca Sacra* 138 (January—March, 1981): 4-13.

Ott, Craig, and Stephen J. Strauss. *Encountering Theology of Mission: Biblical Foundations, Historical Developments, and Contemporary Issues.* Grand Rapids, MI: Baker Academic, 2010.

Packer, J. I. "The Faith of the Protestants." In *Introduction to the History of Christianity,* ed. Tim Dowley. Minneapolis: Fortress Press, 1995, (374-75).

Pennington, M. Basil. *Bernard of Clairvaux: A Lover Teaching the Way of Love.* New York: New City Press, 1997.

_____. "The Cistercians." In *Christian Spirituality*, edited by Bernard McGinn and John Meyendorff. New York: The Crossroad Publishing Company, 1985.

Pentecost, Edward C. *Issues in Missiology: An Introduction*. Grand Rapids, MI: Baker Book House, 1982.

Peters, George. *A Biblical Theology of Missions.* Chicago: Moody Press, 1972.

Pierson, Paul E. *The Dynamics of Christian Mission.* Pasadena, CA: William Carey International University Press, 2009.

Platt, David. *Radical.* Colorado Springs, CO: Multnomah Books, 2011.

Plummer, Alfred. *An Exegetical Commentary on the Gospel According to S. Matthew* Grand Rapids, MI: Wm. B. Eerdmans Publishing Company, 1953.

Randolph, Justus J. "A Guide to Writing the Dissertation Literature Review." *Practical Assessment, Research & Evaluation* 14: 13 (June 2009). <http://pareonline.net/getvn.asp?V=14&n=-13.hym> (accessed June 2, 2010).

Raymer, Roger M. "1 Peter," in *The Bible Knowledge Commentary: New Testament.* eds. John F. Walvoord and Roy B. Zook. Wheaton: IL Victor Books, 1983.

Reed, Eric. "New Ownership." *Leadership* 28:1 (Winter 2007): 19-22.

Renn, Stephen D. ed. "*Hagiasmos.*" in *Expository Dictionary of Bible Words*. Peabody, MA: Hendrickson Publishers, 2005.

"The Rich Young Ruler Who Said Yes." *Christian History* 1:1 (1982): 7-9.

Riche, Pierre. "Spirituality in Celtic and Germanic Society." *Christian Spirituality, Origins to the Twelfth Century*. New York: Crossroad, 1988.

Robinson, Mitchell W. *Mission: A Mark of the Church? Toward a Missional Ecclesiology*. Master's Thesis, Reformed Theological Seminary, 2008.

Robinson, William Childs. "Lord." In *Baker's Dictionary of Theology,* Grand Rapids, MI: Baker Book House, 1960, (328-29).

Robson, Stephen. *With the Spirit and Power of Elijah (Lk.1,17): The Prophetic-Reforming Spirituality of Bernard of Clairvaux as Evidenced Particularly in His Letters*. Rome: Editrice Pontificia Universita Gregoriana, 2004.

Rogers, Cleon, "The Great Commission." *Bibliotheca Sacra* 130: 519 (July-September 1973): 261-67.

Roxburgh, Alan J. and Fred Romanuck. *The Missional Leader: Equipping Your Church to Reach a Changing World*. San Francisco: Jossey-Bass, 2006.

Rusaw, Rick & Eric Swanson. *The Externally Focused Church*. Loveland, CO: Group, 2004.

Ryan, John. *Irish Monasticism: Origins and Early Developments*. Ithaca, NY: Cornell University Press, 1972.

Ryrie, Charles C. *Basic Theology: A Popular Systematic Guide to Understanding Biblical Truth.* Wheaton, IL: Victor Books, 1987.

_____. *Dispensationalism Today.* Chicago: Moody Press, 1965.

The Saintly Triad of the Lives of St. Patrick, St. Columbkille, and St. Bridget, Commonly Known as the Three Patron Saints of Ireland. Dublin: Sold to the Booksellers, 1844.

Samra, James G. "A Biblical View of Discipleship." *Bibliotheca Sacra*, 160, No. 638 (April-June 2003), 219—34.

Sattler, Gary R. *Nobler Than the Angels, Lower Than a Worm: The Pietist View of the Individual in the Writings of Heinrich Muller and August Hermann Francke.* Lanhan, MD: University of Press of America, 1989.

Schaff, Philip. *History of the Christian Church*, Vol. V. Grand Rapids, MI: Wm. B. Eerdmans Publishing Company, 1952.

Scherer, James A. "Church, Kingdom, and Missio Dei." In *The Good News of the Kingdom. Mission Theology for the Third Millennium,* edited by Charles Van Engen, Dean S. Guilliland, and Paul Pierson. Maryknoll, New York: Orbis Books, 1993.

Sellner, Edward C. *Finding the Monk Within: Great Monastic Values for Today.* Mahwah, NJ: HiddenSpring, 2008.

Sergeant, Curtis. *Planting Rapidly Reproducing Churches.* <http//www.churchplantingmovements.com.html> (accessed July 26, 2010).

Shirley, Chris. "It Takes a Church to Make a Disciple: An Integrative Model of Discipleship for the Local Church." *Southwestern Journal of Theology* 50: No. 2 (2008): 207-224.

Sills, David M. *Reaching and Teaching*. Chicago: Moody Press, 2010.

Shenk, Wilbert R."Lesslie Newbigin's Contribution to the Theology of Mission." *TransMission*, Special Edition, 1998: 3-6. <http://www.Newbigin.net/general/bilography, cfm.html> (accessed July 28, 2010).

"Short-Cycle Church Planting." <http://www.avantministries.org/short-cycle.html> (accessed December 1, 2010).

Sommerfeldt, John R. *The Spiritual Teaching of Bernard of Clairvaux: An Intellectual History of the Early Cistercian Order*. Kalamazoo, MI: Cistercian Publications, 1991.

Spener, Philipp Jacob. *Pia Desideria*. Minneapolis: Fortress Press, 1964.

_____. "Pia Desideria." In *Pietist: Selected Writings*, edited by Peter C. Erb. New York: Paulist Press, 1983, (31-49).

Stein, K. James. *Philipp Jakob Spener: Pietist Patriarch*. Chicago: Covenant Press, 1986.

Stevenson, Phil. "Fit Churches Missionally Engaged." *Journal of the American Society for Church Growth* (Winter), 2009.

Stoeffler, Ernest F. *German Pietism During the Eighteenth Century*. Leiden, Netherlands: E.J. Brill, 1973.

_____. *The Rise of Evangelical Pietism*. Leiden, Netherlands: E. J. Brill, 1971.

Swensson, Eric Jonas. *August Hermann Francke, Lutheranism's Forgotten Hero*. <http://pietist.blogspot.com/2010/09/august-hermann-francke-lutheranism.html> (accessed June 6, 2011).

Tasker, R. V. G. *The Gospel According to St. Matthew*. Tyndale New Testament Commentaries. Grand Rapids, MI: Eerdmans, 1961.

Thayer, Joseph Henry. *Greek-English Lexicon of the New Testament*. New York: Harper Brothers Publishers, 1899.

Thiselton, Anthony C. "An Age of Anxiety." In *Introduction to the History of Christianity First Century to the Present Day—A Worldwide History*, edited by Tim Dowley. Minneapolis, Fortress Press: 1995, (610-27).

Thom, Catherine. *Early Irish Monasticism: An Understanding of its Cultural Roots*. New York: T&T Clark, 2006.

Thompson, Michelle Sung-Mee. *Disciple-Making Congregations*. Doctoral Dissertation, Anderson University School of Theology, 2004.

Thomas, Cal. interview in *Christianity Today*, April 25, 1994, quoted in Greg Ogden, *Transforming Discipleship: Making Disciples a Few at a Time*. Downers Grove, IL: InterVarsity Press, 2003.

Tokyo 2010 Declaration: Making Disciples of Every People in Our Generation. <http://www.tokyo2010.org/conference/html> (accessed August 5, 2010).

Toussaint, Stanley D. *Behold the King: A Study of Matthew.* Portland, OR: Multnomah Press, 1981.

_____. "Israel and the Church of a Traditional Dispensationalist." In *Three Central Issues in Contemporary Dispensationalism: A Comparison of Traditional and Progressive Views*, edited by Herbert W. Bateman IV. Grand Rapids, MI: Kregal Publications, 1999, (227-261).

Tozer, A. W. *I Call it Heresy: And Other Timely Topics From First Peter.* Camp Hill, PA: Christian Publications, 1991.

Trueblood, Eldon. *The Company of the Committed.* San Francisco: Harper & Row, 1961.

Van Engen, Charles. *Mission on the Way.* Grand Rapids, MI: Baker Books, 1996.

_____. "The Relation of the Bible and Mission in Mission Theology." In *The Good News of the Kingdom: Mission Theology for the Third Millennium*, edited by Charles Van Engen, Dean S. Gilliland, and Paul Pierson. Maryknoll, NY: Orbis, 1999, (27-36).

Van Gelder, Craig. *The Essence of the Church: A Community Created by the Spirit.* Grand Rapids, MI: Baker Books, 2000.

_____. *The Ministry of the Missional Church: A Community Led by the Spirit.* Grand Rapids, MI: Baker Books, 2007.

_____. ed., *The Missional Church and Denominations: Helping Congregations Develop a Missional Identity.* Grand Rapids: William B. Eerdmans Publishing Company, 2008.

_____. *The Missional Church: Helping Congregations Develop Contextual Ministry.* Grand Rapids, MI: William B. Eerdmans Publishing Company, 2007.

Vine, W. E. *The Expanded Vine's Expository Dictionary of New Testament Words.* Minneapolis, MN: Bethany House Publishers, 1984.

Waggoner, Brad J. *The Shape of Faith to Come: Spiritual Formation and the Future of Discipleship.* Nashville, TN: B&H Publishing Group, 2008.

Wagner, Peter C. *Strategies for Church Growth.* Ventura, CA: Regal Books, 1987.

Walvoord, John F. and Roy B. Zook, eds. *The Bible Knowledge Commentary: An Exposition of the New Testament Scriptures by Dallas Seminary Faculty.* Wheaton: IL: Victor Books, 1983.

_____. *Jesus Christ Our Lord.* Chicago: Moody Press, 1969.

_____. *Matthew: Thy Kingdom Come.* Chicago: Moody Press, 1974.

Wan, Enoch. "Ethnohermeneutics: Its Necessity and Difficulty for All Christians of All Times." *Global Missiology*, January,

2004. <http://www.Globalmissiology.net.html> (accessed February 18, 2010).

Way, Scott W. *The Value of Theology: Philipp Jakob Spener's Doctrine of Sanctification*. Master's Thesis, Dallas Theological Seminary, 2006.

Whiteside, Lesley. *The Spirituality of Patrick*. Harrisburg, PA: Morehouse Publishing, 1996.

Wilkins, Michael. *Following the Master: Discipleship in the Steps of Jesus*. Grand Rapids, MI: Zondervan, 1992.

_____. *Matthew*. The NIV Application Commentary: From Biblical Text to Contemporary Life, edited by Terry Muck, Grand Rapids, MI: Zondervan, 2004.

_____. "The Use of 'Disciple' in the New Testament." Cited in Michael Wilkins, *Following the Master*. Grand Rapids, MI: Zondervan, 1992, n. 19. Unpublished Master's Thesis, Talbot Seminary, 1977.

Willard, Dallas. *The Divine Conspiracy*. San Francisco: Harper, 1998.

_____. "The Gospel of the Kingdom and Spiritual Formation." In *The Kingdom Life: A Practical Theology of Discipleship and Spiritual Formation*. Colorado Springs, CO: NavPress, 2010.

_____. *The Great Omission: Reclaiming Jesus' Essential Teachings on Discipleship*. San Francisco: Harper & Row, 2006.

_____. *Renovation of the Heart: Putting on the Character of Christ*. Colorado Springs, CO: NavPress, 2002.

_____. *The Spirit of the Disciplines*. San Francisco: HarperCollins Publishers, 1991.

Willard, Dallas and Don Simpson. *Revolution of Character: Discovering Christ's Pattern for Spiritual Transformation*. Colorado Springs: NavPress, 2005.

Wittberg, Patricia. *The Rise and Decline of Catholic Religious Orders*. Albany, New York: The State University of New York, 1994.

Wood, Rick. "A Discipleship Revolution: The Key to Discipling All Peoples," *Mission Frontiers,* 33.1 (January-February 2011): 4-5.

Wright, Christopher J. H. *The Mission of God: Unlocking the Bible's Grand Narrative*. Downers Grove, IL: IVP Academic, 2006.

_____. *The Mission of God's People: A Biblical Theology of the Church's Mission*. Grand Rapids, MI: Zondervan, 2010.

Made in the USA
Charleston, SC
02 December 2012